FOR MY LEGIONNAIRES

BOOKS FROM CLEMENS & BLAIR
— www.clemensandblair.com —

Myth and Sun, by Martin Friedrich
Unmasking Anne Frank, by Ikuo Suzuki
Pan-Judah! Political Cartoons of Der Stürmer, by Robert Penman
Passovers of Blood, by Ariel Toaff
The Poisonous Mushroom, by Ernst Hiemer
On the Jews and Their Lies, by Martin Luther
Mein Kampf, by Adolf Hitler
Mein Kampf (Dual English-German edition), by Adolf Hitler
The Essential Mein Kampf, by Adolf Hitler
The Myth of the 20th Century, by Alfred Rosenberg

BOOKS BY THOMAS DALTON
— www.thomasdaltonphd.com —

The Steep Climb: Essays on the Jewish Question
Classic Essays on the Jewish Question: 1850 to 1945
Debating the Holocaust
The Holocaust: An Introduction
The Jewish Hand in the World Wars
Eternal Strangers: Critical Views of Jews and Judaism
Hitler on the Jews
Goebbels on the Jews
Streicher, Rosenberg, and the Jews: The Nuremberg Transcripts

FOR MY LEGIONNAIRES

by

CORNELIU Z. CODREANU

Clemens & Blair, LLC
— 2023 —

CLEMENS & BLAIR, LLC

Clemens & Blair, LLC, is a non-profit educational publisher.
www.clemensandblair.com

Library of Congress Cataloging-in-Publication Data

Codreanu, Corneliu Zelea
For My Legionnaires

English translation of *Pentru legionari* (1937)

p. cm.
Includes bibliographical references

ISBN 979-8986-7250-62
(pbk.: alk. paper)

1. Romania, history of
2. Jewish Question, the

Printing number: 9 8 7 6 5 4 3 2 1

Printed in the United States of America on acid-free paper.

DEDICATION

TO THE LEGIONNAIRES
6 December 1935

LEGIONNAIRES,

I write for our legionary family. For *all* legionnaires: those in villages, in factories, and in the university. I pay no attention to any regulation imposed on book authors. I have no time for that. I write hastily on the battlefield, in the midst of attacks. At this hour, we are surrounded on all sides. The enemies strike us treacherously and treason bites us.

For two years, we have been bound by the chains of an infamous censorship. For two years, our name and that of the Legion are tolerated by the press, only to be insulted. A rain of treacheries is heaped upon us while our enemies applaud and hope that we will perish. But these knights of cowardice, as well as their masters, will be convinced—soon, in fact—that all the attacks in which they pooled their hopes of destroying the legionnaire movement, all their agitation and desperate efforts, will remain fruitless.

Legionnaires do not die. Erect, immovable, invincible, and immortal, they look forever victorious over the impotent convulsions of hatred.

*****

The opinion created in the non-legionary world by the words that follow is of no consequence to me, and their effect upon that world does not interest me. What I want is for you, soldiers of other Romanian horizons, while reading these recollections, to recognize in them your own past and remember your own battles; that you re-live the suffering you endured and the blows you took for our people; that you fill your hearts with fire, and stand firm in the difficult and righteous struggle in which you are engaged, and out of which we all have the command to emerge either victorious or dead. I think of you as I write.

Of you who will have to die, receive the baptism of death with the serenity of our ancestral Thracians. And of you, those who will have to step over the dead and their tombs, carry in your hands the victorious banners of the Romanians.

Corneliu-Zelea Codreanu

CONTENTS

ACKNOWLEDGMENT

The editor would like to acknowledge the extensive assistance in text preparation by WC, who has put in considerable time and effort on behalf of this (and other) books produced by Clemens & Blair. His work is greatly appreciated.

FOR MY LEGIONNAIRES

INTRODUCTION
THOMAS DALTON

It is something of a miracle that a man such as Corneliu Codreanu ever lived. Then as now, the mass of men are, shall we say, small individuals: they think small, they feel small, and they act small. They are concerned with mundane things, trivial material rewards, small pleasures. They have little concept of the higher human virtues—of honor and dignity, of vision and courage, of strength and resolve. Codreanu was, in every way, the opposite of such men; he had a kind of depth and spirit, a sense of God and nation, a greatness of soul, and a feel for his fellow countryman such as we rarely see in history. His difficult, painful, and tragically short life shines like a beacon—for his Romanian compatriots and for all humanity. It is his life that we celebrate in this book, and it is his life from which we hope to learn and draw inspiration.

Codreanu (pronounced 'ko-DRAH-nu') was born on 13 September 1899 in Husi, a small town in the far east of present-day Romania, near the Moldovan border. His mother was an ethnic German and his father a teacher and, later, politician. He was too young to officially fight in World War One, but his father was directly involved and young Corneliu provided some minor and ancillary support for Romanian troops. The Bolshevik Revolution in Russia occurred in late 1917, at which time that nation was ruled by a largely Jewish cohort headed by quarter-Jew Vladimir Lenin and full Jew Leon Trotsky. The Bolsheviks promptly withdrew from the war and embarked on a reign of terror within Russia, eventually killing millions. Codreanu, aged 19 when the war formally ended, was well aware of the Judeo-Bolshevik danger to his east, and he greatly feared that it may spread to his own nation.

Moving to the city of Iasi the following year, he began his studies in law at the University of Iasi. There he learned much about the nature of Soviet Bolshevism and began his first efforts to organize students. He also made a number of acquaintances with influential professors, including especially the economist Alexandru Cuza (1857-1947). Cuza was a prominent Romanian nationalist, one who placed special emphasis on the dangers posed by the thousands of Jews that had migrated to Romania in the previous several decades. Cuza would later become an important national politician, initially working closely with Codreanu but eventually falling away.

The next several years in Codreanu's young life are thoroughly covered in the text; this autobiographical book naturally gives the most intimate and detailed account possible of the years from 1918 through his completion of the book in April 1936, when he was 36. In brief, we find an astonishing story of a courageous and principled young man battling against the combined power of the corrupt Romanian state and the wealthy and well-organized Jewish community. We can scarcely imagine the experiences and trials that this man, only in his 20s, had to endure: ostracism, hatred, beatings, imprisonment, ingratitude, verbal abuse—on and on. It is a story of a relentless attack on a man and his small movement that evidently threatened to expose the rot and decay at the heart of a Romanian political system that had sold its soul to the Jews. It is almost inconceivable that one might find a similar young man or woman today, college-aged, who would be willing to endure intense suffering, hardship, imprisonment, and potentially death, in order to free their society from the grip of Judaism.

In 1927, Codreanu and colleagues created a new organization, "The Legion of Michael the Archangel," named after the Biblical warrior-angel Michael, who was said to fight evil in the name of God. Members of the Legion became known as 'legionnaires' (or in some translations, 'legionaries'), and they eventually acquired a well-earned reputation for honesty, morality, and integrity, all in the name of defending the Romanian people from Jews, Bolsheviks, and other potential invaders.

Most troubling to Codreanu, though, were the many Romanian sellouts and lackeys who, for the money and power offered by the Jews, betrayed their own people by acting in the most appalling, traitorous, and unjust manner conceivable. As evil as the Jews might be, they were simply acting in their own collective self-interest and in solidarity with their own people. The Romanian traitors, by contrast, were acting solely in terms of their individual, personal interest, to the profound detriment of the common people and the nation. This, for Codreanu, was far worse—indeed, the height of corruption and depravity. On his view, such men deserved nothing less than death. In one of the most notable passages of this book, Codreanu writes:

> The Jews are our enemies and, as such, they hate, poison, and exterminate us. Romanian leaders who cross into their camp are worse than enemies: they are traitors. The first and fiercest punishment ought to fall on the traitor, second on the

enemy. If I had but one bullet and I were faced by both an enemy and a traitor, I would let the traitor have it.[1]

This was not mere talk; Codreanu was good to his word. In October 1924, at the age of 25, he shot and killed a horribly corrupt and sadistic local official by the name of Manciu. Put on trial, Codreanu was acquitted; jurors found it to be 'justifiable homicide.'

In early 1930, Codreanu decided that the Legion needed a new, quasi-military unit specifically designed for "combatting Jewish communism." Thus he formed the Iron Guard—which was promptly banned by the federal government. At that point, Codreanu decided to enter national politics in order to pursue all legal options to political change; in mid-1931, he and a number of other legionnaires were elected to the national Parliament. This angered prime minister Ion Duca—a Freemason and Jewish sycophant—and he ordered the arrest of several legionnaires prior to the 1933 elections. In response, a faction of the Iron Guard assassinated Duca in December of that year. Codreanu was eventually arrested for involvement in the killing, but was again acquitted.

C. Codreanu (undated)

---

[1] Chapter 2, section "The October 1923 Student Plot."

In the 1937 elections, the Legion came in third, with steadily-growing support from the public. King Carol II strongly opposed the Legion and envied, and feared, their growing parliamentary power; thus, in February 1938 he dissolved the Parliament and declared himself royal dictator. Carol then directed his right-hand minister, Armand Calinescu, to arrest Codreanu on April 16 on the basis of contrived charges of "slandering the king." After six months, Carol decided to "decapitate" the movement once and for all; he issued an order for the murder of Codreanu and 13 other legionnaires on 29 November 1938. Calinescu's men carried out the deed, allegedly dissolving the bodies in acid to destroy all remains. Thus ended the life of Corneliu Codreanu, at the age of 39.[2]

Now under control of Horia Sima, the Legion would be subsequently banned yet again, and then later, in an ironic turn, invited into government. They were members of a ruling coalition from late 1940 to early 1941, when they were thrown out of power by military strongman Ion Antonescu. The Legion and Iron Guard would carry on for some years in a diminished capacity, but they never again rose to high levels of political power.

*****

C. Codreanu (center, first row) with five colleagues

---

[2] Carol would eventually reinstate civil government, installing Calinescu as prime minister in March 1939. But he would serve only six months—assassinated that September by the Iron Guard, in retaliation for Codreanu's killing.

During his short and frantic life, Codreanu produced only a small number of writings, the most significant of which was *Pentru legionari*—"For My Legionnaires." It was written between December 1935 and April 1936, in great haste and with little regard for literary norms, and published in 1937. Even so, it is a truly remarkable book, befitting a man with a truly remarkable life; equal parts autobiography, worldview, and political manifesto, it compares favorably with Hitler's *Mein Kampf*, though being less detailed and less exhaustive. Roughly three-quarters of the book covers the decade of the 1920s, coincident with Codreanu's life in his 20s.

Codreanu's account is striking in many ways. Simply on the level of a life story, it is compelling; one is always anxious to turn the next page, to discover how some particular incident gets resolved or to find out who will receive his just (or unjust) desserts. Secondly, we get the impression of a profoundly moral and principled young man, one who is willing to commit everything, to risk all, in order to avenge injustice and to make life better—or indeed, simply tolerable—for his fellow Romanians. But to combine principled morality with political vision and raw courage, all in one man, is truly exceptional. One is tempted to say: we will not see the likes of such a man again.

Throughout the book there are two themes of note: *religion* and *anti-Semitism*. Codreanu was deeply religious, raised as he was in a small rural village by Orthodox Christian parents, who certainly imparted their theological beliefs to the young man. Evidently, he uncritically accepted this worldview, as did most young people of the time. Throughout the book, we read of his efforts to combat secular society, to restore nominally Christian values, and to oppose non-Christian (or anti-Christian) religious views—especially of the Judaic variety. He frequently calls on God for support and wisdom, and prays to the saints for courage. He clearly sees his religion as a source of strength, but I suspect that, had he been agnostic or atheistic, he would have been just as courageous and just as driven in the cause of justice.

For me personally, all this is somewhat problematic. First, as a free-thinking and rational individual, I have a very hard time accepting religious mythology as truth without some very compelling evidence. And in the case of Christianity, we have, sadly, none at all. But again, Codreanu, like most Christians throughout most of history, became Christian simply because they were raised so; they certainly did not come to the religion through rational or skeptical thought. So, on the one hand, I cannot blame Codreanu for how he was raised, and yet I can blame him for not becoming a more thoughtful, inquisitive, and skeptical adult.

Still, Codreanu's religious stance is not oppressive or overweening. From his Orthodox standpoint, we see most emphasis on God and the saints. Jesus plays very little role here, garnering only a single mention in the book. The Virgin Mary is cited on just two occasions. And worldly leaders like the pope play no role at all. Priests are seen as shepherds and guardians of the peoples' moral well-being, and thus as important to social integrity.

C. Codreanu (undated)

Second and more awkward is the fact that Christianity, of any stripe, is in fact *Judeo*-Christianity, founded by Palestinian Jews and rooted in the centuries-old Jewish teachings of the Old Testament. Jesus, if he existed, was an ethnic Jew, as was Mary and Joseph. All the apostles, and Paul of Tarsus, were Jews, as were all of the anonymous Gospel writers. Virtually all the New Testament was written by Jews and directed either at other Jews—who were trying to build the new church—or at Gentiles who were being implored to accept this new, radical, and "superstitious" religion based on a savior who died on the cross. Gentiles were, in effect, being asked to accept a deceased Jewish rabbi (Jesus) as their personal savior, and to accept the Jewish God (Jehovah or Yahweh) as their divine creator. And they were asked to do so, simply based on the word of Jews—Paul most of all, but also the Gospel writers. Given the long-standing Jewish conflict with the ruling power at the time, Rome, it is not hard to see this as a strategy for steering the Gentile masses in a pro-Jewish, anti-Roman direction.[3]

Thus, Christianity is intrinsically problematic—but doubly so, if you are a Christian anti-Semite like Codreanu. He could see the pernicious effect that Jews had on Romanian society, as could most perceptive individuals of the time. He saw that they operated in a callous and venal manner, corrupting any aspect of society if it might serve to increase their wealth or power. Bribes, slander, moral degradation, paid criminals, hired hitmen—nothing was beneath them. Despite seeing clearly the Jewish root cause of human suffering in his land, Codreanu nonetheless persisted in openly revering the Jewish God, the Jewish rabbi Jesus, and the Jewish woman Mary. To call this a paradox is an understatement in the extreme.[4]

Despite all this, the central theme of anti-Semitism recurs throughout the book. This is both illuminating and instructive. All the negative characteristics that Codreanu saw around him, all the corrupting and indeed criminal activities, all the crude disregard for justice and Gentile well-being—all these hold true today. Time after time, he recounts an incident of Jewish malfeasance that finds its counterpart in the contemporary world. One constantly gets the feeling that, yes, this is exactly how it is today. When Codreanu sees Jews monopolize and lie via the press; when they deploy their funds to corrupt politicians; when they lure people into ruinous financial schemes; when they deal in alcohol and licentious "culture" that degrade human existence, we see a mirror image, in simpler form, of the present-day Jewish Lobby. In fact, it was the smaller and simpler social setting of 1920s Romania that allowed even a moderately perceptive individual to see the reality. Codreanu not only saw things clearly, he was disgusted to his core and hell-bent on doing something about it.

In the present world—say, the USA or Europe—Jewish influence is much more subtle and much more insidious than it was then. It operates on such a vast scale that the ordinary man has a hard time grasping what is happening. Jews manipulate billions of dollars, operate hugely complex corporate schemes, employ armies of Gentiles as cover, and create and promote the most degrading culture, all while they literally own or run the

---

[3] For more on this topic, see chapters 4 and 25 in my book *The Steep Climb* (2023).

[4] There were, of course, many Christian anti-Semites throughout history, Martin Luther being among the most influential. For details, see my book *Eternal Strangers* (2020).

mass media (liberal *and* conservative) and have most federal politicians in their back pocket. They are experts at stifling critics via censorship, defunding, and 'cancellation,' even as they proclaim the loftiest of values and intentions. Today, the average person has little hope of untangling the many arms of the Jewish hydra. But in 1920s Romania, one young man could see what was happening, travel around his small country, speak the truth, and earn the respect of the masses. From his example, operating in a much simpler time and on a much smaller scale, we see in microcosm the world that we face today. And we see the same root cause of so many social problems.

Thus the short and tragic life of Corneliu Codreanu stands today as both a fascinating life story and a vitally urgent life-lesson. His open, explicit, and justified anti-Semitism stands in marked contrast to the situation today in the West, where the word 'Jew' can scarcely be mentioned without repercussion—so pervasive and so powerful is the Jewish Lobby. Fortunately, today, the facts are finally starting to get out. The nature and effects of Jewish domination are slowly becoming known. Jewish control over media, Hollywood, government, and academia are no longer disputed. No one argues about the facts, because the facts are clear. The Jews can only hope that their censorship will hold and that most people will remain in the dark regarding Jewish power. And they must hope that those who do know the facts are too timid to act. This remains their only chance to sustain their grip on power.

The Jews' greatest fear is that someone—some small group, or some individual man or woman—will not only realize the truth of their malicious dominance but will, like Codreanu, summon the courage to act. This is why Codreanu and his book are almost completely unknown in the West today; no one discusses it, no one analyzes it, no one cites him, no one quotes him. Jews and their lackeys in media and academia know when a wire is too hot to touch. So they keep their distance and pray to Jehovah that no one hears of this brave young man who, 100 years ago, found the courage to confront and eventually defeat the Jewish serpent that was strangling his nation. They pray that no one reads this book, talks about it, or shares it with friends. They pray, and they quiver with fear at the thought of what may come.

In the end, and though he did not live to see it, Codreanu did succeed in his battle. At least 750,000 Jews lived in Romania in the 1920s.[5] World

---

[5] In the text, Codreanu cites estimates of up to 2 million Jews, although this appears to be an exaggeration.

War Two devastated Jewish populations throughout Europe, causing many to flee. Today, Romania has only around 3,000 Jews—just 0.02% of the population of some 20 million. The Jewish serpent has truly been defeated, at least in this one European nation.

Perhaps other nations around the world, currently in the grip of Jewish power, will learn from history, summon their collective courage, and act. Perhaps a new "Legion of Michael the Archangel"—an international legion, or even a global one—will emerge, and bring an end to the decades, even centuries, of suffering under the Jewish thumb. And perhaps Corneliu Codreanu and his book will serve as one more small step of encouragement along the way.

C. Codreanu (undated)

CHAPTER 1
MARCHING INTO LIFE

At the Dobrina Forest

Here we stand, gathered together one afternoon in the spring of 1919 in the Dobrina Forest, which stands guard on the hills around the city of Husi. Who are we? A group of about 20 high school students—sophomores, juniors, and seniors. I called these young comrades together to discuss a grave problem, though our life was just beginning. What are we going to do if the Bolsheviks invade us?[1] My opinion, with which the others agreed, was this: If the Bolshevik army crosses the Dniester River, and then the Pruth, reaching our region, we will not submit, but will take refuge in the woods, armed. There we will organize a center of Romanian action and resistance, and by skillful action shake up the enemy. We will maintain a spirit of non-submission, and keep alive a spark of hope amidst the Romanian masses in villages and towns. To this, we all took an oath in the middle of the ancient forest. This forest was a corner of that famous woods of Tigheciu, on whose paths, throughout Moldavia's history, many an enemy found death.[2]

We decided to acquire weapons and ammunition, to maintain total secrecy, to engage in scouting and battle exercises there in the forest, and to establish a façade that would mask our intentions. We quickly and easily established this façade: a cultural-national association of the students at the high school of Husi that we named "Mihail Kogalniceanu".[3] It was approved by the high school principal. Then we began meetings and lectures in town. We addressed the usual subjects in public, while in the woods we simulated battle exercises. In those times, one could find weapons everywhere, so that within about two weeks we collected all we needed.

---

[1] The Soviet Bolsheviks, a predominantly Jewish militant group led by Lenin and Trotsky, had succeeded in their revolutionary plans in Russia in 1917, eventually murdering Czar Nicholas and his family in mid-1918. There were legitimate fears that they might move into Romania.
[2] Moldavia (also called Western Moldavia or Romanian Moldavia) is a region of present-day Romania. It borders, but is distinct from, the nation known as the Republic of Moldova.
[3] Former prime minister of Romania in the mid-1800s.

Even though we were still children, barely over the age of 18, we understood all too well the chaotic state of affairs in the country. Everyone was thinking about the Bolshevik Revolution, which was well underway only a few steps over the border [in Russia]. The peasantry was instinctively opposed to this destructive force, but they were completely disorganized and could not put up a serious resistance. Industrial workers, though, were sliding toward communism at a dizzying pace, being systematically fed the cult of these ideas by the Jewish press and generally by the entire Jewry of the cities.

It seemed that every Jew, merchant, intellectual, or banker-capitalist was, in his sphere of influence, an agent of these anti-Romanian revolutionary ideas. The Romanian intelligentsia was undecided, and the state apparatus disorganized. One could expect at any moment, either an internal eruption of some determined and organized elements, or an invasion from across the Dniester. External action, coordinated with that of the Judeo-communist bands within—who could bear down on us, destroying bridges and blowing up ammunition dumps—could have then decided our fate as a people. It was in such circumstances, our thoughts in turmoil, worrying about the life and liberty of our country just unified at the end of a difficult war,[4] that our youthful minds conceived the oath in Dobrina Forest.

I had just completed five years at the Military Academy in The Cloister on the Hill, where the head of Michael the Brave reposes, under the searching eye of Nicolae Filipescu. There I received a strict soldierly education and a healthy confidence in my own powers.

In fact, my military education will be with me all my life. Order, discipline, and hierarchy, fused into my blood at an early age, along with the sentiment of soldierly dignity, will constitute a guiding thread for my entire future activity. Here too, I was taught to value silence and to speak little, a fact that later was to lead me to hate those who were "all talk." Here I learned to love the battlefield trench and to despise the living room.

The notions of military science I learned back then cause me to view everything through the lens of this science. This spirit of the sentiment of human and military dignity, in which the officers raised me, was to later create for me difficulties and expose me to suffering, in a world oftentimes lacking in both honor and dignity.

I spent the summer of 1916 at home in Husi. My father had been recalled into the military for the last two years and left with the regiment for

---

[4] Codreanu refers to the "Great Union" of 1918 that saw a large expansion of Romanian territory after WWI.

the Carpathians. One night my mother woke me up, crying and crossing herself, and said: "Wake up, all the bells of all the churches are ringing." It was 15 August 1916, the Feast of St. Mary. I understood that mobilization had been decreed and that at that moment the Romanian army had crossed the mountains. Seized by emotion, my whole body trembled.

Three days later I left home to trail my father, pushed by my yearning that I, too, be among the fighters on the front. Finally, after many adventures, I reached the regiment in which my father was commanding a company, the 25th Infantry Regiment, as it was advancing into Transylvania on the Oituz valley. But my misfortune was great, for, being only 17 years old, the regimental commander turned me down as a volunteer. Yet I took part both in the advance into, and the retreat from, Transylvania, and on 20 September, when my father fell wounded above Sovata on the Ceres-Domu Mountain, I aided him ahead of the enemy's advance. Though wounded, he refused to be evacuated, leading his company throughout the retreat and later in the heavy fighting that followed at Oituz.

At two o'clock one night, the regiment received orders to advance. The officers inspected their troops massed in a tomb-like quiet on the highway. My father was asked to report to the colonel. Returning after a short while, he told me: "Wouldn't it be better for you to go back home? We will soon be engaged in battle and it is not good that both of us die here, leaving Mother with six small children and no support. The colonel called me and told me he does not want to take the responsibility of your remaining here on the front."

I could tell his heart was in doubt; he hesitated at leaving me alone in the middle of the night, out in the open, on unfamiliar roads, 25 miles from the nearest railroad. Noting his insistence, however, I turned in my carbine and the two cartridge holders while the columns of the regiment moved on, disappearing into the quiet and darkness of night. I remained alone on the edge of a ditch, then started in the direction of the old frontier and home.

When, a year later, on 1 September, I entered The Military School of Infantry at Botosani, I still had thoughts of reaching the front. It was here that I completed my education and military training, from 1 September 1917 to 17 July 1918, in the Military School's Active Company. The four distinguished officers—Col. Slavescu, Capt. Ciurea, Lieut. Florin Radulescu and Maj. Steflea—guided my steps in the ways of battle and sacrifice for my country.

Another year passed—1919 brought peace, and we, the children ready to die, were scattered, each to his home. My father, a teacher in secondary schools, had been a lifetime nationalist fighter. My grandfather was a forester, and likewise my great-grandfather. The people of my nation have been, from the very beginning, in any difficult historical times, a people of woods and mountains. That is why my soldierly upbringing and the blood in my veins impressed a note of seriousness on our actions at Dobrina, which our tender age would not have presupposed. In those moments, we felt in our hearts, with their advice and experience, the presence of all our ancestors who had fought for Moldavia on the same paths that our enemies never penetrated.

At the University of Iasi (September 1919)

The summer passed. I completed my high school graduation in the fall and our group parted ways, each directing his steps toward a university. From Dobrina, we retained only the memories of defending our country against the waves of enmity menacingly raised against us, both from without and from within our borders.

I left Husi at this crossroad for every youth: enrollment into a university, the long-awaited enrollment at the university! As preparation, I had the benefit of knowledge acquired in high school. Fortunately I had not been affected by sensationalist literature or that of spiritual perversion which today occupies such an important place in the formative years of a high school student. In addition to the customary literature of the Romanian classics, I had read all the articles by Nicolae Iorga and Alexandru Cuza in the *The Sower* and *The Romanian People*.[5] My father had these in some boxes in the attic. That is where I went in my free hours to busy myself with such literature.

The essence of these articles contained, in a lofty form, the three ideals of life for the Romanian people:

1.   The unification of the Romanian people.
2.   The elevation of peasantry through land reform and
     political rights.
3.   The solution to the Jewish Question.

There were two maxims printed on the jackets of all nationalistic publications of that time:

---

[5] Iorga (1871-1940) was a prominent politician, historian, and social critic. Cuza (1857-1947) was an influential politician and economist. Cuza in particular would become an important figure in Codreanu's life.

"Romania for the Romanians, only for the Romanians, and for all Romanians." — N. Iorga.

"Nationality is the creative power of human culture; culture is the creative power of nationality." — A. C. Cuza.

I approached Iasi with great reverence—the Iasi loved and understood by every Romanian, the city everyone at least wants to visit. Many towns in Moldavia have some fragment of glory, but above all these rise Suceava and Iasi. Suceava, the fortress of Stefan the Great; and Iasi, the city of Cuza-Voda—the city of the Union of 1859, which, through the founding of the university, became the city of youth and that of its noblest aspirations. Here, like a lighthouse in the field of political economics, shines the great personality of Professor Cuza. The university became a school of nationalism; and Iasi, the city of the great Romanian thrust forward, became a symbol of our national greatness, ideals, and aspirations. It is great from the sorrow of 1917 when, in his troubled hours, the tormented soul of King Ferdinand found refuge; great through its destiny of being in 1918 the city of union of all Romanians; great by virtue of its great past; and great by its present tragedy: the city of the 40 churches dies daily, forgotten under the merciless Jewish invasion. Iasi, like Rome, built on seven hills, is and remains the eternal city of Romanianism.

How many glorious memories! Here, as nowhere else, the student feels the spirits of our ancestors hovering in the air over silent Iasi, with their mysterious appeals and their sacred urgings. The Iasi student, in the quiet of the night, hears, as if maddened by pain, the phantom of Mihai Eminescu running through the tortuous streets of the city, moaning like a ghost: "He who takes strangers to heart / May dogs eat his heart / May decay eat away his home / May ill-fame devour his family".[6] This is the town I approached with profound reverence in the fall of 1919, being attracted by its great aura, but moved also because it was here that I was born 20 years earlier. And just like any child, I was moved to again see and kiss my native earth.

I registered in the School of Law. Iasi University, closed during the war years, had reopened a year earlier. The old students, returned now as veterans, retained the line of the traditional nationalism of student life before the war. They were divided into two camps: one under the leadership of Labusca from Letters, and another under that of Nelu Ionescu, from

---

[6] Eminescu (1850-1889) was a leading Romanian novelist and poet.

Law. These groups, small in number, were overwhelmed by the immense mass of Jewish students coming over to school from Bessarabia,[7] all communist agents and propagandists. The university's professors, excepting a very limited group headed by A. C. Cuza, Ion Gavanescul, and Corneliu Sumuleanu, supported the same leftist ideas. Professor Paul Bujor, one of the majority's exponents, stated quite clearly in the country's full Senate: "The light comes from the East," namely, from beyond the Dniester.

Such an attitude on the part of professors who considered "barbarous" any nationalistic idea or tone, resulted in the total disorientation of the students: some openly supporting Bolshevism, others—the greater part— saying: "Say what you will, nationalism is passé, mankind moves toward the left." The Labusca group slid totally in this direction. The Ionescu group, to which I adhered, scattered in time, following some elections in the university which they lost.

The advancement of these anti-Romanian ideas, supported by a compact mass of professors and students, and encouraged by all enemies of unified Romania, found no Romanian resistance among the student body. The few of us who were still trying to man the barricades were surrounded by an atmosphere of scorn and enmity. On the streets or in the halls of the university, colleagues holding other opinions—those with "freedom of conscience" and who preach every other kind of freedom—spat behind us as we passed and became increasingly aggressive. Thousands of students, in meeting after meeting in which Bolshevism was propagated, attacked army, justice, Church, and Crown. The university, traditionally nationalistic since 1860, became a nest of anti-Romanianism.

Preparation for Revolution

But it was not wholly in the university that this situation existed. Iasi's mass of workingmen, almost entirely immersed in Communism, was always ready to erupt into revolution. Little work was done in factories. For hours on end, they held meetings and councils; most were about politics rather than work. We found ourselves systematically sabotaged, according to plan and by command: "destroy machinery and create a state of general material misery which leads to the eruption of revolution." And indeed, the more this command was obeyed, the more the misery spread, hunger threatened menacingly, and rebellion grew in the souls of the multitude.

---

[7] A region of Moldova.

Every three or four days on the streets of Iasi, there were huge communist demonstrations. Some 10,000 or 15,000 starved workers, maneuvered by the Judaic criminal hand from Moscow, paraded the streets while singing the *Internationale*, and yelling: "Down with the King!," "Down with the Army!," and carrying placards on which one could read "Long live the communist revolution!" and "Long live Soviet Russia!" If these people had been victorious, would we have had a Romania led by a Romanian workers' regime? Would the Romanian workers have become masters of the country? No! The next day we would have become slaves of the dirtiest tyranny: the Talmudic, Jewish tyranny. Greater Romania, after less than a moment of existence, would have collapsed. We, the Romanian people, would have been mercilessly exterminated, killed, or deported throughout Siberia: peasants, workers, intellectuals, all in a headlong chaos. The land from Maramures to the Black Sea, snatched from Romanian hands, would have been colonized by Jewish masses. Here they would have built their true Palestine.

I was perfectly aware that, in those hours, the life and death of the Romanian people was at stake. And so were the Jews, who were pushing the Romanian workers into revolution. They had no sympathy with the anguish that gripped our hearts in those moments or with the anxiety betrayed in our eyes. They knew what they were doing. Only the Romanian intellectuals were unconscious; the intellectuals, who had gone to school and were supposed to enlighten the people in difficult times, were absent from their duty. These worthless beings, in those decisive moments, maintained with a criminal unconsciousness that "the light comes from the East."

Who was supposed to oppose the revolutionary columns that marched menacingly through the streets of all our towns? The students? No! The intelligentsia? No! The police? The Romanian Security Service? Upon hearing the columns approach, these groups panicked and vanished. Not even the military could block their way. One spoke not of 1,000 men, but of 15,000 or 20,000, organized and hungry.

The Guard of the National Conscience

One rainy evening in the fall of 1919, in the cafeteria of The School of Arts and Crafts, where I was a counselor, a friend of mine showed me a newspaper notice. "The Guard of the National Conscience holds a meeting this evening, Thursday, 9 o'clock, No. 3 Alecsandri St." I left immediately, running with great impatience to know and to enroll in this organization whose anti-communist flyers I had read several months earlier.

In the room on No. 3 Alecsandri St., set up with newly-made bench-es, I found only one man already there. He was about 40 years old, brawny and downcast, sitting at a table, waiting for people to come. A big head, two strong arms, heavy fists, of middle stature. He was Constantin Pancu, the President of The Guard of the National Conscience. I introduced my-self, telling him I was a student and that I wished to be admitted as a fight-er into the Guard. He accepted me.

I sat in at that meeting. About 20 persons came: a typesetter; a stu-dent; about four mechanics; two from the railways; several tradesmen and workers; the lawyer Victor Climescu; and a priest. Several questions were discussed in connection with the momentum gained by the communist movement in various factories and part of the city, and with the problem of organizing the Guard.

From that evening on, my road bifurcated: one half in the fight at the university, the other half with Constantin Pancu and among the workers. I became attached to this man and I stood with him under his leadership constantly until the organization disbanded. Pancu, whose name was on the lips of all Iasians in both camps, uttered hopefully by Romanians, in horror by the others, was not an intellectual. He was a tradesman, plumber, and electrician. He never went beyond fourth grade. He had a lucid, balanced mind which he himself enriched with adequate knowledge. For 20 years, he had been occupied with workers' problems. For several years, he was the president of the metallurgical union. And he was a first-class speaker. At the podium, before a crowd, he was impressive. He had a soul and a conscience that were clearly Romanian. He loved his country, the military, and the King. He was a good Christian.

Physically imposing, he had the muscles of a circus fighter and truly Herculean strength. Iasians had known him for a long time. Before the war, a circus came to Iasi which held fighting shows. Among the combatants were men from all nations: Hungarians, Turks, Romanians, Russians, etc. One evening, when one of them won over all the other fighters, from among the spectators a citizen stood up asking to fight the winner. He was permitted to do so. He undressed and the fight started. In two minutes, the Hungarian circus strongman was thrown to the ground, defeated. The Ro-manian who won amidst the crowd's enthusiastic admiration was none other than Constantin Pancu. That's why, when his call to battle appeared for the first time on the streets of Iasi, the public, which worships strength, accepted it with trust.

His effort lasted one year, increasing as the Bolshevik menace grew, then decreasing as it diminished. Small meetings were held at first, then rallies that reached 5,000, 6,000, even 10,000 people. These took place weekly in the Prince Mircea Hall, or sometimes in Union Square. I was among those who spoke regularly. This is where I learned how to speak before a crowd. Undeniably, The Guard of the National Conscience raised the conscience of Romanians at a critical time, in an important place as that of Iasi, and placed it like a barrier before the communist wave.

This activity however, was not limited only to Iasi. We went to other towns. In addition, the paper *The Conscience*, which was regularly published, penetrated with its cry of alarm into nearly all the towns of Moldavia and Bessarabia. Almost daily out in the field between the two camps, inevitable bloody clashes occurred, with our side sustaining the most wounded. This tense situation lasted until spring, but after two great victories for our side, the offensive power of our adversaries declined.

(1) The occupation of the Agency of State Monopolies

It was either on the 10th or the 11th of February 1920. For two weeks, there was talk of a nationwide general strike. The decisive battle was approaching. It was rumored in town that sometime around noon at the Agency of State Monopolies, where about 1,000 workers were employed, the strike would be declared, the red flag raised, and the King's picture lowered and trampled underfoot, to be replaced by those of Karl Marx, Leon Trotsky, and Christian Rakovsky.[8]

A riot ensued; our people, including the mechanics and members of The Guard, were beaten and badly wounded. At 1 o'clock, about 100 of us got together at our headquarters. What to do? Pancu chaired the discussion. There were two opinions. Some claimed we should send telegrams to the government, requesting military intervention. My opinion was that those present should head for the Agency and tear down the red flag at any risk. My point of view was agreed upon. We took our flag and, at 1 o'clock, led by Pancu, we started marching on Lapusneanu and Pacurari singing "Awaken, Ye Romanian."

Close to the factory, we broke up several groups of communists. We entered the factory's courtyard and went into the building, carrying our flag all the way to the roof, where I planted it. From there I gave a talk. The military appeared and occupied the factory.

---

[8] Marx (1818-1883) was the long-dead Jewish founder of modern communism. Trotsky (1879-1940; born Lev Bronstein) was a then-41-year-old Jewish leader of Soviet Bolshevism. Rakovsky (1873-1941) was a then-47-year-old Bulgarian Bolshevik (non-Jewish) who collaborated closely with Trotsky.

We retreated, singing, then returned to our headquarters, considering our rapid incursion a success. The news of our attitude flashed through the town like lightning, yet the strike continued. The military could only defend the flag, it could not make the plant run.

What was to be done? An idea occurred to us to search the city for workers in order to open the plant. In three days, 400 new workers, gathered from all quarters of Iasi, entered the plant. It began to run; the strike had failed. Two weeks later, half the strikers demanded that they be returned to work. Our victory was great. The first step toward a general strike was rejected. The plans of the Judeo-communist consortium began to be frustrated. Our action had a resounding echo within Romanian ranks, raising their morale.

(2) The tricolor flag over the Nicolina Works

The most powerful communist center was formed by the Romanian railway works at Nicolina. Over 4,000 men worked there, nearly all bolshevized. Residential areas around these works had been invaded by a considerable number of Jews. That is why the leader of the communist movement in Iasi, Dr. Ghelerter, focused their resistance here. A month had not passed since their defeat at the Agency, and as a signal to begin the general strike and the decisive battle, the red flag was hoisted, fluttering over the works. A strike was declared. Thousands of workers poured out. The authorities were powerless.

Through flyers, we called all Romanians to a meeting in the Prince Mircea Hall. After the speeches, we left the building with our flags and the whole crowd headed for Nicolina. In Union Square, we were stopped by the authorities who advised us against continuing, for there were over 5,000 armed communists there waiting for us and much bloodshed would occur. So we turned from Union Square toward the railway station, where we hoisted flags over the engine roundhouse and over the station.

Then we commandeered a train on the track and went to Nicolina. Someone threw the switch in the Nicolina station, and train and all entered the Nicolina complex. We got off. No one was in the shops. On one of the buildings, we saw the red flag. I climbed up a fire escape, holding a tricolor flag between my teeth. With some difficulty, for it was at a great height, I reached the roof. I got on the roof and crawled to the top. I snatched the red flag and, amidst truly tremendous hurrahs, lasting several minutes, I hoisted and secured the tricolor flag. Then, from there, I spoke. Outside the walls, the communists, increasing in numbers, steadily grew into a compact mass and demonstrated menacingly.

Then arose an infernal racket. Inside, hurrahs; outside, boos and cursing. Then I slowly descended to the ground. Pancu ordered our departure. But at the gate, the communists barred our exit, yelling: "Let Pancu and Codreanu come forward!" We stepped 30 yards in front of our crowd and headed for the gate. In the middle, Pancu, on his right a tradesman, Margarint, with myself on the left. All three of us advanced saying nothing, keeping our hands in our pockets on our revolvers.

Those at the gate watched us, quiet and unmoving. Now we were but a few steps away. I expected the whiz of a bullet going past my ear. But we kept on, straight and determined. However, this was a very unusual, soulful moment. We were now but a couple of steps away. The communists stepped aside, opening up for us! For about ten yards we walked in tomblike silence through their midst. We looked neither to the left nor to the right. Nothing was heard, not even human breathing. Our men followed us.

But as they came through, the silence was broken. Cursing began, with threats on both sides. But no fighting. As a body, we headed along the railroad toward the station. Behind us, over the works, the blowing wind fluttered the cloth of the victorious tricolor.

The moral effect of this action was incomparable. The whole of Iasi was in an uproar. Everyone on the streets spoke only about The Guard of the National Conscience. A current of Romanian awakening was felt in the air. Trains carried news of this resurrection to the four corners of the country. We realized that Bolshevism would be defeated because a barrier of conscience had been raised on all sides that would prevent its expansion. All roads to its further encroachment were now closed.

(3) National-Christian socialism—the national syndicates

The Guard of the National Conscience was a fighting organization designed to knock out the enemy. I spoke with with Pancu many times those evenings in 1919, for we were together constantly and I almost regularly ate at his table. And I told him:

> It's not enough to defeat Communism. We must also fight
> for the rights of the workers. They have a right to bread
> and a right to honor. We must fight against the oligarchic
> parties, creating national workers organizations that can

gain their rights *within* the framework of the state and not *against* the state.

We cannot allow anyone to raise another flag on Romanian soil other that that of our own national history. No matter how right the workers' class may be, we cannot tolerate that it rise up against the country or that it make common cause with foreign movements outside our borders. No one will accept that, simply for your bread, you lay waste to the nation and hand over everything to a foreign people of bankers and usurers—everything that has been earned, for two millennia, by the sweat of working people and brave individuals. You have rights, yes—but within the rights of your people. It is inadmissible that, for your right, the historic right of the nation to which you belong be trampled underfoot.

But neither will we admit that, under the guise of 'color formulas,' an oligarchic and tyrannical class may install itself on the backs of the workers of all categories and literally skin them alive, while continually waving banners through the air for the Fatherland—which they do not love; for God—in whom they do not believe; for the Church—into which they never enter; and for the military—which they sent to war empty-handed.

These are realities that cannot be used as false emblems for political fraud in the hands of some immoral prestidigitators.

Then we began organizing the workers into national unions, and even created a political party: "National-Christian Socialism." It was then that Pancu wrote:

The Creed of National-Christian Socialism[9]

I believe in the one and undivided Romanian State, from Dniester to the Tisa. This state is the holder of all Romanians and only of Romanians, lover of work, honor, and God, concerned about the country and its people; giver of equal rights, both civil and political, to men and to women; protector of the family, paying its public servants and workers on the

---

[9] Codreanu's note: At that time, we had not heard of Adolf Hitler and German National Socialism.

basis of the number of children and the work performed, in quality and quantity; and in a State, supporter of social harmony through minimizing of class differences; and in addition to salaries, nationalizing factories—the property of all workers—and distributing the land among all farmers.

It will distribute benefits between owner (state or private) and workers. The former, in addition to his own salary, will get a percentage inversely proportional to the size of his original investment; furthermore, the State will ensure his original investment; furthermore, the State will insure the workers through a 'risks fund.' The State will provide storehouses for food and clothing for workers and civil servants who, organized in national unions, will have their representatives in the administrative boards of the various industrial, agricultural, and commercial institutions.

I believe in a great and strong 'father of the workers' and King of the peasants, Ferdinand the First,[10] who has sacrificed all for the happiness of Romania and who, for our salvation, became as one with the people; who, at the head of his troops at Marasti and Marasesti, vanquished the enemy; who ever since, looks lovingly and trustingly upon the soldiers owing him allegiance—soldiers who will find their military duty to be a real school of their nation which they can finish in a year.

I believe in one tricolor flag surrounded by the rays of National-Christian Socialism, symbol of harmony among the brothers and sisters of Greater Romania.

I believe in one sacred Christian Church, with priests living the Gospel and for the Gospel, and who would, like the apostles, sacrifice themselves for the enlightenment of the many.

I recognize the election of the Ministers by the Chamber, the abolition of the Senate, the organization of rural police, a progressive income tax, schools of agriculture and crafts in the villages, 'circles' for housewives and adults, homes for invalids and old folks, national homes, the determination of paternity, the encouragement of private initiative in the interest

---

[10] Ferdinand I of Romania (1865-1927) was king from 1914 until his death.

of the Nation, and the development of the peasant's home industry.

I await the resurrection of national conscience even in the humblest shepherd, and I await the descent of the educated into the midst of the tired, to strengthen and help them in true brotherhood, the foundation of Romania of tomorrow. Amen![11]

Then we began the organization of the national unions.

(4) A truthful picture of the situation in 1919

I will try to report on the period of 1919-1920, taking from newspapers and manifestos what I consider to be significant. The first manifesto issued by Constantin Pancu at Iasi in August 1919, posted on all walls everywhere in Iasi, in a moment of general disorientation, is the call to battle for the Romanian workers:

Appeal to the Romanian tradesmen, workers, soldiers, and peasants

Brothers,

Following years of frightful battles, the world celebrates peace among men; the wise leaders in all civilized countries endeavor to do away with war by establishing a law to guarantee a peaceful existence in the future.

But lo, from the East one hears voices of hatred that indicate the attempt by our enemies to rip us apart through discord and misunderstandings. From Russia, ruled by the darkness of erroneous teachings, we are urged to battle and to kill our brothers of like blood.

From Hungary, which weeps over her former grandeur, one hears the same urgings. The enemies in the East have united with those in the West to disturb our peace so that they can invade us.

Foreigners beyond our borders try to pass the poison chalice among us, through the aliens living in the bosom of our country. They dare to say that they prod us forward in the name of peace, justice, and liberty, and in the name of the

---

[11] Published in *The Conscience*, 9 February 1920.

workers. Their word is a lie, their urgings a killing poison, for:

They say they want peace, but they themselves destroy it, killing the worthiest;

They demand freedom, but by death threats, oblige people to submit to them;

They wish brotherhood, while they sow hatred, injustice, and licentiousness within nations. Moreover, they say they want to abolish capital earned by the sweat of one's brow.

They tell us they do not want war, but they conduct war.

They demand the army be abolished, but they arm themselves. They urge us to discard the tricolor flag, while in its stead they hoist the red flag of hatred. Do not lend any credence to their manifestos and urgings, just as you did not believe that of the enemy when you were fighting at Oituz, Marasti, and Marasesti.

The duty of every good Romanian is to see to it that in the future, too, the seed of dissention that the enemy endeavors to sow among us does not take root.

Perfect the work you began by your labor and your honor. Your enemies are indolence, hatred, and dishonor, which rule across the borders and which threaten us as well.

Beware! Keep your soul clean, and do not forget that our salvation is work, unity, and honor.

Brother soldiers,
With faith in God, you have broken the enemy's power. With your weapons, you have eternally etched the country's borders. With your blood, you have perfected and sealed your sacrifice.

That is why you must not allow foreign and lawless bands to destroy that which you perfected. Continue to hold your love of country and faith in your King. You took an oath to defend the Fatherland's borders with the last drop of your blood. Guard them attentively against the evil intentions of the enemy, for that is what our parents and ancestors did.

Brother peasants,
The God of our parents took mercy on our suffering and gave us as bountiful a year as was rarely seen. Be grateful to

the good Lord, through your labor and your faith. Renew your working powers, gather assiduously the yield of the land. Rest assured that the land from the Tisa, the Danube, and the Black Sea, was entirely won by you. Keep it in sacredness, defend its riches through your labor and your love.

Brother Romas,
It is in you that the hopes and strength of this country lie. You are also the happiness of tomorrow. Do not gather for yourselves curses, but blessings.

The enemy is attacking at the Dniester and at the Tisa. He also tries to disrupt the inner peace of our country. Our deliverance is in labor, honor, love of country, and faith in God.

Be careful, call onto the righteous path also those who, straying, have crossed over to those without a people and without a faith. United around the throne and under the shadow of the tricolor banner, stand watch for the peace of the country. Tell the foreigners and foreign-lovers who try to disturb us, that a national guard has formed around us, one that watches and will fight those wishing to sow discord among us.

Romanians everywhere, workers, craftsmen, soldiers, and peasants, be worthy of our ancestors and of the call of these times in which we live.[12]

(5) Leaders of the Romanian workers

The leaders of the Romanian communist workers were neither Romanians nor workers. At Iasi: Dr. Ghelerter, Jew; Gheler, Jew; Spiegler, Jew; Schreiber, Jew, etc. At Bucharest: Ilie Moscovici, Jew; Pauker, Jew, etc. Around them, groups of lost Romanian workers.

Had the revolution been successful, the new president of the republic, the one that would have usurped the great King Ferdinand, would have been Ilie Moscovici. In Greater Romania's Parliament in 1919, while the deputies and senators of all reunited Romanian provinces, thrilled by the great act of the Union, stood up and applauded the unifier and great King, this Mr. Ilie Moscovici refused to stand up, conspicuously sitting down.

---

[12] Published in *The Conscience*, 30 August 1919.

The Attitude of the Jewish Press

It is necessary to underscore the attitude of the Jewish press in those perilous times for the Romanian people. Every time the Romanian nation was menaced in its existence, this press supported the theses that best suited our enemies. As in fact, following the events, it can easily be seen that the same theses were doggedly opposed any time they favored a movement of Romanian revival. For them, our worries were days of joy, while our joys for them were days of mourning.

Consider the following important themes:

FREEDOM
Freedom, so much today denied to the national movement, was back then considered dogma because it was to serve the cause of our destruction. Here is, for instance, what *The Truth* of 28 December 1919 wrote under the byline of Emil D. Fagure (real name Honigmann): "By granting the Socialist Party the right to freely demonstrate, one cannot maintain that said party is granted a privilege. No matter which party wants to demonstrate, this right will have to be respected..."

HATRED
We can read in the same paper: "Hatred must forever be the guide against the ruling party of murderers, headed by Ion Bratianu".[13] Judaic hatred of the Romanians is holy; it is supported; one invokes it. It is not a crime. It is not a medieval shame. But when it comes time for the Romanians to defend *their* infringed rights, their action is labeled "hatred," and hatred becomes a sign of barbarism, a debasing sentiment on which nothing can be built.

LEGAL ORDER
As we read in *The Truth* (5 October 1919):

> It is finished! By the 'high' decree-law, for the duration of the electoral period, a new regime is instituted, much rougher than before, one of siege and censorship, the opposition and the whole country being taken outside of the law. It is pure and simple, a regime of military dictatorship in which the Crown alone is all-powerful; the crown and the Liberal Party, and as an executor of these two wills, you have a government

---

[13] Romania's Prime Minister during WWI.

of generals… [T]hus the decree-law forbids us to attack the Crown. If telling the truth be taken as an attack, i.e., that the Crown took onto itself the heavy burden of governing the country with the Liberal Party, then still, we must make this attack.

The decree forbids us from attacking the present form of administration, if by this is understood that we have no right to protest with all vehemence against the present government which is the result of the unconstitutional will of two persons, we will protest...

If there is no other way open against this state of affairs, if we knew that the incitation to revolt or against the so-called legal order would have any effect—this unfortunately is not the case—we would not hesitate a single moment to do it, for there is no other means of fighting against such a dictatorial and tyrannical regime.

We consider ourselves facing an armed band which places itself outside the law and uses brutal force...

Despite all this, we will raise this banner and we will yet cry: "Down with tyranny," "Long live freedom."

This then is the Jewish press of 1919. In other words: inciting to rebellion against the Crown, against the form of government, and against the legal order.

INCITING REVOLUTION
As we read in *The Truth* (11 October 1919):

The madmen! Where are the madmen? … As we said, we have too many well-behaved men and no madmen. Or rather, madmen is what we need. Those of 1848 were madmen and they uprooted the boyars' 7 regime of the time .... We too, need madmen. With well-behaved men who split a hair into 14 strands, not arriving at a decision, there is nothing to be done. We need at least one madman, if not more of them. What is this madman going to do, how do I know? ..... One madman then is asked for. Let then the madmen come.

Even the socialists have become well-behaved. In reality, they have a party behind them and men who should fear no one. I see they are not afraid, but they are nevertheless well-behaved. As I. Nadejde did of old, they stubbornly stay within the legal framework. Those in power, 30 civilians and military, wish to take them out, a useless endeavor. Their tactic is the legal state. Even when they are shot at, as on 13 December 1918, when they are beaten to a pulp, when Frimu is lowered by his henchmen into his grave, the socialists protest-granted, with great dignity-but they do not step outside the law.

In any case, we need madmen. Let the madmen who would begin the illegal action, or that against the law, against today's state of affairs, come forward.

THE CROWN

To the Romanians, the Crown always constituted a dear patrimony. As the guarantor of our unity and resistance facing any dangers, the Jews never hesitated to attack it, to insult and compromise it by any means. Here is, for example, how *The Morning* of 16 November 1919 treats King Ferdinand:

An animal has need of limited preoccupations, but its brain suffices to fulfill them. Rarely, extremely rarely, is the animal wrong. Likewise, his intelligence, no matter how small, prevents it from falling into gross error.

It is not the same with the King. "I want to speak of the king of creation. "The king of creation is much more intelligent than a dog, a horse, an ass. This is certain. But whereas none of these animals would step off the edge of a precipice, would not throw themselves into the waters to drown or would not attempt an unsafe move, the king of creation daily commits unpardonable errors.....

Wisdom demanded that the King not permit himself to fall prisoner into the hands of a single man or party. "With all due respect I am duty-bound to tell His Majesty he erred. The situation which is so unclear is the work of His Majesty. For His Majesty, giving in to some guilty and interested obsessions, has run away from the natural solutions that the internal situation demanded. "If even today the crown will not decide to enter into the natural ways which are divorced from future interests, nature will exact its rights with even greater determination." Let the king of creation be advised.

THE CHRISTIAN CHURCH
As we read in *The Opinion* (10 August 1919):

> The nationalists of Iasi begin to agitate. There are too few of
> them and they are too scoundrelly, that is why their agitating
> which in times past was revolting, is today ridiculous, pure
> and simple. "The nationalists formed a 'Guard of the Nation-
> al Conscience.' Manifestoes were issued; meetings were
> held… Chauvinistic students were also invited. The custom-
> ary priests also came... At a time when everywhere, out of
> the most despotic laws, differences among nationalities are,
> being abolished, in our country nationalists want to accentu-
> ate these differences.... this particularly at the moment when
> the peace conference wants to impose by treaty the control of
> minorities....
>
> "When everywhere the church is being separated from
> the state, remaining the private concern of every individual,
> in our country the nationalists appeal to the clergy for orga-
> nized religious propaganda of principle...
>
> "Then the priest intervenes: he gently grasps the people
> by the hair of their heads and beats their foreheads against
> the stones of the church until they are dazed. It is in the
> church that the people learn humility and resignation. Such is
> the will of God.
>
> "No one is fooled by lies any longer. It is in vain that the
> nationalists pin tricolor bands on their sleeves, that they in-
> cite the plebeian intellectuals against the Jews, that they have
> the priests anathemize us in church. No one today fears their
> anathema.
>
> "We preach love among people. And kick at the door of
> the temples which shelter hatred and revenge...."
>
> Signed: M. Sevastos

THE PROCESSION
From *The Opinion* (26 October 1919):

> To the appeal of the 'Guard of the National Conscience,' the
> honorable clergy placed at the disposal of the demonstrators,
> their beards, vestments, and church banners.

"But the luxury of having at one's disposal a God with a whole staff must be paid for. We prefer that from our taxes a professor be hired, not a priest. We wish therefore the separation of church from the state. For we do not wish that our forced contribution serve to encourage obscurantism, renunciation and the spirit of resignation, thanks to which police regimes are maintains maintained.

"Back to the Middle Ages? To the Inquisition? We are exasperated by the terror in striped pants and tails, and military tunic, nor can we any longer tolerate the terror 32 wearing the religious habit. It hurts us to see street demonstrations prompted by political intrigues and the military, and no longer wish to witness parades of mitres and of red neckkerchiefs...

"Enough! The cupolas of the churches weigh heavily upon the shoulders of humanity; the prostrations pull it to the ground. This procession is going to be an insipid one. One will see on the streets museum vestments, brilliant-studded scepters, miters... Crosses will be seen, and stoles. Beards will pass, Orators with contorted gestures will bare their chests showing the crowd their bloodied side-sucking between teeth sponges soaked in vinegar..."

Signed: M. Sevastos

It is clear. From here to attacking officers and tearing off their stripes is but one step. Also one step to knocking down the churches with picks, or to their transformation into stables or places of sadistic parties for the little Jewish reporters from *The Opinion, The Truth, The Morning*, and their people. I saw in the columns of these newspapers, at a time of great Romanian hardship, all the hatred and foxy plotting of an enemy race, settled and tolerated here only by the pity of the Romanians. I saw how they flaunted their lack of respect for the Romanian Army's glory and for the hundreds of thousands who died in its sanctified uniform; their lack of respect for the Christian faith of an entire people.

No day passed without venom being poured into our hearts from each page. By reading those newspapers that burned my soul, I came to know the real feelings of these aliens, which they revealed without reticence, at a time when they thought we had been knocked to the ground. I learned enough anti-Semitism in one year to last me three lifetimes. One cannot strike the sacred beliefs of a people or what their heart loves and respects, without hurting them to the depths and without blood dripping from their wound. Seventeen years have passed since and the wound is still bleeding.[14]

May I be permitted once again to fulfill a sacred duty, mentioning here this hero, an athlete of Christian workingmen, the craftsman Constantin Pancu, under whose command I stood and by whose side I would stay until the "Red Beast," as he called it, was defeated. It is to this man—to his courage and steadfastness—that is owed the deliverance of the city of Iasi from destruction. Seven years later, this giant, weakened by suffering and poverty, was walking the streets of Iasi like a shadow, seeking aid for the treatment of a heart ailment. He died ill and poor, forgotten and unaided, in the midst of a country that cared not, and in a city that he defended with his own body in its most trying hours.

The First Student Congress after the War (Cluj, September 1920)

This congress was held in the National Theater in Cluj, in an atmosphere of great enthusiasm, as a result of the unification of the Romanian people by force of arms and their sacrifice. This was the first meeting of the young intellectuals of a people who had been, up to then, scattered to the four winds by destiny and misfortune. Two thousand years of injustices and suffering were coming to an end. What enthusiasm! How many sacred emotions! How many tears did we all shed!

But as great as our enthusiasm was for the present, which overwhelmed our hearts through its majesty, just as great was our disorientation with respect to what line to follow in the future. It was from this uncertainty that the Judaic power sought to profit, via pressure on the ministries. Masonry and compliant politicians placed on the congress agenda the possible admittance of Jewish students into the students' associations. In other words, they attempted to transform the Romanian associations into mixed Romanian-Jewish ones. The danger was serious: On one hand, Bolshevism was knocking at the door; on the other, the probability of being overwhelmed numerically by Judeo-communist elements in our own groups. In at least two of the groups, Iasi and Cernauti, the situation was tragic.

Despite this, the leaders of the congress—Labusca, the president of the Iasi student association, and his entire committee—and Nazarie, Bucharest's president with his whole committee and all associations; and Puscaru, Cluj's president, were all won over to this idea. Young students are influenced very easily, particularly when they lack a faith. They let

---

[14] That is, in 1936, the time of this writing.

themselves be lured, not so much by the immediate material advantages they might be offered, but more particularly by flattery and by the prospect of a great future they were promised. But the youth must know that, no matter what position he will hold, he is a sentinel in the service of the nation; permitting himself to be bought, flattered, or lured means a dereliction of duty, and could even lead to desertion or betrayal.

A small unofficial group of us from Iasi, unshakeable in our determination, and united with that of the Bucovinans, fought fiercely for two days. And ultimately we won. The congress passed the motion I proposed, by nominal vote, as opposed to the motion supported by the entire student leadership. I believe the congress voted thus not so much out of conviction as out of admiration for the determination and desperation with which our fight was conducted.

The students from Cernauti, no more than 60, behaved admirably. Our small group of Iasians, not more than 20, likewise. If we add the Ciochina group of 20, also from Iasi, the two-day battle was won by 100 versus 5,000.

That victory of ours was decisive. Had our point of view lost, the student associations would have also lost their Romanian character, and in contact with the Jews would have turned toward Bolshevism. The Romanian student body was at a great crossroad. And later, in 1922, we would not have had the eruption of a Romanian students' movement, but perhaps an eruption of the communist revolution.

The Opening of Iasi University in the Fall of 1920

In the other university centers, there was quiet. Only ours in Iasi was condemned to continuous struggle. For the first time in the history of Iasi University, the University Senate announced the opening of the academic year without the customary religious service. In order for someone to understand our sorrow, one must know that this solemn ceremony has been, without interruption, for half a century, the University's most beautiful event. This occasion embraced the entire University Senate, all professors, all newly-registered students, and the intellectual elite of Iasi. The service was always celebrated in the auditorium by Moldavia's Metropolitan or his vicar, blessing the start of a new year in the education of the Romanian people. But now our university was casting aside, by a gesture of the University Senate, this jewel of its half-century tradition.

Graver still, the university of our Christian Iasi, the highest institution of Romanian learning, was thus proclaiming, in those difficult times, a fight against God and the banishment of God from schools, institutions, and country. The university professors, excepting four or five known to oppose this trend, welcomed with great satisfaction the heathen decision of the Senate as a step forward, one that would take "Romanian science" out of "barbarism" and "medieval preconceptions."

Communist students were jubilant, Jewry triumphant. Meanwhile, a few of us pondered sorrowfully: we wondered how long it would be before churches were torn down and priests in their vestments crucified on their altars? About eight of us nationalist students knocked in vain at the doors of many of the professors, trying to convince them to rescind the Senate measure, but our repeated attempts failed.

And then, on the evening before the start of the academic year, we decided to take a grave step: we would forcibly oppose the opening of the university. In order to stay grouped, we all slept at No. 4 Suhupan St., the headquarters of our action. At six in the morning, Vladimir Frimu and my-self left for the university—the others were to follow. We closed and barri-caded the rear door of the university, leaving Frimu there to guard it. I put up a poster in red pencil on the large entrance door, reading, "I bring to the attention of the students and the professors that this university is going to open only following the traditional religious service."

The rest of our comrades came late—too late. Students started arriv-ing already at 8 o'clock. Alone at the entrance, I resisted until about 9:30, by which time over 300 students had gathered. When mathematics Profes-sor Muller wanted to force his way in, I told him: "You swore on the cross when you became a professor at this university. Why do you now raise yourself against the cross? You are a perjurer, because you had sworn on something you did not believe in, and now you break that oath."

Then the students, headed by Marin the communist leader and Hritcu and Ionescu from Botosani, dashed at me, opened the university's main entrance, took me into the lobby hitting me over the head with sticks and fists. No defense, no riposte was possible, for I was caught in the middle, pushed from all directions, getting blows from everywhere.

Finally, I was left alone. As I stood in a corner, reflecting upon the misfortune of my defeat, in came the six students. However, the victory of the enemy did not last very long, for shortly afterward, the university's secretary came down from the rectorate and posted the following notice: "It is brought to everyone's attention that the rectorate has decided that this university will remain closed until Wednesday, when it will open with the religious service." This was a great victory, one that we welcomed with unsurpassed joy.

Wednesday morning, two days later, in the auditorium filled to capacity by city people, the religious service was held. I was congratulated by everyone. Professor A. C. Cuza spoke with unsurpassed eloquence. It was at that moment that the belief took hold in me—and it has never left me—that one who fights for God and his people, even if alone, will never be defeated.

In the public opinion at Iasi, these battles, especially those at the Agency and the Railway Works, and lastly that at the university, have had a powerful echo. The enemy began to realize that Bolshevism cannot advance without serious obstacles, even when it is supported by nearly all the university's professors, the entire press, all Jewry, and the largest proportion of workingmen—while on the other side there is only a minimal group of youth opposing these huge waves, armed only with their great faith in the future of their country. These youth presented the barrier of their wills, comparable to some jagged rocks in the ground that one can easily see but cannot climb over without great pain. The enemies feared not so much us, but our determination. The sane part of the population, the Christian and Romanian Iasi, encouraged us and sympathetically watched us.

The 1920-1921 University Year

Begun in the conditions mentioned above, this year was an unending series of battles and clashes. We, the fighting students, organized ourselves around the student group "Stefan Voda," of which I was the president. From here we attacked our adversaries, defeating them time and again. Despising Romanian culture, they looked down upon the university and everything we had in this country with pretensions of being savants and advisors, like someone arriving from a great country upon this sinful and backward Romanian soil. They may have been right in certain points, but soon they would clash in our little country with a great centuries-old common sense, something that they in their large empire beyond the Dniester, proved never to have had at all.

At the university, meetings became impossible. No decisions could be made. The great majority of students were communists and their sympathizers. But they could not take one step forward because our group, never over 40, was always present; we attacked, and did not permit the airing of communist ideas and practices. When the communist student Spiegler was arrest, the communists attempted to implement a general strike at the university. But this failed after one day, thanks to our efforts. Our group occupied the mess hall, forbidding strikers entrance to meals on the grounds that "Whoever does not work, does not eat." All pleadings by the rector and the professors to convince us that these students ought to be permitted to enter for their meals, were made in vain.

Shortly thereafter, our group was to win another victory. Communist students were wearing Russian caps—not that they had no other caps, but as an ostentatious sign of affirming Bolshevism. On the occasion of a clash at the university, these caps were grabbed and burned in Union Square. Then daily, at the university, on the streets, through the pubs, the hunt began. All caps were burned. After one week, they completely disappeared.

Our group went even further and engaged the Judeo-communist press in battle. We had no printing presses to spread our word. Thus, following several disrespectful articles about the King, the Army, and the Church, our group, running out of patience, invaded the offices and printing premises of the newspapers *The World* (published by the Jew Hefter) and *The Opinion*, and wrecked the presses that had spewed poison and insult. We provoked disorder, no doubt, but those disorders would stop the Great Disorder: the irreparable disorder that the lackeys of communist revolution were preparing for our country.

But all this activity made me the principal object of their revenge. The Jewish press attacked us; I violently responded. Meeting the editors of *The Opinion* one day on the street, following a verbal exchange, after I demanded they account for their insults, we had a fight. My adversaries were soundly beaten up. But the next day, all newspapers in Iasi made a common front against me.

Expelled from Iasi University Forever

Things did not stop here. The university Senate took action immediately; it met and, without giving me a hearing, permanently expelled me from Iasi University. Finally, both the university and the city of Iasi would be rid of the disturber of the public order—someone who, for two years, disrupted the peace of the Judeo-communists and opposed all their endeavors to unleash a revolution for the dethronement of our king, the burning down of churches, the shooting of the officers, and the massacre of hundreds of thousands of Romanians. In the eyes of the university Senate, the communists were the men of order; and I was the disrupter of this order.

But their plans fell flat, because a truly unique event intervened in the ordinary course of our student life. The Council of the Law Faculty took issue with the expulsion pronounced by the Senate, led by Professor Cuza, its Dean, and Professors Matei Cantacuzino and Dimitrie Alexandrescu.

The Council's attempts to moderate the fury of the University Senate failed. The Senate did not rescind the expulsion order.

Then, a remarkable event: the Faculty of Law withdrew is representative from the Senate. They no longer opposed its decision and declared themselves independent. I was then informed by the Law Faculty that I could continue to attend classes, for the professorial council refused to recognize the decision of the University Senate. Thus, I continued to remain on as a student at Iasi University after all.

As a result of this incident, the council of the Faculty of Law refused to send its representative to the University Senate for three years. The conflict continued for years longer, even after I left the university. Later on, when I obtained my degree, the rectorate refused to issue my diploma. And to this day, they have not issued it. To register in the bar and to continue my studies abroad, I made use of the certificate issued to me by the Faculty of Law.

The 1921-1922 University Year

The new academic year opened under normal conditions—that is, with a religious service. Again, the university and the city of Iasi were in a festive mood. This great event passed almost unnoticed in Bucharest. There, when students arrive, their number is lost in the multitude of hundreds of thousands of people, in the noise, the lights, and the many conflicting interests. In Iasi, when students leave, a general melancholy descends on the city, as when the cranes and the birds leave in the fall. When students return, the youth returns, and the life. It is a holiday. In Bucharest, the student feels alone amidst an immense world that does not see him, does not appreciate him, has no interest in him, and does not love him. The student's education at Iasi bears no similarity to that at Bucharest; in Iasi, he develops like a child under the love of his mother, in the shelter of the Romanians' love. Here, the nation raises her students.

I myself owe this Iasi an important share of gratitude for anything that I was able to do in my life. I have always felt the concern that this spirit of Iasi held for me. I have felt the ray of its love, I have felt its admonition, encouragement, urging, its call to the fight. These are following us—the students of Iasi—even now, and they will follow us to the end of our lives, like the ever-present memory of my mother's urgings and love. Out of all the student generations who passed through Iasi, how many were not stimulated all their lives by Iasi's call to fight! How many were not accompanied all the way to their graves! How many are, even today, haunted by its reproaches!

It was noticeable at the beginning of the year that Judeo-Communism backed down, disoriented, its morale practically nil, and it put up no resistance. All the newly-enrolled students had heard of our battles and had, for a long time, been waiting to witness our side. Once here, they joined our ranks.

(1) President of the Law Students' Association

That fall, I was elected president of the Association of Law Students. The University Senate refused my validation on the pretext that I had been expelled from the university. I validated myself.

Our Law Students' Association, like the associations in all the other colleges, had as its purpose the scientific activity of completing and deepening studies in their respective fields. For instance, under the presidency of Nelu Ionescu, two years ahead of me, the Association held meetings almost every week. Some student read a book on law or a related field, condensed it, and in a meeting presented a critique. Competing discussions then took place.

I retained this general format but I also added something new. All these themes and reports could not be treated unless they delved scientifically into the Jewish Question. Works treating this problem in Romania and abroad were read, on international Jewish power, and on the history of this problem at home and abroad. We studied not only their methods of fighting us, but the Judaic spirit and mentality as well. We then proposed various means of fighting back and defending ourselves. Then, after each exposition, there followed discussions, completions, and lastly, the formulation of an established truth so that everyone could leave enlightened.

Furthermore, in the same meetings, we sought to accomplish: (a) the identification, at every step, of this Judaic spirit and mentality that have stealthily infiltrated the thought and feeling patterns of a large portion of Romanians; (b) our detoxification—namely, the elimination of Judaism that was introduced in our thinking through schoolbooks, literature, professors, lectures, theater, and motion pictures; (c) an understanding and unmasking of the Jewish plans hidden under so many forms. For we have political parties, led by Romanians, through which Judaism speaks; Romanian newspapers written by Romanians, through which the Jew speaks for his interests; and Romanian lecturers and authors, thinking, writing, and speaking Jewish in the Romanian language.

Studying all these, we began to realize that, for the first time in his history, the Romanian had come into contact with a people that uses slyness and deceit as weapons—as *national* weapons. The Romanian has always known only the honest fight. Faced with the new Jewish method, he was at a loss. We realized that everything comes down to knowing the enemy, and that as soon as we Romanians know him, we will vanquish him.

Our meetings continued regularly for the whole year. They attracted larger and larger numbers of students from other colleges, so that the General Association of the Iasi students became almost nonexistent. The entire student body gravitated around the activity of our law group. The auditorium became too small for the crowds of students who wished to take part in these meetings.

In particular, the Bessarabian students were participating in greater and greater numbers. One half-year of activity brought us a real miracle: three-fourths of the Christian Bessarabian students woke up, felt themselves called to a new life, and became enlightened. In a short time, they were to become the most faithful soldiers in our fight, reaching positions of leadership through faith, devotion, purity of heart, and spirit of sacrifice. This moment of brotherhood in the same faith and of pledging to fight for our Christian country against the Judaic hordes will never be forgotten. We who were fighting each other but yesterday, were now embracing.

The orienting material for our meetings were the writings of our national geniuses Bogdan Petriceicu Hajdeu, Vasile Conta, Mihail Eminescu, Vasile Alecsandri, etc. but especially the writings and lectures of Professor Cuza, the writings of Professor Paulescu, and the lessons in national education by Professor Gavanescul.

All the writings of Professor Cuza were read not only once, but three or four times, and they were studied carefully. Of special importance was his course in political economy, which brilliantly treated the Jewish Question from his prestigious position, asking Romanians to understand this as their gravest present problem. Our greatest good fortune, and that of Romanians, was thus having Professor Cuza at our institution—he was, indeed, one of the most knowledgeable men on the worldwide Jewish problem. It was thanks to him that we were able to orient ourselves to any Jewish maneuver. His courses, of the highest academic standard, were followed by all students with hitherto unprecedented attention. The auditorium of the School of Law always proved to be too small. For a long time to come, this University of Iasi will not have another professor with sermons on nationalism that will inspire the same enthusiasm.

During this time, for many of us, life began to reveal a unique purpose, above all other interests: that of fighting for our people, whose very existence was threatened.

(2) Visiting Cernauti University

At the other universities, quiet prevailed. Since the spring of the previous year, 1921, Cernauti witnessed stirrings around the Romanianization of the theater. Several days of fierce battle ended with the students' victory.

Now, in the spring of 1922, under the auspices of the Association of Law Students, I organized a visit of the Iasians to Cernauti. We were well received by both professors and students. We 100 visitors did nothing else for three days than impart to our colleagues in Cernauti the new faith that was taking shape in our souls. This was not difficult because Cernauti, just like Iasi only more so, suffered from a Jewish invasion, with its streets, its commerce, its dilapidated churches, its land, and its Romanians all groaning under Jewish domination. Briefly, a new and tight spiritual kinship was created between us, one based on a yearning and our common dream to see for once our people awakened to the consciousness of dignity, power, and rights as master of their own fate and that of their country.

This kinship then grew stronger through the visit repaid us by the Cemauti students one month later. It was then that I first met Tudose Popescu, that handsome figure of a young fighter who was later one of the 44 leaders of the student movement, but who today rests in a poor cemetery under a forgotten cross.

(3) The *National Defense*

On 1 April 1922, the bimonthly journal *The National Defense* was first published under the editorship of Professors Cuza and N. C. Paulescu. Anyone can imagine what the publication of this magazine meant for us in the midst of our thoughts and concerns. In it we found everything that we needed for our own full comprehension and useable arguments. The articles of Professors Cuza and Paulescu were religiously read by all the youth and had a resounding impact everywhere upon students, both in Bucharest and in Cluj. We considered the publication of each issue a triumph, because it was for us another munitions transport for combating the arguments in the Jewish press.

Below I reproduce two articles—a short one by Paulescu and a longer piece by Cuza.

The Divine Spirit of Truth will Forever Defend Mankind

As the politico-religious legislation of the Hebrews, the Talmud—unlike the Gospels, which oppose ownership and domination—by contrast pushes these vices to an unheard-of peak in order to accomplish Judah's dream of being at the same time both the owner of the entire earth and the master of all mankind.

But while the Christian apostles preached their ideal in the open, the Talmud hides; and its two appendages, the Qahal[15] and Freemasonry, are even more invisible. In order to remain in the dark, the three of them use a scabrous and accursed means, namely the lie. In other words, the lie is the basis of the system used by Jews, to whom one can say: 'You speak, therefore you lie.'

But the lie has a mortal enemy, namely the truth. The truth is the distinctive trait of Christianity. Christ said: "I am the truth" and that's why His doctrine is in hated by Israel. The lie, on the contrary, characterizes what is called the spirit of evil or of the Devil. Thus Jesus, speaking to the Hebrews, said to them:

> You are of your father the devil, and your will is to do your father's desires. He was a murderer from the beginning, and does not stand in the truth, because there is no truth in him. When he lies, he speaks out of his own character, for he is a liar and the father of lies. (John 8:44)

Leaving this world, Christ sent his disciples an invincible weapon, namely His Ghost—the divine spirit of truth, which will defend mankind forever against the devilish spirit of the lie. I bow before this Spirit of Truth, saying from the bottom of my soul: I believe in the Holy Ghost!

— Prof. Dr. N. C. Paulescu[16]

---

[15] The Qahal (or Kahal) is the collective Jewish community.
[16] From *Philosophic Physiology*, vol 2, 1913 (pp. 300-301).

The Science of Anti-Semitism

Another horrible pairing of words: the science of anti-Semitism. "How can anti-Semitism be a science?" asks the scientists, indignantly, with their mathematics, their symbols, their rocks, and their supposed 'fixed' ideas about culture.

Anti-Semitism? For these scientists, it is only a savagery, a blind manifestation of brutal instincts, vestiges of prehistoric times, the shame of our civilization, something which is condemned both by science and the enlightened conscience of man, free of preconceptions and passion.

This is the atmosphere created particularly by the Jews—and by the Judaized—around anti-Semitism, fooling the naive or exploiting the naivete of the stupid with pretensions that they too be 'on par with modern civilization.' And who does not want to be?

For example, there is this interesting case of a Judaized individual, himself half-Jewish, speaking several years earlier, with the air of a professional scientist, about our anti-Semitism, which was then, as it is today, unchanged. And here is what this author, Nomen Odiosum, tells us in *The Romanian Life* (November 1907, pp. 186, 204-207)—a man who was then a traitor of national thought as he was later a traitor of our national action during the war:

> I want to talk about the Jewish Question...totally de-natured by the vulgar and ferocious Judeophagy of our anti-Semites, who thus...compromise us before the civilized world... With rusted weapons dug out from the arsenal of medieval persecutions, with hatred propaganda, with impassioned incitement to excesses, with the stirring of bestial instincts in popular masses...one can only compromise a just cause—but the cause of anti-Semitism is not a just one...
>
> But, to give this conflict...a false air of persecuting a race, of religious persecution, in a word, of anti-Semitism, can serve only the enemy's cause, only too glad to exploit the divagations of some maniacs...

[Some] anti-Semitic scandalmongers, prematurely places on the order of the day the entire question...

No people, let alone our own, can fence itself in *ad infinitum* free of repercussions, against modern ideas, nor against external political action...

Therefore, to place our question in the realm of anti-Semitism, of racial hatred, means for us being led to a shameful and fatal defeat... Asiatic urgings...violent demagoguery, unhealthy agitation... [A]n endeavor of speculating dark passions...

I quoted this typical conception, typical of all who sold themselves to the Jews. And one sees what it comes down to: cliches ('the civilized world,' 'modern ideas'), and particularly to slander ('vulgar and ferocious Judeophagy,' 'rusty weapons,' bestial instincts,' 'divagations of some maniacs,' 'anti-Semitic scandalmongers,' 'Asiatic urgings,' 'dark passions'). We find such 'appreciations' not only coming from the vulgar Jew lovers but sometimes even from some otherwise distinguished representatives of culture in other fields.

Thus, for instance, the eminent jurist, university professor, orator, man of politics, and former minister of public instruction, Mr. A. C. Arion, attacked me because of my anti-Semitism, in the full session of the Chamber of Deputies, calling me a caveman.

As for the Jews, their explanation of anti-Semitism is more characteristic yet. In addition to the usual cliche "with hatred and savagery"—naturally with no motive, as they do not care to discuss motives—according to them, anti-Semitism is a madness, an intellectual degeneration, an affliction of the spirit. This is how we are considered by one of the most distinguished modern 'intellectuals' of the Jews, Dr. K. Lippe—he of illustrious origin as great-grandson of the famous commentator of the Talmud in the Middle Ages, Rashi,[17] who said *tob sebegoim barog* ("kill the best of the Goyim"). Lippe came our way from Galicia, settling down in Iasi where he served time in prison for having killed a woman while performing an abortion on her. He authored a special

---

[17] Lived in France, circa 1100 AD.

work in German entitled: *Symptoms of the Mental Illness: Anti-Semitism* (1887).

And as proof that the arguments used by the parasitic Jews against anti-Semitism are very poor and repetitive, just as are those of the Judaized, here is what *The Israelite Courier*, the official organ of the Union of Naturalized Jews, says in the editorial of its issue of 15 September 1922, under the slanderous title "A Band of Rascals":

> There exists with these anti-Semites a state of intellectual degeneration that reached the perversity of the senses, some kind of mental sadism by which those touched are pushed to lies and calumnies.

As you can see, this is a very simple explanation as well as an extremely naive one: all that is said against the Jews is lies and calumnies, due to a specific intellectual degeneration.

The definition of anti-Semitism—according to Jews and those Judaized—is, then, summed up in these two words, *savagery* and *madness*, naturally, of the so-called anti-Semites. As for the Jews as a social phenomenon, they do not even enter into this 'explanation'—as if they did not exist.

It was this "savagery" and "madness" that compelled all peoples of all time—Egyptians, Persians, Romans, Arabs, as well as the modern nations up to this day—to consider Jews as a national menace and thus to take measures against them. It was this "savagery" and "madness" that darkened the understanding of the most prominent representatives of the culture of all nations, such as Cicero, Seneca, Tacitus, Mohammed, Martin Luther, Giordano Bruno, Frederick the Great, Voltaire, Josef II, Napoleon I, Goethe, Herder, Immanuel Kant, Fichte, Schopenhauer, Charles Fournier, Ludwig Feuerbach, Richard Wagner, Bismarck, Rudolf Virchow, Theodor Billroth, Eugen Dühring—and countless others in all fields to come out against the Jews.[18]

Savagery and madness, finally, explains the anti-Semitism of the most distinguished representatives of our

---

[18] For a recent and comprehensive review of many of these individuals and their criticisms of the Jews, see T. Dalton, *Eternal Strangers* (2020).

culture, such as Simion Barnutiu, B. P. Hajdau, Vasile Alecsandri, Vasile Conta, and Mihail Eminescu.

Savage and mad: all these. Civilized and well-behaved:
those Judaized. And the Jews: nonexistent. And the venality
of those Judaized is incapable of explaining anti-Semitism as
a social phenomenon; thus we will call it The Anti-Semitic
Theory. According to this theory of ours, anti-Semitism may
be decomposed into three aspects: *instinct, consciousness,*
and *science.*

Instinct makes the masses—initially preoccupied by
immediate material interests—oppose Jewish parasitism
through popular movements. This is often times widespread
and bloody, as it was among many others all over, e.g., the
terrible movement of the Cossacks in the Ukraine led by
Bohdan Khmelnytsky in 1649, in which over 250,000 Jews
perished.[19]

Consciousness of the Jewish menace is awakened gradually, first in the educated classes. Then it spreads and pene-
trates the masses. The former group unites with the people in
supporting their demands. The latter thus become progressively aware themselves.

Science begins with sporadic research until it reaches—
only now, in our day—the determination of its objective:
studying Judaism as a social phenomenon, lifted out from the
medium in which it seeks to hide. Such a science determines
that this is a human problem, in fact the largest problem,
whose solution must be found.

We could say, by virtue of the conclusions reached by
partial studies so far, that they form the "anti-Semitism of
science." This is the basis, which is not to be confused with
the "science of anti-Semitism." What distinguishes these two
is their different objectives. And here is the definition as determined by the objective of this science, which clearly
demonstrates it to be a true science with its own domain: The
science of anti-Semitism has as its object Judaism as a social
problem; thus, it is necessarily a synthesis of all sciences that
can contribute to its solution. And this is the way in which

---

[19] Khmelnytsky (1595-1657) was a Ukrainian military leader. His 'uprising' of
1648-1649 included the massacre of up to 300,000 Jews.

the science of anti-Semitism uses its findings in order to arrive at a solution.

History establishes that, from the earliest times, the Jews have been a people wandering among others, nomadic and stateless. The science of anti-Semitism establishes that this nomadism is contrary to the well-being of agricultural, sedentary peoples and cannot be tolerated.

Consider five domains of science. *Anthropology* establishes that Jews are a mixture of unrelated races, as differing among themselves as the Semitic, Aryan, Negro, and Mongolian. The science of anti-Semitism explains the sterility of the Jewish nation in the domain of culture as a result of this mongrelization. It shows that this mongrel cannot contribute anything to the culture of other nations, which they only falsify by denaturing their characteristics.

Theology establishes that the Jewish religion is an exclusivist religion, based on the special covenant made between their God, Yahweh, and the Jews considered as a chosen, sacred people, apart from other. The science of anti-Semitism rigorously deduces that such a concept excludes the possibility of any peaceful cooperation or any assimilation with the Jews.

Politics establishes that everywhere within other nations, Jews have their unique social organization, constituting a state within the state.[20] The science of anti-Semitism concludes that Jews are an anarchic element, dangerous to the existence of all states.

Political Economy establishes that Jews have always lived, even in Palestine, as a superimposed people over other nations, exploiting their labor, while themselves producing nothing. The science of anti-Semitism says that any people

---

[20] Compare to Johann Fichte (1794): "Throughout almost all the countries of Europe there is spreading a mighty hostile state that is at perpetual war with all other states, and in many of them imposes fearful burdens on the citizens: it is the Jews. I do not think, as I hope to show subsequently, that this state is fearful—not because it forms a separate and solidly united state but because this state is founded on the hatred of the whole human race… Do you not remember the state within the State? Does the thought not occur to you that if you give to the Jews, who are citizens of a state more solid and more powerful than any of yours, civil rights in your states, they will utterly crush the remainder of your citizens?"

has the right to defend its productive labor from exploitation by Jews who cannot be tolerated, who live like parasites, jeopardizing peoples' existence.

Philosophy establishes that Judaism's concept of life is an anachronism contrary to human advancement. The science of anti-Semitism imposes, as a duty toward civilization, that this cultural monstrosity be eliminated by the united efforts of all nations.

The science of anti-Semitism bases its conclusions on what various, but differing, special sciences objectively established, all of which lead necessarily to the same conclusion: *the elimination of Jews from the midst of other people*, putting an end to their unnatural, parasitic existence that is due to an anachronistic concept opposed to the civilization and peace of all nations who can no longer tolerate it.

This anti-Semitic theory differs, as one can see, from the theory of the Jews and the Judaized, which reduced anti-Semitism to the two individual expressions—savagery and hatred. And in fact, the minute these two are manifested *en masse*, they become themselves a social problem.

The instinct of anti-Semitism can indeed sometimes be accompanied by savagery and hatred. For instinct is blind—so they say—though it is essential in defending life. The consciousness of anti-Semitism is added, however, to the instinct, enforcing its urges, no matter how 'savage.' For in order to be 'civilized' one must first exist.

The science of anti-Semitism finally arrives to explain this phenomenon, enlightening further the consciousness of people, fully satisfying their instinct and its violent eruptions, thus legitimized by revealing their cause—the parasitism of the Jews. Thus it gives us the formula of the scientific solution for the problem of Judaism.

Modern anti-Semitism, then, pools all energies: the energy of instinct, conscience, and science, of fully revealed truth. This creates a formidable social force, certainly capable of solving the greatest problem of civilization of our times, which is the Jewish problem.

And what do the Jews and the Judaized put up against this great power, seeking to prolong the detested existence of their parasitism? We have seen it: cliches, slander, and whims. "The vulgar Judeophagy of our anti-Semites," "they compromise us in the eyes of the civilized world," "Rusty weapons, dug out of the arsenal of medieval persecutions," "The stirring up of bestial instincts in the popular masses," "Asiatic urges," "madness," "mental sadism." These are the only arguments they oppose to our anti-Semitism, for they have no others, thinking they can do away with it by their stupidities.

And all the while, within all nations revolted by the nomadic Judah's parasitism, revenging energies reach the boiling point…"

— A. C. Cuza (15 Nov 1922).

(4) Founding the Association of Christian Students

On 20 May 1922, in a restricted meeting, we abolished the General Students Association of Iasi which was still in the hands of a remnant of adversaries supported by the rectorate. In its place, we founded "The Association of Christian Students" which is still alive today. We were a small group when we started, initially a student circle, evolving later into the Association of Law Students, and now finally, from our labors, a real general student association was being born under the name of the Association of Christian Students. This was a group for which the hearts of all the Iasi students were beating, but a different student body, unlike that of 1919.

By now, and not without considerable melancholy in my soul, following three years of battle and dear friendships hardened in the fire of so many trials, I was approaching the day of my departure from the university, from student life, and from my comrades in battle. I only had one month before taking my degree exam and I could not resign myself to the idea of having to leave—that we, the 1919 high school graduates, so tightly bound in heart, would scatter, God only knows to which corners of the country. That's why, after designating my successors, we comrades who felt ourselves closer together, took a vow aiming to fight no matter where we were, for the creed that bound us together while students at the university. We all signed this vow, placed it in a bottle, and buried it in the ground.

After I passed my degree exams, another vow was taken from a second group of 46 students, newer in battle. These were my guests in Husi where, for four days, we held meetings, clarifying in our minds the minutest details regarding our future activity. Here, my father spoke to my comrades on several occasions, urging them to fight. Then we parted ways, carrying in our soul the yearning for better and more just days for our people.

(5) Obligation of honor

We took the following vow:

> The undersigned students at the University of Iasi, realizing the difficult situation in which the Romanian people finds itself, menaced in its very existence by an alien people that grabbed our land and tends to grab the leadership of the country; *in order that* our descendants not wander through foreign lands, chased from their land by poverty and misery; *and in order that* our people not bleed under the tyranny of an alien people, *we determinedly rise* around a new and sacred ideal: that of defending our Fatherland against Jewish invasion.
>
> It is around this ideal that we formed the Association of Christian Students at the Iasi University.
>
> It is with this ideal in our hearts that we leave the school halls today. To fight wherever we may be, for our justice, for the threatened life of our people, we consider as our foremost honor-bound duty. That is why, congregated today, 27 May 1922, we pledge ourselves to a common obligation—one that, despite scattering throughout the country, we take with us everywhere the fire that animated us in the times of our youth, and to light in the saddened hearts of our people the torch of truth, that of their right to a free life in these lands.
>
> We shall maintain the closest contact with the Association that we leave behind today and in which we remain supporting members, it being the central point that shall always unite us in our common struggle. We will meet again in eight years, namely in 1930, May 1 to 14, at Iasi University. The Association's Committee will see to it that all members shall be notified two months before this day and will prepare for their arrival.
>
> We invite all student generations following us through this Association—those who show an understanding of consecrating their labor on the Fatherland's altar—to join us that year and that day at Iasi University.
>
> (signed) 27 May 1922, Corneliu Zelea-Codreanu of Husi.

(6) At the end of my university studies

At home, the three years spent at the university passed before my eyes. I asked myself: How could we overcome so many obstacles? How could we defeat the mentality, the will, of thousands of men? How could we vanquish university senates? How could we weaken the audaciousness of an entire enemy press? Did we have money to hire mercenaries, to publish papers, to go out into the countryside, to sustain this real war? We had nothing.

When I threw myself into that first battle, I did not do it because of someone else's urging, or as a result of some meeting, or some earlier decision that I was charged to execute, or even under the impulse of the great, prolonged, inner turmoil or deep thinking in which I had considered this problem. Nothing of the sort. I could not describe how I entered this fight. Perhaps it was as a man who, walking down the street with his worries and thoughts, is surprised by a fire that consumes a house, takes off his coat, and jumps to the aid of those engulfed by flames.

I, with the mind of a youth of 19-20 years of age, understood from all that I saw that we were losing our country, that we were no longer going to have a country, and that, by the unconscious collaboration of the poor and exploited Romanian workingmen, the ruling and devastating Jewish horde would engulf us. I acted on orders from my heart, from an instinct of defense possessed by even the lowest crawling worm—not out of an instinct for mere personal preservation, but one for defending the people of whom I was a part.

That's why, all the while, I had the feeling that the whole people was behind us—with all the living, with all those who have died for their country, and with its future generations. I felt that our people fights and speaks through us, and that the enemy numbers, no matter how large, faced with this historic entity, are but a handful of human wretches that we will scatter and vanquish. That's why all our adversaries have failed, beginning with the thoughtless university senates who, believing they were fighting a handful of crazy youth, in reality fought against their own people.

There exists a law of nature that puts everyone in his place. Rebels *against* nature—from Lucifer to the present day, all these rebels, oftentimes very intelligent, though always lacking wisdom—have fallen thunderstruck. Within the framework of this natural law, of this wise order, anyone can fight; everyone has the right to fight for betterment. Outside it, against it, over this order, no one can go unpunished and unvanquished.

In the human organism, blood cells must remain within the body's framework and in its service. A rebellion would exist not only if a cell were to rouse itself against the organism but also when it would do even less, namely, when it would be in its own employ, when it would only satisfy itself, when it would have no other purpose and ideal outside itself—in other words, when it became its own God.

The individual lives within the framework and in the service of his people. The people lives within the framework and in the service of their God and of God's laws. Whoever understands these things will be victorious even if he is alone. Whoever does not understand will be defeated. I finished my final university year under the reign of these thoughts.

From an organizational viewpoint, we had settled on the idea of leader and discipline. Democracy was excluded, but not out of speculation or theoretical conviction. We had lived anti-democracy from the very start. I always led. In three years, it was only once that I was elected president of the Association of Law Students. At all other times, it was not the fighters electing me leader, but I choosing them to follow me. I never had committees and I never put propositions to a vote. However, whenever I felt a need, I consulted with everyone. But I took decisions on my own responsibility.

That's why our small group was always an unshakeable unit. Factions of divided opinions, majorities or minorities, clashing among themselves on questions of action or theory, did not exist. With all the other groups, the opposite was true. That's why they fell defeated.

One great faith, like a flame continuously burning in our hearts, lighting our way; a great and unforgettable love for one another; a great discipline; decisive action during battle; and a balanced weighing of the battle plan—these things, along with our Fatherland's blessing and God's, assured us of victory for those three years.

(7) The summer of 1922

The summer of 1922 did not pass peacefully. On the stages of Romanian national theaters or communal ones in Moldavian towns, Jewish plays began to be performed in Yiddish. We youth considered this a threat, for we saw a beginning of the alienation of the theater, which was meant to be for the national and moral education of the Romanian people. Alienated in commerce, industry, in the richness of the Romanian soil and subsoil, and in the press, we will one day see ourselves also alienated from the stages of our national theaters.

The theater, together with the school and the church, can elevate a decayed nation to the consciousness of its rights and historical mission. It can prepare and motivate a nation to liberating struggle. Now even this stronghold will be taken away from us. Our theaters, which were built by the Romanians' sweat and money, will serve Jewry for the preparation and strengthening of their forces in the fight against us. And, on the other hand, from these Romanian stages, the Jews will serve up to us Romanians, as "spiritual nourishment," everything that will contribute to our national demoralization, moral decadence, and destruction.

It was the duty of others—namely, the government, or any authority, or the professors—to take a stance against this new anti-Romanian attack. But none was taken. Only we youth reacted as best we could, risking blows, being showered with countless insults, finding no support anywhere.

This struggle was pursued in every town: Husi, Bariad, Botosani, Pascani, and so on, by the group of Iasian students who were everywhere helped by high school students. They entered halls full of Jews, throwing anything they could grab at Satan's artists, thus chasing them off the Romanian stage. Perhaps, some may say, it was in an uncivilized manner. I too, say, perhaps.

However, how civilized is it that an alien nation dispossesses me of all the goods of my country, one by one? How civilized is it that the same nation poisons my culture, then serves it up on the stage to kill me? To what extent were the means used by Jews in Russia civilized?[21] How civilized is it to slaughter millions of people without trial? To what extent is it civilized to set fire to churches or to transform them into cabarets?

For myself, in my poverty and with my limited powers, I defend myself against such an assault as best I can—by the printed word, if I can; with the aid of authorities, if they are still Romanian; by voice, if someone listens; by force, as a last resort, and if everyone keeps quiet. Unworthy and traitorous is he who does not defend his country, either because of selling out, or because of innate cowardice, or who simply does not react in any way.

Anyway, this fight was a protest—the only protest amidst a cowardly and terrifying silence. The next day, our comrades returned, full of blows and wounds, for it was no easy matter for a group of 15 youth to enter a theater with 3,000 or 4,000 Jews; and especially when they returned borne down with the opprobrium and invectives from our own Romanians. Many a time, I ask myself: What kept us going, such a small group, faced with so many blows, so many rebukes heaped upon us from all directions? We found no support anywhere. In this fight against everyone, we found the

---

[21] During the Bolshevik Revolution, when thousands, even millions, of ethnic Russians were killed.

only support in ourselves; in our belief that we were on the great path of our national destiny, side by side with all those who fought, suffered, and died as martyrs for our land and its people.

(8) In Germany

I returned to Iasi in the fall of 1922. There, I shared with my comrades an old thought of mine: that of going to Germany to continue my studies in political economy, while at the same time trying to realize my intention of carrying our ideas and beliefs abroad. We realized very well, on the basis of our studies, that the Jewish problem had an international character, and the reaction therefore should have an international scope; that a total solution to this problem could not be reached except through action by all Christian nations, awakened to the consciousness of the Jewish menace.

But I had neither money nor clothing. My comrades got me some clothes and they borrowed 8,000 lei from engineer Grigore Bejan, which they were to repay monthly, each contributing according to his ability. With this money in hand, I left for Berlin, accompanied to the station by all those from whom I parted, who now were staying behind at home to fight on.

When I arrived in Berlin, two student friends, Balan and C. Zotta, were of great help. I registered at the university. On registration day, I donned my national costume and went to that beautiful ceremony wherein the rector, following an old tradition, shakes the hand of each new registrant. In the university's halls, I was the subject of general curiosity because of my Romanian costume.

Two questions in particular might interest the reader, regarding Germany of 1922: a look at the general situation there, and the status of the anti-Semitic movements.

The wounds left by a war just ended in defeat were still raw and bleeding. Material misery blanketed both Berlin and the rest of the country alike. Lately the Ruhr valley, an important center of riches, had been occupied too. I witnessed the vertiginous and catastrophic downfall of the German mark.[22] In the workingmen's quarters, there was a lack of bread, lack of foodstuffs, and lack of work, while hundreds of children were accosting passers-by, begging.

The fall of the mark also threw the German aristocracy into the same misery. People who had money were, in a few days, left penniless. Those

---

[22] The Jewish-dominated Weimar Germany suffered extreme hyperinflation between 1921 and 1923, effectively wiping out the savings of millions.

who sold their land and real estate holdings, being attracted by the mirage of high prices, became impoverished in the course of a few weeks. Domestic and foreign Jewish capitalists closed colossal business deals. Those possessing strong currency became owners of huge buildings of 50 apartments for only a few hundred dollars. Speculators combed through the entire city, scoring formidable coups.

Sharing this great misery were also many foreigners, among them myself, for I had no money at all. The 8,000 lei I came with were spent. Then came the hunger. But in the midst of general suffering, your own suffering is easier to bear.

Being a type who does not bend easily when faced by difficulties, I did not submit to misery but tried to fight it. I studied all possibilities and decided to engage in commerce. I needed a very little capital to procure a stock of food items in the countryside, to bring them into Berlin to sell to restaurants. This idea inspired me to move to Jena before the holidays, where life was cheaper. There, in the midst of the misery in which the German people struggled, I was impressed by their spirit of discipline, their capacity for labor, sense of duty, rectitude, power of resistance, and faith in better days. They were a healthy people, one that would not permit itself to be knocked down and that would, with unsuspected powers, resurrect itself from under the rock of all the difficulties burdening it.

The anti-Semitic movement. There were in Germany several anti-Semitic political and doctrinaire organizations, with papers, manifestos, and insignia—but all of them feeble. Students in Berlin, as those in Jena, were divided in hundreds of associations but numbered very few anti-Semites. The student mass knew the problem only vaguely. One could not speak of an anti-Semitic student action or even of a doctrinaire orientation similar to that of Iasi. I had many discussions with the students at Berlin in 1922, who are certainly Hitlerites today, and I am proud to have been their teacher in anti-Semitism, imparting to them the truths I learned in Iasi.

I heard of Adolf Hitler for the first time around the middle of October 1922. I went to visit a worker in North Berlin with whom I established a good relationship, who was making "swastikas." His name was Strumpf and he lived at 3 Salzwedeler Strasse. He told me: "They say that an anti-Semitic movement has been started in Munich by a 36-year-old painter, Hitler. It seems to me he is the man we Germans have been waiting for." The foresight of this worker was fulfilled. I always admired his intuitive powers, by which he could select, with the antennae of his soul, a stranger among scores of men, ten years before his time, the one who would succeed in 1933, uniting the entire German people under a single great command.

It was also in Berlin at that time that I heard the news of the huge Fascist eruption: the march on Rome and Mussolini's victory. I rejoiced as much as if it were my own country's victory. There is, among all those in various parts of the world who serve their people, a kinship of sympathy, as there is such a kinship among those who labor for the destruction of peoples. Mussolini, the brave man who trampled the dragon underfoot, was one of us, which is why all dragon heads hurled themselves upon him, swearing death to him. For us, the others, he will be a bright North Star giving us hope; he will be living proof that the hydra can be defeated; proof of the possibilities of victory.

"But Mussolini is not anti-Semitic. You rejoice in vain," whispered the Jewish press into our ears. It is not a matter of what we rejoice in, say I; it is a question of why you Jews are dismayed at his victory, if he is not anti-Semitic. What is the rationale of the worldwide attack on him by the Jewish press? Italy has as many Jews as Romania has Csangos[23] in the Siret valley. An Italian anti-Semitic movement would be as if Romanians started a movement against the Csangos.

But had Mussolini lived in Romania, he could only have been anti-Semitic, for fascism means, first of all, defending your nation against the dangers that threaten it. It means the destruction of these dangers and the opening of a free path to life and glory for your nation. In Romania, Fascism could only mean the elimination of the dangers threatening the Romanian people, namely, the removal of the Jewish threat and the opening of a free way to the life and glory to which Romanians aspire.

Judaism has become master of the world through Masonry, and in Russia through Communism. Mussolini destroyed these two Judaic heads that threatened death to Italy. There, Judaism was eradicated through its two manifestations. In our country, it will have to be eradicated through what it is there: Jews, communists, and freemasons. These are the thoughts that we, the Romanian youth, oppose to Judaic endeavors to deprive us of joy in Mussolini's victory.

The Student Movement (10 December 1922)

I was still in Jena when, one day, I was surprised by the news that the entire Romanian student body from all universities arose to battle. This col-

---

[23] The Csangos are a Catholic group of ethnic Hungarians living in Moldavia.

lective demonstration of the Romanian youth, unsuspected by anyone, was a volcanic eruption rising from the nation's depths. It first manifested itself in Cluj, the heart of that Transylvania that took a stand any time the nation experienced an impasse. It then almost concomitantly erupted, violently, in all other university centers.

In fact, on December 3rd and 4th, great street demonstrations took place in Bucharest, Iasi, and Cernauti. The entire Romanian student body rose to its feet, as in a time of great peril. For the thousandth time, this earthy race, menaced so many times throughout history, threw up its youth to face the threat in order to save its being. A great collective electrifying moment, with no preparation beforehand, without any pro and con discussions, without any committee decisions, without those in Cluj even knowing those in Iasi, Cernauti, or Bucharest. It was a great moment of collective enlightenment, like the lightning in the middle of a dark night, in which the entire youth of the country recognized its own destiny in life as well as that of its people.

This destiny runs brightly through our entire national history. It extends into our whole Romanian future, pointing the way to life and honor—both things that we and our grandchildren will have to follow, if it is life and honor we wish for our people. Generations can follow this destiny, can stay close to it or depart from it, having thus the capability of giving to their nation a maximum of life and honor or a maximum of dishonor and shame.

Sometimes only isolated individuals, abandoned by their generation, can reach this destiny. In that moment, they *are* the people, they speak in its name. All the millions of dead and all of the martyrs of the past are with them, as well as the nation's life of tomorrow. Here, the majority, with its opinions, does not matter, though it might be 99 percent. It is not the opinions of the majority that determine this destiny of life for our people. They, the majorities, can only get nearer or farther away from it according to their state of consciousness and virtue or that of unconsciousness and decadence.

Our people have not survived by the millions of Romanian slaves who put their necks under the foreigner's yoke, but through Horia, Avram Iancu, Tudor, and Iancu Jianu, who, faced by the alien yoke, did not submit but put their muzzle-loaders on their backs, heading up the mountain paths, carrying with them honor and the spark of freedom. It was through them that our people spoke, not through cowardly and well-behaved "majorities." They would conquer or die, no matter what. For when they die, the whole people lives from their death and is honored by their honor. They shine in history like golden beacons on the heights, bathed at sundown in the sun's rays; while over the vast lowlands, no matter how extensive and numerous, settles the darkness of forgetfulness and death. The one who belongs to our national history is not he who *wins* by sacrificing the destiny of his peoples' lives, but only he who, whether he wins or loses, holds himself to this destiny.

Our Romanian destiny is predetermined by God's wisdom; this could be seen on December 10, in the Romanian students. And it is in this that the value of the day resides: the entire Romanian youth saw the light. On December 10, delegates from all student centers congregated in Bucharest, establishing, in ten points, what they thought formed the essence of their movement. They then declared a general strike for all universities, demanding the realization of these points. December 10 is not great through the value of the formulation of points agreed upon, as much as the delegates could formulate of the truth's essence that then troubled the entire Romanian youth. It is great by virtue of the miracle of this youth's awakening to the light its soul had seen; by its decision for common action to declare the holy war that was to demand so much strength of heart, so much heroism, so much maturity, so much known and unknown sacrifices, and so many graves! December 10, 1922 called the youth of this land to a great test.

Neither those in Bucharest, nor I who was far away, nor others who were perhaps high school students, but who today languish in so many prisons or sleep under the earth, could believe that this day would carry us through so much danger, and would bring us so many blows and so many wounds in battles to defend our country.

In Bucharest, Cluj, Iasi, and Cernauti, formidable eruptions of student masses took place, which, led by their own power of intuition—not by leaders—turn toward the enemy.

They eye first the Jewish press: *The Truth, The Morning, The Redemption, The Opinion*, and *The World*—hot-beds of moral infection, poison, and confusion for the Romanians. They turn to these in order to destroy them, but also to show the Romanian people the danger of the enemy's front line, against which they must be on guard. Demonstrating against the press means: declaring it an enemy of national interest and thus calling the attention of Romanians so that they not permit themselves to be fooled, blinded, or led by the press written by Jews or Judaized Romanians. This press attacks the religious idea, thus weakening Romanian moral resistance and breaking their contact with God. This press disseminates anti-national theories, weakening faith in their nation and separating them from their country's land, of their love for it—land that was, at all past times, an urge to battle and sacrifice.

This press falsely presents our Romanian interests, disorienting people and directing them onto paths opposed to national interests. This press elevates mediocre elements and corrupt men, so that the alien can satisfy his interests, and downgrades the moral people who will not stoop to doing favors for Judaism and its interests. This press poisons the soul of the nation, daily and systematically publicizing sensational crimes, immoral affairs, abortions, and adventures. This press murders truth and serves up lies with diabolical perseverance, using slander as a weapon to destroy Romanian fighters. That is why Romanians must be careful when they read a Jewish paper, being on guard against every word, not one of which is haphazardly printed; they must strive to decipher the Jewish plan behind it.

It was these matters that the student movement wanted to call to the attention of all Romanians when it turned against Jewish editorial offices, declaring them enemies of the Romanian people. I emphasized that the formidable eruptions of the student masses were led by their power of intuition and not by leaders. It's easy for someone to direct several individuals towards someone's house to stage a hostile demonstration, but when great multitudes turn on someone with hostility by command of their instinct, then that person is condemned, with no right of appeal, as an enemy of the nation.

The "Numerus Clausus"

The phrase *numerus clausus* passes from mouth to mouth during student battles, but not as a saving formula; masses do not issue phrases, they point out threats. *Numerus clausus* means that the Jewish menace, being great in numbers, can no longer be supported, either in schools, in commerce or industry, or in the independent professions. "Attention to their great number" is what *numerus clausus* intends to say, for it exceeds our powers of national resistance; if we do not take any measures, we die as a people. This is the whole value of this formula. Or, if you wish, as a saving measure, it has the value of an emergency formula, of necessary first aid, though totally inadequate to cure the illness.

Numerus clausus per se, means: the limitation of Jews in schools, professions, etc. To what numbers? To the proportion between the number of all Jews in relation to that of Romanians within Romania. Namely, if there are 15 million Romanians and 3 million Jews, the proportion is 20%. According to the *numerus clausus* formula, Jews are to be admitted into schools, medical professions, the bar, etc. in the proportion of 20%.

Numerus clausus is thus only a formula of redistribution of the Jews within nations, and not a formula for resolving the problem. This formula resolves almost nothing, for it addresses proportions but does not cut down the high number of Jews. If the Jews are 3 million, that is what they remain. Especially it does not treat the cause of this high proportion and does not show the means by which it can be diminished; in sum, it does not constitute the means for resolving the Jewish problem.

CHAPTER 2

THE JEWISH PROBLEM

The Number of Jews

The large number of Jews raises a series of problems:

1. The problem of the Romanian land;
2. The problem of the cities;
3. The problem of the Romanian school and of the leading class;
4. The problem of national culture.

All these are impeccably treated by Professor A. C. Cuza in his writings: *The Peoplehood, Nationality in Art, Articles, Parliamentary Discourses,* and *Course in Political Economy.* The ideas that I give below belong essentially to Professor Cuza's thought.

The number of Jews in Romania is not known exactly. This is because the statistics were taken were with the greatest lack of interest on the part of Romanian politicians so that they could cover up their work of national treason, and because Jews everywhere run away from the truth of statistics. A proverb says: "Jews live by lies and die when coming in contact with truth." As a matter of fact, for a long time, the Director of the State's Statistics in the Ministry of Finance had been a Jew, Leon Colescu, real name Leon Coler.

And from their viewpoint, they are right; if Romanians were faced with the exact number of the Jewish population, they would realize they are confronted by a real national menace and would rise up to defend their Fatherland. In other words, in the face of statistical truth, Judaic power flickers out and dies. It can live only by hiding the truth, falsifying it by lies.

We believe that there are from 2 to 2.5 million Jews in Romania.[1] If there were but one million—as they claim—the Romanian people would still face mortal danger. This is true because it is not only the number per se that matters, the quantity, but also the quality of that number; particularly

---

[1] In a population of around 16 million Romanians. If Codreanu is correct, that would mean a Jewish percentage of around 15%—astonishingly high. Figures for Iasi at that time are as high as 45% Jewish. Modern sources, however, estimate only some 750,000 Jews in Romania in the 1920s, rather than 2 million or more.

important are the positions occupied by Jews in the functional structure of the state and in the life of the nation in all its aspects.

Our land has been a land of invasions. But it has never, throughout its long history, known an invader to reach such formidable numbers as those of the present-day Jew. Past invasions eventually ended; the present-day invaders never leave. They settle down here on our land in greater numbers than ever before and hold on like scabies to this land's body and people.[2]

When did this Jewish invasion begin? Only several thousand Jews were found around 1800 in all of Moldavia. In 1821, there were 120 families in Bucharest. Such late settlement on our land is due to the fact that Jews have always engaged in commerce, and commerce demands freedom and security in which to develop. But two conditions were lacking in Romania: a lack of freedom to exploit Romanian soil, and a lack of stability and security. Romanian land was the most insecure land in the world. The Romanian peasant had no security of home, cattle, his labor, or his crops from year to year. Our country was ravaged by invasions, serving as a theater of war for centuries, oftentimes with the aftermath of foreign domination and bloody tribute. What was Jewry to do on this land? Fight the Huns, Tartars, and Turks?

The Jewish invasion began only 100 years ago. As a result of the peace of Adrianople in 1829, freedom of commerce was granted and visions of a more peaceful life began to appear. It was then that their invasion began, increasing year by year over our Romanian heads, especially those of the Moldavians, draining us of wealth, destroying us morally, and threatening us with extinction.

In 1848, Moldavian merchants and industrialists began to complain to Mihail Sturza, the ruler, demanding measures be taken against Jewish merchants and their dishonest competition. Since then, the invasion has steadily increased. 'Invasion' may not be the right term, for it presupposes the idea of violence, and of moral and physical courage. 'Jewish infiltration' is a more suitable term, for it better encompasses the idea of sly penetration—cowardly and perfidious penetration. For it is no small matter to steal the land and wealth of a people without justifying it through battle, through risk-taking, and through great sacrifice.

Little by little, they took over Romanian small commerce and industry; then, by using the same fraudulent tactics, they attacked big commerce

---

[2] With the coming of World War Two, Jewish numbers in Romania dropped precipitously, by half or more. Today there are only some few thousand Jews in the entire nation.

and big industry, thus acquiring control over the towns in the northern half of the country.

The attack on the Romanian middle class was conducted with a precision found only in the case of some predatory insects, which, to paralyze the enemy, sting it in the spine. They could not have chosen a more suitable spot. Successfully attacking the middle class meant breaking the Romanian people in two. It is the only class having a double contact: *down*, with the peasant class, being superimposed on it and exercising authority over it; and *up*, with the governing class that it supports on its shoulders. A successful attack on the middle class, namely its destruction, brings in its wake: a) The collapse of the ruling class, b) The impossibility of its reconstitution, and c) The confusion and animalization, the vanquishing and enslavement, of the peasant class.

In the last analysis, the Judaic attack on the Romanian middle class means death. The death of the Romanian people does not mean the death of the last Romanian, as some imagine. This death means life in slavery— the lowering to slave life of several million Romanian peasants, who would work for Jewry.

Here are the findings of Professor Nicolae Iorga regarding the number of Jews and their arrival in our parts. Professor Iorga in his paper "The History of Jews in our Principalities," delivered before the Romanian Academy on 13 September 1913, which exposed this question, he states, among other things:

> [I]n Neamt, several Jews settle on the lands of the Monastery between 1764-1766... In Botosani, no ruler's document like that of 1757 mentions Jews among the other inhabitants of the town. ... Sometimes a Jew pops up in Suceava as tavern-keeper on church land; others as small merchants in Ocna, Harlau, Siretiu, Galati, Barlad (there was a time when one could say that Christian Barladians were engaged in commerce more than in any other occupation)... [T]hen in Roman, where in 1741 only 'Moldavians' and 'Armenians' were known; in Targul Frumos, where two taverns and a Jewish one are mentioned as existing there in 1755.

In Bucovina about the time of its annexation in 1775:

> In the regions of Cernauti and Campulung, to which were annexed parts of Hotin and Suceava before the Austrian

imperial domination, there were only 206 'Jewish' families. ... In 1775, through overflow from Galicia, their number reached 780-800 families. ... The country's first governor, Gen. Ehzenberg, learned that they engage primarily in tavern-keeping, with wine, whiskey, beer... They are, says the general, "the most outright wicked people, inclined to laziness, living, without much trouble, from the sweat of Christian workingmen."

A commission operating in 1781 shows that:

In this country, Jews are in the habit of buying from the peasant the chick in the egg beforehand, the honey in flower, and the lamb in its mother's womb, for a pittance; and through this usury entirely sucking the inhabitants dry, bringing them to poverty, so that the peasants, thus burdened by indebtedness, find no recourse for the future to save themselves but by fleeing from the country. ... We see the administration of this country (Moldavia), then the boyars, particularly Constantin Moruzi, desperately defending themselves against them. ... The Qahals offered Enzenberg, in writing, 5,000 pieces of gold annually to tolerate the old state of affairs... Corrupting our Ruler was also tried, but he rejected the money rather than expose his country to total destruction.

And later, around 1840-48, this is what Professor Iorga determines:

One could count these establishments of exploitation and depravation by the score, tavern by tavern, with bottles of potato whiskey and other poisons, all across Moldavia, exhausting a race, for the feeding of the civilized vices of the domineering class.

And Professor Iorga writes on:

Still, the intervention by foreigners, fostered by Jewish elements in the country, did not cease. In 1878 they imposed conditions before they would recognize Romania's independence (won with so much sacrifice of Romanian blood) and heaped indignities on independent Romania that cannot but commit suicide by politically yielding half of itself to the power of the Moldavian Jews... And as Kogalniceanu defended villages from Jewish alcohol and usury, so Mr. Maiorescu defends Romania's dignity from the insult of granting civil rights to foreigners in the country as a result of the pressures of their coreligionists abroad.

I cite these examples as reported by a great, recognized, and uncontested scientific authority, to clarify the start of Jewish settlements on Romanian soil.

I now turn to the four problems cited at the beginning of this chapter.

1) The problem of Romanian land

There cannot be any people in this world, even a tribe of savages, that, faced by a foreign invasion, would not consider the predicament of its land. All peoples of the world, from history's beginnings to this day, have defended the soil of their Fatherland. The history of all peoples, as ours, is replete with battles in defense of its land. Would it be an anomaly, a state of illness of ours, the Romanian youth, that we stand to be counted in the defense of our menaced land? Or an anomaly if we did not defend it when we see it endangered? It would be an anomaly for us *not* to defend it, namely, not doing what all nations have done. Placing us in contradiction to the entire world and our entire history would be an anomaly and a state of illness.

Why is it, I wonder, that all peoples have fought, and will always fight, for the defense of their land? Land is a nation's basis for existence. The nation has its roots, like those of a tree, deep in the country's soil whence it derives its nourishment and life. There is no people that can live without land, as there is no tree which can live hanging in air. A nation that has no land of its own cannot live unless it settles on the land of another nation—on its very body, sapping its sustenance. There exist God-given laws that ordain the life of peoples. One of these laws is the territorial law. God gave each people a definite territory to live and grow in, and on which to develop and create its own culture.

The Jewish problem in Romania, as elsewhere, consists of the infringement by Jews on this natural law of the territory. They trespassed on our territory. They are the violators; and it is not we, the Romanian people, who are called to bear the consequences of their infraction. Elementary logic tells us: the infractor must bear the consequences of the committed infraction. Will he have to suffer? Let him suffer! All infractors suffer. No logic in the world will tell me that I should die for the infraction committed by others.

Thus, the Jewish problem is not born of "racial hatred." It is born of an infraction committed by Jews against the laws and natural order in which all peoples of the world live.

The solution to the Jewish problem? Here it is: *the re-entry of violators into the universal natural order and their respecting natural law.*

But the laws of the land too, prohibit the Jewish invasion. Article 3 of the Constitution says: "The territory of Romania cannot be colonized by a population of foreign origin." What does the fact of two million Jews settling on Romanian territory mean, if not colonization? But this territory is the inalienable property of the Romanian people. And as someone wrote, not after 50, not after 100, but even thousands of years later, we will claim the right over this land, as we reconquered the Transylvanian land following 1,000 years of Hungarian occupation.

2) The problem of the cities

Within the breadth of this Romanian land, Jews did not settle just haphazardly. They placed themselves in towns, forming within them real islands of compact Jewish populations. At first it was the cities and market towns of northern Moldavia that were invaded and conquered: Cernauti, Hotin, Suceava, Dorohoi, Botosani, Soroca, Burdujeni, Itcani, Briceni, Secureni, etc. The Romanian merchant and tradesman gradually disappeared—today one street, tomorrow another, the day after tomorrow, a whole neighborhood. In less than 100 years, Romanian centers of ancient renown lost their Romanian character, taking on the likeness of real Jewish fortresses. Other Moldavian towns too, fell quickly: Roman, Piatra, Falticeni, Bacau, Vaslui, Bariad, Husi, Tecuci, Galati.

Even Iasi, the second capital of Moldavia—after the first one, ancient Suceava—was purely and simply turned into a dirty Jewish nest that surrounds the poor glorious ruins of Stefan the Great's fortress. In Iasi now, one can walk through whole streets and sectors never meeting a Romanian, or seeing a Romanian home or a Romanian store. People pass by famous churches, today in ruins and decay: the Church of Talpalari, built by the Romanian cobblers' guild, and the Church of Curelari, built by the Romanian harness-makers' guild. Everything is falling apart. In that large city of Iasi, there is no longer a Romanian cobbler or harness-maker.

The Church of St. Nicholas the Poor of the old Moldavian nobility has totally collapsed; and over the tombs around it, the Jewish eating places discard their slop, garbage, and refuse. The Church in Main Square, where one finds the greatest agglomeration of people, is closed, due to lack of churchgoers.

And it is the Jewish population that constitutes that agglomeration of people now.[3] On Lapusneanu St., Cuza Voda's palace, which almost groans as if in pain, has been transformed into a Jewish bank, and in its former garden a Palestinian-style Jewish theater can be seen. The foreign invader tramples underfoot everything we hold most sacred. Our hearts groan in anguish.

We youth, our souls rent, ask ourselves: How could there be Romanians who behave with so much enmity toward their people? How could there be so many traitors? How come they were not lined up against the wall or burnt alive at the moment of their betrayal? How come everyone is impassive? How come we do nothing? These are problems of conscience that weigh upon us, that disturb our souls and upset our lives. We know that in no way will we find our peace but in battles, in suffering, or in graves. Our silence covers us with cowardice, and every minute of delay seems to kill us.

We do not even mention the cities and market towns of Bessarabia, which are open sores on the country's exhausted and squeezed body. Nor do we even mention Maramures, where Romanians, in a state of slavery, daily die. There are no words that can describe the great tragedy of Maramures. But the illness spread like a cancer; it reached Ramnicul-Sarat, Buzau, Ploesti and it penetrated the capital. In 15 years, Vacaresti fell, an old Romanian quarter; Dudesti fell entirely; likewise, the Romanian merchants on Calea Grivitei. The famous merchants in the Obor quarter die and are replaced by 73 Jews; Calea Victorieil[4] has fallen. Today it has become in reality only a Romanian road of 'defeat'; three-fourths of the properties on Calea Victoriei are now Jewish owned.

In the last ten years, the Jews spread westward up the Danube plain into Oltenia and entered Michael the Brave's capital city of Craiova. They went into Ramnicul-Valcea and Severin under the protection of the Romanian politicians who, well paid, pretend there is no Jewish problem.

This betrayal by these politicians of their people is so frightening that, if they are still alive, the people should gouge their eyes out; if they are dead, their bones should be disinterred and burnt in public squares. Their

---

[3] Recall the earlier estimate that 45% of Iasi's population at that time was Jewish.
[4] "Victory Way," a fashionable shopping street.

children and grandchildren should be prosecuted, their wealth confiscated, and they should be stigmatized with the epithet of "traitors' children."

The loss of our Romanian towns has had devastating consequences for us, since towns are the economic centers of a nation. The entire richness of the country is accumulated in them. Whoever controls the towns controls the means of subsistence, the wealth of a nation. Could it be an indifferent matter to we Romanians, regarding who are the masters of our national wealth—ourselves or the Jews?

All people everywhere must care about this question because a population reproduces and develops within the means of subsistence at its disposal. The fewer these means are, the less will be the growth of the population and the fewer the chances for its development, and vice versa. These truths regarding the law of population were studied by all economists and formulated by Professor Cuza with unequalled clarity. The passing of Romanian riches into Jewish hands does not only affect our economic or political independence—for, whoever has no economic freedom, has no political freedom—but it means more: a national menace that crushes our very ability to grow in population.

To the extent that our means of subsistence vanish, to that extent, we Romanians will die off on our own land, leaving our property in the hands of a Jewish population whose number increases day by day. This happens both because of the invasion from abroad and because of seizing our means of subsistence, our riches.

Secondly, the towns are the cultural centers of a nation. Here in our towns, one finds schools, libraries, theaters, and lecture halls, all of them serving the townspeople. A Jewish family can easily support five or six children in school, whereas the Romanian peasant, in some remote village far from town, can hardly manage to send one child to school. And in this case, he is completely exhausted of strength and wealth so that he endangers the well-being of the other four or five children at home. Thus, whoever controls the towns controls the possibilities for partaking in the culture.

But that is not all. It is through towns and schools that a nation fulfills its cultural mission in the world. How is it possible for the Romanians to fulfill their cultural mission through Jewish voices, pens, hearts, and minds?

Finally, towns are the political centers of a nation. Nations follow the lead of the towns. Whoever controls the towns, directly or indirectly, has political leadership of the country. What is left of the country, outside of the towns? A crowd of several million peasants, lacking humane means of existence, drained and impoverished, cultureless, poisoned by alcohol, led by the enriched Jews now become the masters of Romanian towns.

Or worse, they are led by Romanians—prefects, mayors, police officers, gendarmes, cabinet ministers—who are administrators in name only because they are nothing but supine executors of Jewish plans. These officials are supported, flattered, showered with gifts, co-opted in administrative councils, and paid monthly by the Judaic economic power (Judas was paid but once). Their lust for money is roused, they are urged on to luxury and vice, and when disobeying Jewish directives and stances, are purely and simply thrown out, even though they be cabinet ministers. Their pay and subsidies are cut, their thieveries brought to light, and shady business deals exposed, implicating them, in order to compromise them.

This is what remains of the Romanian Fatherland since we lost our towns: a dishonest leader class, a people of peasants without freedom, and all Romanian children effectively stateless and futureless.

3) (a) The problem of Romanian schools

Whoever controls the towns, controls the schools; and whoever controls the schools today, controls the country tomorrow. Here are some 1920 statistics:

The situation at the University of Cernauti—
   School of Philosophy: Summer Semester,
          Romanians: 174;
          Jews 574.
   School of Law: Summer Semester, according to denomination:
          Orthodox: 237 (Romanians and Ruthenians)
          Catholics: 98
          Lutherans: 26
          Other Religions: 31
          Hebraic: 506

From *The Demographic Situation of Romania*—
   In Bessarabia:
   Rural Elementary Schools:
          Boys: 72,889 Romanians, 1,974 ethnically non-Romanian
             Christians, 1,281 Jews.
          Girls: 27,555 Romanians, 1,302 ethnically non-Romanian
             Christians, 2,147 Jews.

Urban Elementary Schools:
    Boys: 6,385 Romanians, 2,435 non-Romanians, of which 1,351
        were Jews.
    Girls: 5,501 Romanians, 2,435 non-Romanians, of which 1,492
        were Jews.

Secondary and professional schools:
    1,535 Orthodox,
    6,302 Hebraic.

Coeducational secondary schools:
    690 Orthodox,
    1,341 Hebraic.

The situation at the University of Iasi:

	Romanians	Jews
School of Medicine	546	831
School of Pharmacy	97	299
School of Letters	351	100
School of Sciences	722	321
School of Law	1,743	370

The Romanian system of education thus being destroyed by the large number of Jews raises two problems:

1) The problem of the Romanian leading class, because schools form the leaders of tomorrow—not only the political ones but all leaders in every domain of activity.

2) The problem of national culture, because schools are the laboratory in which the culture of a people is formed.

In order to underscore the tragedy of this Romanian school system overwhelmed by Jews, I consider it particularly important to cite below the distressing findings of one of the most illustrious pedagogues of our nation, Professor Ion Gavanescul of the University of Iasi:

> We no longer wish to see the spectacle offered by the National Lycee of Iasi, where the crushing majority of students is composed of the Jewish element. The few Romanian stu-

dents feel like strangers; during recess, they retreat, uneasy, into corners. They constitute the tolerated minority.

The majority lives apart, talk among themselves about their preoccupations, their games, societies, Macaby, Hacoah, Macoah, etc., of their get-togethers and lectures, their sports, work plans, and good times. And when they are doubtful of the discretion of the Romanians, the Jewish students (a majority in school, though a minority in the country), whisper among themselves or switch directly to Yiddish...

Pity the Romanian professors faced with such student souls! One is involuntarily reminded of the hen that hatched duck eggs. Look at her, how she stands cackling, scared, at the edge of the pond, how she desperately calls her ducklings, her chicks of another species which jumped into the water, gliding off to the other shore where she cannot follow.

What school of nationalism can you teach to such an audience? Can you speak, if you feel in yourself the flame of patriotism, of Romanian aspirations and ideals? Can you even open your mouth? Your jaws lock, your words freeze on your lips.

Even the great Kogalniceanu, in the face of such benches full of foreign students...could he have pronounced his famous discourse introducing the history of Romanians, that he delivered on this very spot, where today the Romanian 'National' Lycee has turned into a Jewish 'National' one? He would have lost the inspiration that derives its force from the sympathy of the shining eyes full of understanding and faith.

— I. Gavanescul,
The Imperative of the Historic Moment.

And further:

To limit ourselves to but one aspect of national life, where did anyone ever see in England, France, or Italy a school, at any level, in which the preponderant number of students belongs to another people than the people constituting the indigenous population of the country and which founded the National State in question?

Can anyone imagine, for instance, that at some school of Law in some English university, there might be 547 Jews versus 234 Britons, the same proportion of Jews to Romanians at the Cernauti School of Law in 1920? Or that, at a school of philosophy in Italy, there could be 574 Jews versus 174 Italians, the same proportion as that of Jews to Romanians in Cernauti?

Are these ratios normal? Are they not inadmissible, inconceivable monstrosities of ethnic biology? Are they not an indication of criminal unconsciousness on the part of the Romanian people's responsible leading class?

— I. Gavanescul, op.cit.

3) (b) The problem of the Romanian leading class

But who are the pupils and students of today? The present-day students are the professors, doctors, engineers, lawyers, prefects, congressmen, and cabinet ministers of tomorrow—in a word, the future leaders of the people in all domains of activity. If present-day students are 50%, 60%, 70% Jews, tomorrow we will logically have 50%, 60%, 70% Jewish leaders for this Romanian people.

Can one still raise the question whether a nation has the right to limit the number of alien students in its universities? Here is how this question is answered in the *Harvard University Bulletin* by Harvard-graduate Morris Gray, after he studied the Jewish problem there—as cited by Professor Cuza in "Numerus Clausus." Gray began by formulating the problem in principle, asking:

> First of all, what is the function of a university? What are its duties? If its duty is a duty to the individual, the admission into the university must be based frankly and manifestly, on the democratic principle: any candidate must be admitted on the condition he pass his entrance examination and pay the first term of tuition. And this with no serious investigation of the candidate's personality or his latent possibilities of progress, his capability, or usefulness to himself or to others.
>
> But, if the university's duty is a duty toward the nation, its attitude regarding student admissions must naturally be based on a different principle. In my opinion, the duty of a university is to form men in the various domains of human thought in such fashion that part of them at least can become leaders in their respective fields, thus serving the nation.

Here, then, is a well-established principle, adds Professor Cuza:

> The duty of universities is toward their nation, for which they must prepare leaders in all fields, and these must be necessarily ethnically native. For it is intolerable that a nation educate for itself alien leaders in its universities.

From the preceding figures, one can deduce the grave problem of the Romanian leading class of tomorrow.

There remains the well-established truth: Romania ought to be led by Romanians. Is there anyone who claims that Romania ought to be led by Jews? If not, then one has to admit that the Romanian student youth are right—that all campaigns, all wrongs, all infamies, all provocations, all plots, and all injustices that are heaped and are going to be heaped upon this Romanian youth, find their justification in the war waged by Jewry for the extermination of Romanians and of their best fighters.

4) The problem of national culture

A people, considering this the gravest of all problems, is like a tree concerned with the problem of its fruit. When it sees itself overwhelmed by caterpillars, it can no longer fulfill its mission in this world, it cannot bear fruit. In such a case, it would have to face the saddest problem, greater even than the problem of life itself, for, seeing its aim in life destroyed, it would be more painful for it than death.

The greatest pains are those of useless efforts, because they are the pains resulting from a frightful awareness of the uselessness of life. Is it not frightening, that we, the Romanian people, no longer can produce fruit? That we do not have a Romanian culture of our own, of our people, of our blood, to shine in the world, side by side with that of other peoples? That we be condemned today to present ourselves before the world with products of Jewish essence? That today, at this moment, when the world expects the Romanian people to show the fruit of our national blood and genius, we present ourselves with an infection of Judaic cultural caricature?

We look at this problem with hearts constricted with anguish, and there will be no Romanian who, seeing his entire history endangered, will not reach for his weapons to defend himself. I quote here from Professor I. Gavanescul's *The Imperative of the Historic Moment*, these immortal lines:

The principal concern of the Romanian people, just as important to its being as its physical preservation, is its affirmation in the realm of humanity's ideal of life: the creation of a culture specifically of Romanian character. It is impossible that a Romanian culture evolve from a school or an economic or political organization of alien character. An institution, as a function of national life, has a Romanian character only when the human factor giving it birth is Romanian.

Faced with this sad situation, faced by the large number of invaders overwhelming us, Professor Gavanescul, filled with anxiety, and posing the question of a national school and culture, asks himself:

Where can Romanian souls seek refuge? Where can they escape the obsessing, painful impression of being exiles in their own country? Excepting the church, where they enter to collect their thoughts in quiet, under the protection of the saving cross, their only refuge is the *school*. School is the ideal nest in which the national genius gathers its progeny to nurture it, to raise it, to teach it how to fly, to show it the way to heights that only that national genius knows and only it is meant to reach. School is the place of refuge where the nation's heartstrings and the spiritual organs of the people are tuned in order to intone a new symphony—one as yet unheard in the world, the first symphony of its natural talents predestined by God exclusively to its being. School is the sanctuary where the great mystery of a people's life unfolds, where the ethnic soul distills, in drops of light, its immortal essence so that it be molded into the ideal form, preordained to it exclusively by the world's creative thought.

The melodic instruments of other ethnic souls cannot harmoniously participate in the symphony of our culture. By virtue of their make-up, they know only how to sound the note of their people. What kind of Romanian symphony could they produce? The essence of national genius of other ethnic souls cannot crystalize in a different form from that determined for them by the creator of peoples. How can one produce a Romanian image from the Jewish, Magyar, or German national essence?

— I. Gavanescul

Not only will Jews be incapable of creating Romanian culture, but they will falsify the one we have, in order to serve it to us poisoned. The Romanian school, being thus macerated, is in the position of renouncing our mission as a people, of renouncing the creation of a Romanian culture, and of perishing from Jewish poison.

Return to Romania

In contrast to our colleagues from the other universities, we Iasian students knew all these things from the lectures of Professor Cuza, the writings of Professors Paulescu and Gavanescul, from our studies and research done at the Association of Law Students, and from what we saw with our own eyes and felt with our own souls.

A problem of great moral urgency confronted us. Every day brought us additional proof. We recognized the perfidiousness of the Jewish press—we saw its bad faith in all circumstances, and we saw its incitement behind everything anti-Romanian. We saw the work of flattery and elevation of political figures, functionaries, authorities, writers, and Christian priests, who stooped to do the bidding of Jewish interests. We saw the ridicule heaped upon those who adopted a correct, dignified Romanian attitude, or those who dared denounce the Jewish peril. We saw the indecency with which we were treated in our own land, as if they had been masters here for thousands of years. We saw, with growing indignation, the daring meddling of these uninvited guests into the most intimate problems of Romanian life: religion, culture, art, politics. Here, they seek to direct the destiny of the Romanian people.

Young as I was, almost a child, I was long troubled by these thoughts, even while searching for a solution. The elements that impressed me most, that then compelled me to fight, and that comforted and strengthened me in times of suffering, were:

- A consciousness of the mortal danger in which our people and its future found itself.
- My love for the land, and my sorrow for every sacred and glorious place, today ridiculed and profaned by Jews.
- Pity for the ashes of those who had fallen for their country.
- A feeling of revolt against the offenses to, and the ridicule and trampling underfoot by this alien enemy of, our dignity—as human beings and as Romanians.

That's why, when, on 10 December 1922, I heard the great news about the volcanic explosion of the student movement, I decided to return home, so that I too might fight alongside my comrades.

A short time later, the train was taking me home. From Krakow, I sent a telegram to the students in Cernauti, who were expecting me at the station. I stayed there two days. The university was closed. The students guarding it seemed like soldiers serving their country, their soul enlightened by God. No trace of personal interest clouded their beautiful and sacred action. The cause for which they banded together and fought as one went far beyond themselves and their constant privations and needs.

In Cernauti, the leading fighters were: Tudose Popescu, the son of the old priest from Marcesti; and Danileanu, Pavelescu, Carsteanu, etc. I inquired about the battle plan. It was decided to declare a general strike until we won, namely, until the government satisfactorily solved the points raised in the motion of December 10, beginning with *numerus clausus.*

To me, this plan seemed wrong. In my head, another one began to form:

- The student movement ought to reach out to all the Romanian people. Limited now to universities, it should be extended into a Romanian national movement. This was because, firstly, the Jewish problem is not limited to the universities but involves the whole Romanian nation, and secondly, the universities by themselves cannot solve it.

- This national movement must be incorporated into an organization under a single command.

- The aim of this organization must be fighting to bring the national movement to power, which will resolve both *numerus clausus* and all other problems; no other rule by political parties outside of this movement will resolve the national problem.

- With these points in mind, the students should organize a great national assembly of Romanians from all social strata, which would then signal the beginning of the new organization.

- In order to implement this assembly, each university should provide as many flags as there are counties in each province. The cloth for each would then be given by a student delegation there to a known nationalist whom the delegation would consider the best qualified person for the job of gathering together a group of town and country leaders. Then, upon receiving a telegram announcing the date and place of a great rally, he would head out for that place with the flag and all his men.

- Lest the government try to prevent the rally, all preparations should be made quietly, keeping the date unknown until the last minute.

I outlined this plan to about 50 fighters in one of the dormitories, and they liked it. Then we all pitched in money, bought the necessary cloth, and female students immediately began making flags for the counties of Bucovina.

(1) At Iasi and Bucharest

In Iasi, I met all my former comrades. I exposed my plan to them as well. Here too, flags were made on the first day, by female students, for all counties in Moldavia and Bessarabia. But I couldn't find Professor Cuza. He had left for Bucharest together with Professor Sumuleanu and my father to attend a meeting in the capital.

The next day, I left for Bucharest. Here, I went to see Professors Cuza and Sumuleanu and my father, who, for over a quarter of a century, fought together against the Jewish menace. Most of this time, they were overwhelmed by ridicule, blows, and even wounds. But today they can experience the great satisfaction of seeing the entire educated youth of the country, numbering over 30,000, raising battle banners for the faith they had served for a lifetime.

But in Bucharest, my thoughts were not received with the same enthusiasm. First, I encountered some opposition from Professor Cuza. Presenting my plan, proposing the creation of a national movement, headed by him as chief, and the rally to be held, he did not consider my plan good because, he said, "We do not need to organize, our movement is based on a formidable mass current." I insisted, comparing a mass movement to an oil well that, unconnected to a pipeline, even when it gushes, it comes to naught, because the oil spills all over.

I left with no success, but the next day, Professor Sumuleanu and my father convinced him.

But I was soon confronted by an unexpected difficulty. It was around the beginning of February 1923. The great body of students overflowed with enthusiasm. Though all its mess halls were closed down and the gates of all dormitories locked against us, being thus left out to starve in the middle of winter, yet the students were enthusiastic. They were admirably protected by the capital's Romanians, who, the very next day, opened wide the doors of their homes, sheltering and feeding over 8,000 student fighters. There was, in this gesture, an approval, an urge to the struggle, a solidarity, a comfort for those being wounded.

But I had no contact with this mass. I knew no one there. Through the student Fanica Anastasescu, who was the manager of the review *The National Defense*, I began to meet a few. I had the impression that the leaders of the student movement in Bucharest were not sufficiently oriented. Though possessed of elite elements endowed with distinguished intellectual qualities—a fact verified by the functions they later occupied in society—they found themselves unexpectedly heading a movement that they had given no prior thought. In fact, each person had a different opinion. Among the valuable elements of the leadership, figured in the forefront: Cretu, Danulescu, Simionescu, Rapeanu, Roventa, and others. The mass was warlike, but part of the leadership thought it wise to calm down such high spirits.

On the other hand, both their insufficient familiarity with the Jewish Question and their inadequate contact with politicians made at least some of them try, to some extent, to reposition the movement onto a material plane. For me, this was unacceptable. It would have been as if someone were to say:

- We fight to take our country back from the Jews.
- We fight for white bread on our tables.
- We fight for two-course meals.
- We fight for more comfortable beds.
- We fight for equipment in our labs, for dissection instruments, etc.
- We fight for more dormitories.

Then, in the end, the authorities would tell us loudly: "Student demands have been satisfied; the government has recognized the pitiful state of students' lot, their great misery, etc. Out of the six points demanded, five were granted: dissection instruments, laboratory equipment, two white loaves of bread daily, two-course meals, three student dormitories with comfortable beds, etc." As to the first point: saving the country from Jewish hands, nothing would be said, on the pretext that the government conceded five points out of six.

From the beginning of the student movement, the entire Jewish press sought to shift it onto this material plane: that the objective of the movement be 'a loaf of bread.' Thus the real objective—the Jew—would escape unnoticed. In fact, if one bothers to re-read the papers, one observes that

Romanian politicians also posed the problem in similar terms: students must be given dormitories, better food, etc.

As I have said, part of the student leadership in Bucharest were inclined toward this view. Had the students taken this course, they would have strayed from their true mission. My opinion was always contrary to this point of view—against any intrusion of a material order into the formulation of student demands. For, I was saying, as I also say today, it was not the immediate needs or material wants that impelled students toward this great movement, but on the contrary, it was the *abandonment* of concern for such things, of selfish interests, of their own or family sufferings: it was the *forgetting* of all these things on the part of the Romanian students, and instead the identification of their whole being with the worries, needs, and aspirations of their people.

It was this abnegation and only this, that lit the holy light in their eyes. The student movement was not one of material demands. It raised itself above the needs of a generation, entwining itself with the superior aspirations of the nation.

On the other hand, here in Bucharest, the idea predominated that the student movement ought to stay within the university's confines, to remain an academic movement, not become a movement of a political nature. But this opinion was a totally incorrect one, for it coincided with the design of the Jews and political parties who had the greatest interest in restricting this fiery movement to the university, so that there, by one means or another, it could be extinguished. Our opinion was not that we had formed a movement in order to agitate, but to gain a victory. Our student forces alone being insufficient for that, we needed to unite with all Romanians.

In addition, the Bucharest leaders opposed having Professor Cuza proclaimed president of an eventual organization, claiming he was not good for such active leadership. I insisted that we must support him, such as he is. Finally, those in Bucharest held great reservations toward me personally. This pained me, for I was coming to them with what a man has as cleanest and most sacred in his heart: with the active desire to cooperate in the best possible manner, for our country. Perhaps, not knowing me, they were justified in having reservations. For these reasons I encountered opposition in Bucharest. Thus I began to work outside the committee.

(2) At Cluj

I left for Cluj together with Alexandru Ghica, who acted admirably throughout the student campaign. The president of the Cluj student center was Alexa, a moderate, good person. He offered me the same arguments regarding both student orientation and proclaiming Professor Cuza as president of the new movement. The student mass was staunch and full of enthusiasm.

It was then that I met Mota, an agile, talented fellow. He held the same opinions as Alexa. I tried to convince him, but unsuccessfully. I had a difficult time, since I knew no one. Yet, I found a few students on my side: Corneliu Georgescu, student in Pharmacy; Isac Mocanu from Letters; Crasmaru, in Medicine; Justin Iliesu, etc. We made only one flag, and then, in Capt Siancu's house—who, from the first moment and with great enthusiasm agreed to our plan of action—we took an oath on this flag.

The Assembly of Iasi: Founding the League of National Defense

Once returned to Iasi, I had before me two roads of parallel activity: (1) Laying the groundwork for the rally, for which flags were made in all universities. (2) Continuing the student movement and keeping the general strike going. Regarding the first point, the biggest difficulty was not the lack of men or lack of organization, or the government's measures. This time, the greatest obstacle was coming from Professor Cuza himself, who, though not disapproving it, showed lack of enthusiasm. He was not sufficiently convinced of the necessity for organizing, and did not believe at all in the possibility of success for the projected rally.

Regarding the second point, I faced serious difficulties with the leaders in the Bucharest and Cluj centers—difficulties that prevented agreement on a single point of view toward a battle plan, around which we could unify and rise up together in defiance of the enemy and all our past errors. Neither the leadership nor the body of these student centers (a) knew the Jewish problem, and particularly did not know the Jew; they were unaware of Judaic power and its way of thinking and acting. In other words, they began to wage a war without knowing the adversary. And (b) they believed that the then-Liberal government, and eventually the one to succeed it, would satisfy our demands.

On this basis, they preferred to engage in diplomacy, believing that ultimately they would convince the politicians of the justice of our cause. Believe me, there is nothing more distressing than discussing a problem with men who are not even familiar with its most elementary aspects.

Regarding this situation, I took the following steps:

1. Ensure that several good delegates from Iasi regularly take part in the meetings of the central committee in Bucharest. As an aside, I note here that

the meetings were regularly held two and three times a week, beginning at 9:00 pm and running to 3:00, 4:00, even 7:00 in the morning, and filled with contradictory discussions. For many of those participating, their only recollections were of these meetings with their rhetorical encounters.

2. Create, at Bucharest and Cluj, a group of the best fighters from the student body, in order to work independently from the directives of their respective centers.

These groups were formed very quickly. In Bucharest, they were present right in the committee, where the leadership bumped into stiff opposition at each meeting. There, Ibraileanu, the delegate from Iasi, was of real help. Likewise, the firm attitude of Simionescu, the leader of the medical students, kept the student body in the true spirit.

Regarding the arrangements for the assembly, according to news received from Iasi, the outlook was as follows: In only two weeks, over 40 flags had been issued in 40 counties, to trustworthy people. It was only natural that, after two months of student movement, of general strike in all universities, the soul of Romanians would boil and that they would be ready to arise everywhere, awaiting but the word. The flags and the news of the rally came on time.

Professor Cuza wanted to fix the date for the rally sometime in May so that more people would come. I suggested that the rally should be held as soon as possible, for the following reasons:

1. All the people, on their feet, rallying around the student movement, were expecting to hear a command from somewhere, in order to form a unit, to know that a plan was established that they could follow.

2. I was afraid that Jewry and Masonry, getting wind of the situation, might initiate a pseudo-nationalist organization in order to tap the people and thus divert the movement onto a dead-end track. In any case, this would have created such confusion in the minds of the Romanians that we dare not contemplate this event.[5]

3. I felt it was necessary to support the front line of the student movement. Waging war is not easy, with blows coming from all directions: government, local authorities, parents, professors; with poverty, hunger, and cold. A mobilization of the Romanian masses coming to their defense, sending them a word of encouragement, would invigorate the entire front of this movement.

---

[5] This is a remarkable anticipation of present-day Jewish tactics of creating false flags, fake news, and especially 'controlled opposition.'

4. Finally, because thousands of students were inactive, not knowing what to do. They demonstrated once, twice; they held a meeting or two. But it had been two months. These youth had to have something to do. Once the new organization was born, the entire multitude would be offered a wide field of activity. They could start working the very next day, heading for villages to organize them and to win them over to the new faith.

March 4, 1923

Deciding in my favor, Professor Cuza determined the rally should be held on Sunday, 4 March 1923; the place, Iasi. He had invited me to dinner. There, the question was raised as to what name should be given the new organization. Mr. Lefter said: "The National Defense Party," as in France. I liked it. Professor Cuza added: "Not party, but *league*—'The League of Christian National Defense'." And so it was. Then I sent out telegrams to Cernauti, Bucharest, and Cluj, containing the same message: "Wedding in Iasi on March 4."

Following this, I busied myself with arranging the smallest details of preparation for the rally. The schedule was determined by Professor Cuza in agreement with Professor Sumuleanu and my father: at the Cathedral, prayer; at the University, homage to Simion Bamutiu and Gh. Marzescu; in the Bejan Hall, public meeting. Posters were printed announcing the great national assembly. The news of a big Romanian assembly in Iasi, having as its purpose the founding of a fighting organization, spread like lightning among the students of the four universities and then among Romanians at large.

On the evening of March 3, full trainloads began arriving, headed by leaders bringing with them the cloth for flags. By morning, 42 groups had arrived with 42 flags. The cloth of these flags was black—a sign of mourning; in the center, a round white spot, signifying our hopes surrounded by the darkness they will have to conquer; in the center of the white, *a swastika*, the symbol of anti-Semitic struggle throughout the world; and all around the flag, a band of the Romanian tricolor—red, yellow, and blue.[6] Professor Cuza had approved the design while in Bucharest. Now we affixed them to poles, wrapped them in newspapers, and all of us left for the Cathedral, where the religious service was conducted before a crowd of

---

[6] The exact design is unknown. A reconstructed image can be found at: https://www.fotw.info/flags/ro}fasc.html. The flag on the cover is modeled after this reconstruction.

over 10,000 people. All 42 flags, at the moment when they were to be blessed, were unfurled before the altar.

Once blessed, they were to be taken throughout the whole country, each to have a real fortress of Romanian souls rallying around it. These flags, sent into each county, would be crystallizing emblems to gather together all those of like thought and feeling. With their solemn blessing, their impressive symbolism, and their placement in each county, a great national problem was being resolved.

From the Cathedral, the thousands of people, banners unfurled, formed a procession through Union Square, heading for the University. There, in a gesture of homage and veneration, wreaths were placed for Mihail Kogalniceanu, Simion Barnutiu, and Gheorghe Marzescu—the last, defender of Article 7 of the Constitution of 1879 and, ironically, father of the liberal minister George Marzescu, defender of the Jews. There in the University's amphitheater, we signed the founding document of The League of Christian National Defense.

That afternoon, the meeting took place in Bejan Hall, presided over by Gen. Ion Tarnoschi. Many people who could not be accommodated in the hall stood in the street. Professor Cuza was proclaimed president of the League of Christian National Defense, with great enthusiasm. The speakers were: Professor Cuza, Professor Sumuleanu, Gen. Tarnoschi, my father, each county delegate, and those of the university centers: Tudose Popescu, Prelipceanu, Alex Ventonic, Donca Manea, Novitchi, Sofron Robota, and myself.

At the end, following the reading of the motion, Professor Cuza, in conclusion, entrusted me with a mission, saying: "I appoint with the organization of the League, for the entire country, under my direct leadership, the young lawyer C. Z. Codreanu." Then he named the county leaders. The rally ended in perfect order and with great enthusiasm.

Other Anti-Semitic and Nationalist Organizations

Small anti-Semitic organizations of an economic and political character existed even before 1900, as well as after. These were weak efforts of people with foresight and love of country, to oppose the ever-growing Jewish invasion.

But the most serious anti-Semitic organization was The Nationalist-Democratic Party, founded on 23 April 1910 under the leadership of Professors Iorga and Cuza. This party had a whole administrative program. Its article No. 45 gave the solution to the Jewish problem: "*The solution to the*

Jewish problem must be accomplished through the elimination of the Jews,
the development of the productive powers of Romanians, and the protection of their enterprises." Following the enumeration of these points, one
reads this solemn statement: "We will keep, spread, and defend this program with all our steadfastness and power, considering this our first honor-
bound duty."

This organization gathered together all veteran fighters since 1900.
Among the prominent ones, one counted: Professor Sumuleanu, Professor
Ion Zelea-Codreanu (my father), Butureanu of Dorohoi, Toni of Galati, C.
N. Ifrim, and then later Stefan Petrovici, C. C. Coroiu, and others. In 1914,
all these were leading the movement that demanded Romania enter the war
for Transylvania's liberation; and in 1916 most of them were on the front
lines, brilliantly doing their duty. Ever since 1910-11, the counties of Dorohoi, under the leadership of lawyer Butureanu; Iasi, under that of Professor Cuza; and Suceava, under that of my father, became fortresses of Romanian rebirth.

By 1912, the current in these counties was so powerful that in the
elections, the administration could not avoid a sound defeat without the use
of terror. On that occasion, my father was seriously wounded. Immediately
after the war, when the peasants returned home from the front resolutely
desiring a new life, the first elections brought into the Parliament Professor
Cuza for Iasi and my father for Suceava. There they engaged in a fierce
parliamentary fight, applauded by the whole country. The fight was waged
against the peace that the Germans, whose armies invaded our country,
wished to impose upon us.

The echo of these truly remarkable clashes gathered the hopes of the
country around the Nationalist-Democratic Party, so that in the elections
that followed, real formidable victories were registered. In Suceava, the
victory was unparalleled. Out of seven deputy seats, the administration
took one, the other groups none, and my father's list, six. In Dorohoi and
Iasi, almost the same. The trains took to Bucharest 34 Nationalist deputies.

But, unfortunately for the Romanian people, this whole troop, coming
up from all corners of the country, ended up in a great defeat. This struck
like lightning over the heads of Romanians. The Judeo-Masonic forces
succeeded in dividing the two party chiefs, Professors Iorga and Cuza. Iorga did not oppose the treaty imposing on us the "minorities' clause," declaring himself ready to sign it. Cuza, on the opposite barricade, showed
that this infamous "minorities' clause" represents a defiance of all the
blood shed by Romanians, an impermissible meddling into our national
affairs, and a beginning of misfortune for us.

In effect, the imposition was placed upon us to grant Jews political rights *en masse*. Iorga was no anti-Semite. It was clear that the break was an irreparable one. And this unfortunate Romanian nation again became heartbroken over its hopes for salvation. The majority of the party's membership and parliamentarians sided with Iorga, believing that Cuza's position placed them farther away from any chances to gain power. Only Professor Sumuleanu and my father stood with Cuza.

"The Romanian National Fascia" and "The Romanian Action"

In 1923, during the student movement and under the impetus of the wave of nationalism, "The Romanian National Fascia" came into being, under the leadership of Vifor, Lunguiescu, and Baguiescu. Meanwhile, in Cluj, "The Romanian Action" was formed, led by Professors Catuneanu, Ciortea, Iuliu Hategan, Em Vasiliu-Cluj and a group of students headed by Mota. The former published the weekly journal *Fascism*, which was well-written and spirited. But they did not know the Jewish problem. The latter published the bimonthly *Romanian Action* and later *Romanian Brotherhood*, also very well written, but they limited themselves only to publishing. They could not initiate any action or create a sound organization.

During this time, the student Mota translated from French *The Protocols of the Elders of Zion*, which were commented upon by Professor Catuncanu and Vasiliu-Cluj, then published in booklet form. Also at about that time, Vasiliu-Cluj published his work *The Demographic Situation of Romania* in which he showed statistically the terrible state of Romanian towns. These two organizations had neither power of action nor organization nor a doctrinal competence like that of The League of Christian National Defense. They survived only until 1925, when they merged with the League.

After the founding of the League, my activity was to continue along two lines: that of the student movement as a separate unit, organized by centers, having as an immediate objective its own battles in which it had been engaged for three months; and that of the League itself, in which I was assigned as organizer under Professor Cuza.

On the student side I was to fight for: (1) Maintaining the posture of the general strike, which involved the honor of the students—quite a difficult job considering the attacks, blows, pressures, and lures that flowed over the heads of students everywhere. In addition, there were defeatist students who, as partisans of believers in defeat, had to be checked. (2) Systematically using available students to recruit among all Romanian masses, thus organizing them into a single army: the League.

On the League side, we had leaders and flags in some 40 counties. We needed: (1) The completion of flags for the remaining counties. (2) As tight a contact as possible with the respective leaders. And (3) the immediate set-up of precise guidelines in organizational matters, thus far nonexistent, but requested by county chiefs who did not know how to proceed.

In sum: *defense* on the student lines; *offence* via the League. The large mass of students acted well, guided by their healthy racial instinct and by the spirit of the dead. They followed their glorious path, overcoming many difficulties.

With the League, the problems were somewhat more serious. County chiefs were asking for clarifications and guidelines for organizing. People who were moved by this current had to be strengthened in their faith, educated, and fully informed regarding the organizing and the objectives they had to attain in their fight. They had to be taught discipline and trust in their superiors. We were not then giving birth to a movement but already had a full-fledged movement, one which had to be organized, disciplined, educated, and led into battle.

When I went to Professor Cuza with the letters and requests received, he was disarmed; they introduced him to a strange new world. As an intellectual, shining like the sun, he was unchallengeable on the heights of the theoretical world; but when he was brought down to Earth on the battlefield, he became powerless. "We have no need of regulations. Let them organize by themselves." Or: "We are not in a barracks, needing discipline"—as he often told us.

Then I began to write up a statute myself, down to the last detail. But realizing this was a tough job for my age, I took it to my father. Working on it for several days, I eventually achieved the needed modifications in form and substance. The organizing system was simple, but different from that of existing political parties. The main difference was that, in addition to the political organization proper, based on county village committees and members, I formed separately a *youth corps*, organized by tens and hundreds. Our political organizations up to then had nothing like these. Later, the others adopted them too, in the form of Liberal Party Youth, National-Peasant Party Youth, etc.

When I presented the statute to Professor Cuza, things really got heated. He wouldn't hear of such a thing. Then an embarrassing discussion ensued, for several hours, between Cuza and my father, which literally froze me. Suspecting that it would possibly lead to an unfortunate conflict, I regretted starting the whole discussion. My father, a violent and rough man, took the statute and left for the printer to have it published without

Cuza's approval. But the latter, exercising more tact and calm, and as much as he was adamant in certain matters, was quite malleable in cases like these, and knew how to quiet things.

He called my father back, telling him: "All right, let's print it, but give me a chance to look it over." He corrected it, rearranged it, added a doctrinaire section, and then sent it to the printer. This, then, became "The Good Romanian's Guide," and later, the fundamental book of the League until 1935.

I was satisfied that I had accomplished something good and absolutely necessary for the organization, but in my heart, I was telling myself: "Things are going to be tough if we need so much discussion for such elementary questions. In such an organization, neither a lack of comprehension by the leader nor too much discussion are good."

Modification of Article 7 of the Constitution: The Granting of Civil Rights to the Jews

It was rumored for a long time that the Liberal Parliament—which was also the Constituent Assembly, thus having the mission of re-writing the Constitution—intended to modify Article 7 in the sense of granting "citizenship and political rights to all Jews present in Romania."

Up to now, this article of the old Constitution prohibited the granting of citizenship to foreigners and thus constituted a real defense shield against the invasion and meddling of the Jews in the administration of our own Romanian destiny. Giving this privilege of meddling in public affairs to as many as two million Jews, and to the just-settled Jew on our land, and granting them equal rights with the Romanian who lived on this land for millennia, was both an injustice crying to high heaven and a great national menace—one that could not but worry and profoundly shake every Romanian who loved his country.

Confronted by this situation, Cuza wrote a series of immortal articles showing the menace threatening the future of this nation. The League distributed petitions throughout the country to be signed by Romanians, by which it was demanded that Article 7 of the Constitution be maintained as is. The petitions were filled with hundreds of thousands of signatures and forwarded to the Constituent Assembly.

I felt that we students, while this grave question was being deliberated, should go from all centers to Bucharest, where, together with the local students and the population, we would demonstrate in order to stop the act of enslaving our future. I left for Cernauti, Cluj, and Bucharest. Students accepted my proposition and began organizing for the departure. In order to communicate the departure date, it was agreed that I would send a casual telegram.

But the plan failed. We had expected that deliberations on this question would last at least three days, during which time we could reach Bucharest. But on March 26, the deliberations lasted less than 30 minutes. Both the Liberal government and the Assembly—seemingly conscious of the act of great shame they were about to commit—sought to cover it up, passing it as unnoticeably as they could.

The day after this great act of national betrayal, the so-called Romanian press, as well as the Jewish one, treated the infamous act with silence. *The Morning, The Fight*, and *The Truth* regularly printed, in bold face, the conflict between landlords and renters in Bucharest. And in one corner, a few words by which they announced simply and perfidiously: "Article 7 of the old Constitution has been replaced by Article 133."

The Liberal Party and the infamous Assembly of 1923 thus laid in the grave and sealed the tombstone over the future of this people. No curse by our children, our mothers, our old folks, or all Romanians suffering on this Earth now and forever, will be adequate to punish these traitors of their nation. Thus in silence and in an atmosphere of general cowardice, this great act of national betrayal was consummated.

Only Professor Cuza's voice, the personality now towering over the entire Romanian nation, could be heard. He wrote:

> Romanians: The 28 March 1923 Constitution must be abolished immediately. Protest against its promulgation. Demand free elections. Organize, in order to insure your victory. A new Constitution must guarantee the Romanian Nation's rights of priority, as the dominant people in the State.

When I heard the news in Iasi, I burst out crying. And I told myself: "It cannot be! At least people ought to learn we protested. For, if the people, on whose neck such a yoke is placed, does not protest, it is a people of imbeciles." Then I edited a brief manifesto addressed to Iasians, calling all Romanians to a protest meeting in the university. The news of the Jews being granted civil rights spread like lightning. The town was seething.

On governmental orders, local authorities brought out the army, the gendarmes, and the police; provocations arose, followed by the interdiction of movement. Then the plan changed. The rally, instead of being held at the university, would occur at 14 locations throughout the city. Clashes began at all these locations, lasting throughout the night. Local authorities, the army, and police forces were completely baffled by the abrupt change of our battle plans, of our meeting place, and by running from one end of the city to another, as they were informed by their agents regarding demonstrations that erupted every half hour at opposite points of the city.

The group under my command met at the toughest point: Podul Rosu and Tg. Cucului, where Jewish impertinence maintained that no anti-Semitic demonstrator would ever set foot and get out alive. No Romanian lives there. Thousands of Jews woke up, running to and fro like a nest of worms. When we were greeted with fire, we responded with fire. We did our duty, toppling everything that stood in our path and showing the Jews that Iasi, Moldavia's ancient capital, was still Romanian and that there, it is *our* arm that rules—which can permit or forbid, which determines peace or war, and which punishes or forgives.

The next day, the cavalry from Bariad arrived in the city to aid the two local regiments, the police, the gendarmerie, and the Jews. The Bucharest papers came out in special editions with headlines such as: "Iasi lived a night and a day of revolution." This showed how much we could do, mere youth; this much we knew how to do, and to do it the moment the yoke was put on our shoulders. We did not accept it serenely, with a slave's resignation, with cowardice. That much we did, and took the sacred oath for all of our life to break this yoke, no matter how many battles and sacrifices we might face.

I went to the police prefecture the following day to take some food to those arrested. There, Iulian Sarbu was just then being interrogated, as he was suspected of being the author of the manifesto. Seeing that, I went up to the investigator and said: "Sarbu is not the author of the manifesto, I am."

My First Arrest

At the police station, I was told: "Mr. Codreanu, you must go to the Court House accompanied by the officer." "Why with the officer?" I replied back. "I will go alone."

This was the first time that my word was doubted. I felt offended. "No, I will not go with the officer. He can, if he wishes, walk 60 feet behind me. I go alone. My word is worth more than 20 police officers." I left, with the officer walking 20 feet behind me. I reached the Court House. The officer came along and took me before the investigating judge Catichi, who told me: "You are under arrest, and I must send you to the penitentiary."

When I heard that, I saw black before my eyes. At that time, "arrested" was something degrading. No one among Iasians was ever arrested and no one heard of a nationalist student being arrested. Let alone me, with the record of a patriot! I approached his desk and told him: "Your Honor, I do not accept being arrested, and no one is going to pick me up and take me to the penitentiary." The poor man, in order to avoid further discussion, ordered the officer to take me to the penitentiary and advised me against opposing it. Then he left.

The officer tried to take me. I told him: "Go home, sir, and leave me alone. You cannot take me from here." Then other officers came in. I stayed there from 11 AM until 8:00 in the evening. All efforts to take me out were fruitless. I was thinking: "I am guilty of no wrongdoing. I did my duty to my people. If there is a guilty party who ought to be arrested, that party is of those who wronged their people: the Parliament that accorded civil rights to the Jews."

Finally, all Court House employees went home one by one, down to the ushers. Only the officers by my side and myself were left. Around 8:00, three officers arrived. "Mr. Codreanu, we have orders to evacuate this Court House." "All right gentlemen, I will go out." We descended the stairs and left the building.

To my surprise, I saw there a company of gendarmes in a semi-circle, with prosecutors, judges, police. At that, I walked ahead and sat down in the middle of the courtyard. The authorities came to me and said: "You must go to the penitentiary." "I will not go." They lifted me up, put me into a vehicle and I was transported to the penitentiary, slowly, followed by the gendarme company on foot.

At the last moment, as we were going through the gate of the prison, our boys attempted to free me, but the officers' revolvers stopped them. Was it a protest against the laws? No. It was a protest against the yoke of injustice. My obstinate refusal to let myself be arrested seemed to be, for me, a foreboding of much suffering to come my way, once taking the path that led me inside the cold walls of prisons.

I was kept there one week, until the eve of Easter. My first days in prison! Morally speaking, I took them very hard; I could not understand that someone could be arrested when he fights *for* his people, and by order of those fighting *against* the people.

Upon being released, I went home. Many Romanians came to meet me at the railroad stations, showing sympathy for me and encouraging me to carry on the fight—which is the people's fight, and which in the end will be won. The entire nation, in all its best elements, from peasant to intellectual, received with great pain the sad news of the Article 7 modification; but it could do nothing, for it woke up sold out and betrayed by the leaders. I wondered what curse on our heads and what sins condemned us Romanians to have such scoundrelly leaders?

Here we have, face to face, two historical moments in two different Romanias, with two sets of people and with the same problem: The Constituent Assembly of 1879 in Little Romania, very small, that had the courage to withstand Europe's pressure; and the Constituent Assembly of 1923, in Greater Romania, emerged from the sacrifice of our blood, and which, out of venal servility, under the pressures of the same Europe, does not hesitate to humiliate and endanger the life of an entire nation.

The Great Men of Romania of 1879: The Veil of Forgetfulness

In the pages that follow, readers of this book will encounter some surprising extracts from the works of several great men: pinnacles of thought, patriotism, and character of our people, who, in 1879, fiercely fought for the right to life of the Romanian people. Though the inclusion of these extracts divert from the normal unfolding of the present volume, disobeying rules customarily followed in such matters, I include them, not so much wishing to use them as historical arguments, but to bring to light anew these pearls of reasoning and of expression of these great forebears. These men were persecuted by the conspiracy of the Judeo-Masonic Occult, locking them up under heavy seals and plaques of forgetfulness, just because they wrote, thought, and fought like true giants of Romanianism.

Our student generation, jumping over 50 years of the abdication practiced by politicians vis-a-vis the Jewish peril, identifies itself with the same convictions, sentiments, and character possessed by those of 1879; in the moment of this sacred union, our generation bows its head in gratitude and reverence in the shadow of their greatness.

VASILE CONTA: Consider the attitude held by our great Conta in the Chamber in 1879. Fifty years earlier, the Romanian philosopher demonstrated, with unshakeable scientific arguments and framed in a system of impeccable logic, the soundness of racial truths that must lie at the foundation of a national state.

From this, one can see the frailty of the arguments of those who attack the national movement as being inspired by the new German ideology—when in reality, after so many years, it is Berlin that has taken up the line of Vasile Conta, Mihail Emineseu, and the others. Conta wrote:

We, if we will not fight against the Jewish element, will perish as a nation.

It is a recognized fact, even by those attacking us today, that the first condition for a State to exist and prosper is that the citizens of that State be of the same race and same blood. This is easy to understand. First, individuals of like race usually marry only among themselves, for only thus can they retain the unity of race. Then marriage creates true family feelings, which are the strongest and the most lasting ties between individuals. And when we consider that these family ties spread out until they take in all the citizens of the State, we see that the latter are attracted to one another by a general feeling of love, by what is called *racial sympathy*.

Moreover, bearing in mind that the same blood flows through the veins of all the members of a people, one understands that all these members will have, through heredity, similar feelings, similar tendencies, and even similar ideas. Thus, in perilous times, on unique occasions, their hearts will beat as one, their minds will adopt one opinion, and the action of all will seek the same purpose. In other words, the nation made up of a single race will have only one center of gravity; and the State made up of such a nation, that and only that one, will be in the best condition of strength, durability, and progress. In consequence, just as in the maintenance of a species, the first requisite for the existence of a State is that its people be of like race.

This is the truth on which the principle of nationalism is based, and which is much discussed in the civilized world. This principle of nationalism, naturally, refers only to race and not at all to what is called 'the subjects of the State, regardless of race'; for then the principle would have no application whatsoever.

This principle is so deeply-rooted in the conscience of all people today, be they statesmen or simple citizens, that nowadays all States in the civilized world come into being or are reconstituted only on this basis.

Let's have no more talk by Jewish publicists or the Jew-lovers, who say that the basis of the State is only a common material interest of its citizens—because, on the contrary, we see that it is exactly this, our century, that gave birth to the principle of nationalism, that prevails today more and more...

True, this does not prevent foreigners from acquiring citizenship in a State, *provided* they assimilate into the dominant nation; namely, to mix totally, so that ultimately the State remains of the same single blood.

These are the only scientific principles of naturalization. For naturalization to be useful, rational, and conforming to scientific criteria, it must be granted only to those foreigners who assimilate or are inclined to do so by marriage to the indigenous. Otherwise, one can easily comprehend that granting citizenship to individuals who lack, or cannot have, this inclination of assimilation into the blood of the dominant race, would result in a State subject to perpetual struggles between opposite tendencies.[7]

I am not saying it is impossible for various races that might exist in some country to sometimes have a common interest, and I am not saying that the hereditary tendencies of one race are just as favored as those of another in the same circumstances. As long as this state of affairs lasted, both indigenous and naturalized would certainly live peacefully.

But circumstances change, and with them the interest of the various races could also change; and if not today, then tomorrow; if not tomorrow, then day after tomorrow the tendencies of the naturalized will be in conflict with those of the natives. In this case, the interest of some will be at odds with that of the others. And then the interests of some could not be satisfied without sacrificing those of the others. And then we would have a fight for existence between two races, with fierce battles that could only be ended either by the total abolishment of the State, or when one of the races is totally crushed, so that again only one dominant race remains in the State....

Our national history and everyday experience have proved to us that, from among all foreigners who come to us, the Turks and particularly the Jews are the ones who never intermarry with us. Meanwhile, other foreigners—Russians,

---

[7] In fact, one continually sees such conflicts play out in all multiracial and 'multicultural' nations today.

Greeks, Italians, and Germans—intermarry and fuse with us, if not on the first then during the second or third generation. Eventually there comes a time when there is no distinction between these foreigners and ourselves, either as regards blood or love of country. But it is not the same with the Jews....

No matter how this question would be posed, or how it would be interpreted, we, if we do not fight against the Jewish element, will perish as a nation.[8]

VASILE ALECSANDRI: While in the Chamber, Vasile Conta delivered the above-mentioned discourse, and in the Senate, Vasile Alecsandri, the poet of the Union, expressed the feeling of Romanians as follows:

What is this new impasse? What is this new invasion? Who are the invaders? Where do they come from? What do they want? And who is the new Moses, leading them to the new promised land, situated this time on the banks of the Danube?

What are the invaders? They are an active, intelligent people, never tiring in the fulfillment of their mission; adepts of the blindest religious fanaticism; the most exclusivist of all the inhabitants of the Earth, the most unassimilable with other peoples of the world...

What do they want from us? To become owners of the land of this people, turning the old masters of this country into slaves, as are today the peasants of Galicia and part of Bucovina.

What is easier than substituting themselves for the inhabitants of this country and thus turning all of it into an Israelite property?

If this is the plan of the present-day invaders, as everything leads us to believe, it once again proves the enterprising spirit of the Israelite people. And far from deserving blame, it is likely to attract the plaudits and admiration of practical men. We Romanians would deserve the blame, if by our indifference or by the application of some fatal and absurd humanitarian theories, we would ourselves be helping

---

[8] From the discourse against the revision of the Articles of the Constitution, delivered in the Chamber of Deputies, held on 4 September 1879, and published in the *Official Monitor* No. 201, dated 17 September 1879.

in the fulfilment of this plan. The blame would fall upon our heads, if fooled by these theories, understanding them inside-out. Or, dominated by an imaginary fright under the influence of imaginary threats, we would forget that the Romanian Fatherland is a sacred storehouse entrusted to us by our parents, to be transmitted whole and unstained to our children...

What then would the whole country say, if we created such a situation? What would the Romanians say who had joyously fought for the independence of the ancestral land? Our country would turn her eyes away from us in pain. The Romanian would say: *Ask no longer for my blood from now on, if the blood that was shed serves nothing but the fragmentation of my country and the demeaning of national dignity.*

For these considerations, when Romania comes before us today, holding her History Book in her hand so that we may inscribe on its pages our veto, for myself, I tear out the page meant for the inscription to humiliate our country; and on the other page, I write with my heart, its dignity, its deliverance![9]

MIHAIL KOGALNICEANU: Here is the dignified attitude regarding the Jewish problem and the pressures exercised from abroad, taken by Mihail Kogalniccanu, Minister of Internal Affairs in 1869. He was titular head of that same ministry that, today, has become the place from which orders emanate for torturing those of us who still fight to defend our people:

> All those possessing a live interest in their country have been preoccupied with stopping Jews from exploiting the people.
>
> In Romania, the Jewish Question is not a religious one, but a national and at the same time an economic one. In Romania, Jews not only constitute a different religious community; they constitute, in the full sense of the word, a nationality, foreign to Romanians by virtue of origin, language, dress, customs, and even sentiment.
>
> It is not a matter then, of religious persecution, for if this were the case, the Israelites would face interdiction or restriction in the exercise of their cult, which is not the case.

---

[9] From the discourse against the revision of Article 7 of the Constitution, delivered in Romania's Senate, on 10 October 1879, and published in the *Official Monitor* No. 230, October 1879.

Their synagogues would not be allowed to rise freely near Christian churches; their religious instruction, and the publicity of their cult, likewise would not be tolerated.

All those who visited the Principalities, in particular Moldavia, were frightened by the sad aspect, not to say worse than sad, revealed by the Polish Israelites populating our towns. And when they looked more closely into the commerce, industry, and this crowd's means of livelihood, these travelers became even more frightened, because they saw that the Jews are consumers only, not producers. And that their principal industry is the retailing of alcohol...

I evicted no Jew from his domicile on the simple basis that, according to all the laws of the land, the Israelites from Romania have no right of domicile in villages, as is also the case in Serbia. I restricted the future rental of taverns and nightclubs by Jews, especially by those called Galicians and Podolians. This measure was justified on the Organic Statute and on the law voted by the General Assembly, then sanctioned by Prince Mihai Sturza, which no succeeding law has to this day abolished—on the contrary, a law that all Ministers of Internal Affairs before and after the convention, maintained and enforced. Proof of this are the orders of my predecessors…

Under these conditions, not one minister, not even ten succeeding one another in office, could do other than myself and my predecessors did.

Ministers of Romania, as a country with a constitutional regime, we cannot govern but according to the will of the people. We are duty-bound to take into account the needs, wishes, and to a certain degree even the prejudices of this nation...

This justifies the great irritation on the part of the Romanian populace, originating out of profound suffering and of a legitimate concern, for it is the voice of a nation feeling threatened in her very nationhood and her economic interests. Foreigners can stifle this voice, but it is impermissible to a Romanian minister, of any party, not to listen to it.

That's why, not only today, but always, in all times and under all administrations, all rulers, all statesmen of Romania, all those who possess a live interest in their country, have been preoccupied by the necessity of stopping the exploitation of the Romanian people by an alien people—the Jews.[10]

ION HELIADE RADULESCU:

Do you not see that the kikes in England and France do not only demand citizenship rights in Romania for their co-religionists, but privileges, and supremacy; do they want to establish an aristocracy of money, of the Golden Calf?

They demand that which we cannot give, were we to die to the last man. Do the kikes in England and France believe, I wonder, do you gentlemen believe with them, that Romanians will watch calmly, while among them will settle the most sordid and filthy, the most vulgar of aristocracies, the domination of clowns, Jews, and ruffians of Mammon? Under what title and on what right could such an abominable domination be established before the atrium, before the gates of the 20th century, where all humanity, except the sons of perdition, will come like a bride before the divine Groom?

Do the kikes of England and France come out with the Right of Man based on 'equality,' and yet have the audacity to pretend privileges and supremacy for themselves? And because they cannot invoke this right, they dare to coin the paradox "Romanian of Israelite Rite," in order to push their specifically Jewish audacity further, so far as to threaten us in the name of Europe's monarchs?

With what then shall the Jews conquer us? By their numbers, their force? For the good that we wish and we have wished them, in the name of the regeneration of peoples and of the Jews themselves in the land of Palestine, we pity them. We advise them, as a Christian would, not to try anything of this sort, or dare to even contemplate it, let alone lay claim to something in our present era of agitation caused by Satan's angels who tempted them. They had better not dare something of the kind, for God only knows how far Romanians may go in their legitimate and most sacred of all tempestuous

---

[10] From the communication of the Minister of Internal Affairs Mihail Kogainice-anu, addressed to the Minister of Foreign Affairs, June 1869, regarding the Jewish Question.

furies, defending their rights as a nation with an instinct of preservation![11]

BOGDAN PETRICEICU HAJDEU:

Two ways of Jewish behavior toward us are specified in the Talmud:

1)   If you are stronger than Christians, exterminate them.
2)   If you are weaker than Christians, flatter them...

But someone weaker than I, in order to become stronger than I someday, has first to pass through a middle stage in which he is equal to me. Do you now understand, I wonder, what it means to grant so-called political rights to the Jews?[12]

COSTACHE NEGRI:

Jewry, one seventh of our total population, is the saddest leprosy to which our weakness, our lack of foresight, and our venality have condemned us.[13]

A. D. XENOPOL: Finally, I permit myself to introduce, in the same selection of extracts, the opinion of the great historian Xenopol, professor at the University of Iasi. This, in view of the uncontestable authority of a scientist who had lived and seen with his own eyes the painful reality of his findings:

If a Romanian decides to open a store, no Jew will cross his threshold. Thus he would be by-passed by a large clientele; while Romanians are not averse to buying from Jews. It is clear that even without price-rigging, the resistance of the Romanian merchant and tradesman can be broken.
A Jew will never take a Romanian into his establishment if the latter stands to learn something thereby; for Romanians

---

[11] From *The Equilibrium Between Antitheses of Spirit and Matter*, by I. Heliade Radulescu, (1859-1869); Part III, entitled "The Israelites and the Jews."
[12] From "Studies in Judaism: The Talmud as a Profession of Faith of the Israelite People," by B. P. Hajdeu (1866).
[13] From the Letter to Lupascu, dated 12 January 1869, published in the volume *Verses, Prose, Letters* by C. Negri (1909).

are received into Jewish homes only as servants or porters. This system of exclusiveness persists strongly. In the innumerable Jewish workshops and stores that cover Moldavia from one end to the other, there is not a single Christian or Romanian apprentice, worker, foreman, accountant, cashier, or salesman.

Jews, then, practice against Romanians the most stringent economic exclusivism, something that they cannot renounce, for it is prescribed by their own religion.[14]

The Student General Strike Continues

After Easter, the fight recommenced. Regarding the League, Professor Cuza continued action via the papers, while the rest of us busied ourselves organizing. The series of meetings in towns and villages began.

On the student front, the modification of Article 7 of the Constitution brought with it changes. Student leaders in Bucharest and Cluj who believed that a student movement would ultimately persuade the government to recognize the just demands of the students, became bitterly disappointed upon seeing that, not only does the government not recognize any of their demands, but that it grants the Jews political rights; the students consequently thought more and more of capitulating. In Cluj, the president called a meeting in which he suggested the best thing to do was to go back to classes. The student mass rejected his proposal, declaring that they were fighting to preserve their honor, and that the fight should be fought to the very last limit of resistance. The supporters of this approach were Ion Mota, Corneliu Georgescu, Isac Mocanu, and all our groups. The president, Alexa, resigned, and Ion Mota was elected to replace him, along with a new committee.

The government's tactic, to make students resume their classes, failed this time also, but the leaders were sacrificed—Ion Mota and six others were forever expelled from all universities for their uncompromising attitude. In Bucharest, a group headed by Simionescu and Danulescu began to replace the leadership that had become increasingly undecided and weak. Here too, the government failed in its attempt to open classes after Easter.

It was now June 1923. Two more months of heroic resistance, misery, and pressures passed, with students exhausted. In Bucharest, the University

---

[14] From *La question israelite en Roumanie* by A. D. Xenopol, a study published in *La renaissance latine* (1902).

was reopened for exams, if only for Jewish and renegade students. On opening day, the army was posted in the university. Student clashes occurred out front but were too weak to deter its opening. The government's plan was to open the universities one by one, leaving Iasi for the last, and presenting Iasi with the *fait accompli* of three operating universities.

A week later in Cluj, several days after that in Cernauti, the universities opened with the army present, under the same conditions as in Bucharest.

In another week, the difficult hour of Iasi was to come. It was isolated by the government, alone, with its student forces considerably diminished. On the opening eve, knowing tomorrow morning the army would enter the University, we planned to occupy it ourselves during the night. Before dark, I sent a trusted student who entered the lobby and pulled back the bolts of two large windows in such a manner that this would go undetected, so that, being pushed from the outside, they would open. Not yet sharing this plan with anyone, I convoked a 9:00 pm meeting of 100 students in the Bejan Hall.

At 10:00 we occupied the University. We raised the swastika banner on its façade. A little later, the Rector of the University arrived, Professor Simionescu. He was let in. He urged us to leave the University. We replied, explaining to him our reasons. Several hours later, he left. We organized ourselves for guard duty and stayed there the whole night.

The next morning, students arrived at the University in large numbers. Invigorated, they unanimously resolved to continue the fight. The Jewish papers furiously attacked us. Two days later, Cluj, in a fight, tried to retake their University from the hands of the gendarmes. After two more days, Bucharest and Cernauti followed suit. These fights led to student risings again and to the closing anew of all universities.

The academic year ended. The Romanian youth had passed a unique exam in resistance, character, and solidarity. Honor to the student body, which, for its steadfastness, taking so many blows, has given an example of collective will yet unsurpassed in the history of the world's universities. No country has ever witnessed students, united in a single soul and assuming unto themselves all responsibility and all risks, being able to maintain a general strike for one year in order to prove their faith. None has witnessed students seeking, through their demonstration, to awaken the conscience of an entire nation, faced by the gravest problem of her existence. This is a beautiful page, a heroic page, written by the suffering of this youth, in the book of the Romanian nation.

The Plans of Judaism against the Romanian Nation

(1) Against the Romanian people

Whoever imagines that the Jews are some poor unfortunates, arrived here haphazardly, brought by winds, pushed by fate, etc., is badly mistaken. All Jews over the entire world form a great collectivity, bound together by blood and by the Talmudic religion. They are constituted into a very strict state, having laws, plans, and leaders making these plans. At the foundation, there is the Qahal. Thus, we do not face some isolated Jews but a constituted power, the Jewish community.

In every city or market town where a number of Jews settle, the Qahal—that is, the Jewish community there—is immediately formed. This Qahal has its own leaders, separate judicial set-up, taxes, etc. and holds the entire Jewish population of that locality tightly united around itself. It is here, in this tiny Qahal of a market town or city, that all plans are made: How to win over local politicians and authorities; how to infiltrate certain circles of interest to them, such as magistrates, officers, and high officials; what plans to use to take over such and such branch of commerce from the hands of a Romanian; how to destroy a local anti-Semite; how to destroy an incorruptible representative of local authority who might oppose Jewish interests; and what plans to apply when, squeezed beyond endurance, the populace would revolt and erupt into anti-Semitic movements.

I won't dive any deeper into these plans here. In general, the following methods are used:

I. For winning over local politicians:

1. Gifts; 2. Personal favors; 3. Financing the political machine for propaganda, leaflet printing, traveling expenses, etc.

If there are several bankers in town or rich Jews, each is assigned to a specific political party.

II. For winning over local authorities:

1. Corruption, bribery. A policeman from the smallest town in Moldavia, in addition to the pay he receives from the state, gets another salary or two each month. Once he accepts a bribe, he becomes the Jews' slave, and if he does not follow orders, then they use on him the second weapon:

2. Blackmail. If he does not comply, his bribe-taking is revealed.

3. The third weapon is destruction. If they realize you cannot be swayed or subjected, they will try to destroy you by searching for your weaknesses. If you drink, they will seek an opportunity to compromise you through alcohol; if you are a skirt-chaser, they will send you a woman who will compromise you or destroy your family; if you are violent by nature, they will send your way another violent man who will kill you or whom you will kill and then go to prison.

4. If you lack all of these defects, then they will employ *the lie*, whispered or printed calumny, and denounce you to your superiors.

In market towns and cities invaded by Jews, local authorities are either in a state of bribery, a state of blackmail, or a state of destruction.

III. In order to infiltrate into various circles or around highly-placed people, they use:

1. Servility; 2. Boards of directors; 3. Base personal favors; 4. Flattery.

Thus, all politicians are given Jewish secretaries, because they are handy at doing the shopping, shining the shoes, rocking the babies, holding the briefcase, etc., while at the same time cajoling and insinuating themselves. A Romanian is not going to be as good, for he is less refined, is not perfidious, comes from the plow, and particularly because he wants to be a faithful soldier, guarding his honor and refusing to be a lackey.

IV. Plans to ruin a Romanian merchant:

1. Flanking the Romanian with either one or two Jewish merchants. 2. Selling merchandise below cost, the loss being made up by special funds given by the Qahal. This is how Romanian merchants were ruined one by one.

To these can be added: a) The commercial superiority of the Jew, resulting from a commercial practice much older than that of the Romanian. b) The Jew's superiority in competing under the Qahal's protection. The Romanian enjoys no protection from the Romanian state but only miseries imposed by the local authorities corrupted by the Jews. The Romanian does not fight the next-door Jew but the Qahal, and this is why the individual will be crushed if he fights the coalition. The Romanian has no one, no parent state to raise him, advise and help him. He is left by himself, to his fate, while faced by the powerful Jewish coalition.

It's easy to repeat the solution of all politicians: "Let the Romanian become a merchant." Let these Romanian politicians show us a single Romanian merchant who was assisted by the state, a single school that was meant to really educate merchants, not bank officials or clerks. Let them show us even one institution built by them that helped with a small loan or guided the young graduate of a commercial school on the road to commerce. It was not the Romanian who deserted the road to commerce, but these politicians who deserted their duty as leaders and counselors of the nation.

The Romanian, abandoned by his leaders, has been left alone to face the organized Jewish coalition, the fraudulent maneuvers and the dishonest competition, and he was defeated. But the hour will come when these leaders will have to account for their wrongdoing.

(2) Against the Romanian land

I repeat once again, we are not confronting some poor individuals who wandered here haphazardly, by themselves, in quest of shelter. We face a Judaic State, an army that comes into our land to conquer us. Jewish population movements are effected against Romania according to a well-established plan. The great Judaic council probably seeks to establish a new Palestine on a section of land extending from the Baltic Sea down through parts of Poland and Czechoslovakia, then covering half of Romania to the Black Sea, whence they could easily establish contact by water with the other Palestine.

Where is the naive person who can believe that the movements of Jewish masses occur unplanned? They come *according to plan*, but they lack the courage to battle, to face risks, to shed their blood in order to justify some right to this land.

How do we know these plans? We know them for certain by drawing conclusions from the enemy's movements. Any troop commander attentively following the enemy's action realizes the plans he is seeking. It is an elementary matter.

Was there ever a leader in all the wars of history who knew the adversary's plans because he sat in on their making? No! He knew them perfectly from what the enemy did.

In order to break all power of resistance of the Romanian people, the Jews apply a truly unique and diabolical plan:

1. They will try to break the spiritual ties of the Romanian to *heaven* and to *Earth*. To break our ties with heaven, they will engage in widespread dissemination of atheistic theories in order to separate the Romanian people, or at least some of the leaders, from God; separating them from God and their deceased relatives, they can destroy them—not by sword but by severing the roots of their spiritual life. To break our ties binding us to the land, the material source of a nation's existence, they will attack nationalism, labelling it 'outmoded.' They will attack everything related to the idea of Fatherland and soil, in order to cut the thread of love tying the Romanian people to their furrow.

2. In order to succeed in this, they will try to get control of the press.

3. They will take advantage of every opportunity to sow discord in the Romanian camp, spreading misunderstandings, quarrels, and if possible, to split it into factions, fighting each other.

4. Will seek to gain control of most of the means of livelihood of the Romanians.

5. They will systematically urge Romanians on to licentiousness, destroying their families and their moral fiber.

6. They will poison and daze them with all kinds of drinks and other poisons.

Anyone wishing to conquer and destroy a people could do it by using this system: Breaking its ties with heaven and the land, introducing fratricidal quarrels and fights, promoting immorality and licentiousness, by material ruin, physical poisoning, and drunkenness. All these destroy a nation more surely than being blasted by a thousand cannons or bombed by thousands of airplanes.

Let the Romanians look back a bit to see whether this system has not been used against them with precision and tenacity—truly a murderous system. Let the Romanians open their eyes to read the press for the last 40 years, ever since it has been under Jewish control. Let them re-read *The Truth, The Morning, The Fight, The Opinion, The World*, etc. and see if, from each page, this plan does not constantly emerge. Let the Romanians open their eyes to see the disunity in present-day Romanian public life; let them open their eyes and see well.

The Jews use these plans like poison gas in a war, to be used against the enemy, not their own people. They propagate atheism for Romanians but they themselves are not atheistic, as they fanatically hold to respecting their most minute religious precepts. They want to detach Romanians from their love for the land, but they grab land. They rise up against the nationalist idea, but they remain chauvinistically loyal to their own nation.

(3) Against the student movement

Whoever believes that the forces of Jewish power have no plans for the student movement is mistaken. Being temporarily thwarted in their expectations, the Jews were disoriented for a moment. They tried to oppose the students by maneuvering the workers in the communist movement, but they were unsuccessful. This was because, on one hand, these workers were drained of strength, and on the other, they too, began to realize that we fight and suffer for their rights and for the Romanian nation. Many of them were, in their hearts, on our side.

The Jews, realizing their failure to turn the workers against us, then set the government and all the politicians against the students. By what means? Political parties need money and loans from abroad; when in power, votes; and favorable press when in opposition. Jews threatened to cut off financing needed for election propaganda of various political parties. They threatened, in conjunction with Jewish international finance, to run down loans to the government. They threatened to direct their mass of votes to compliant candidates, now that they had civil rights, and which might decide victory or defeat in a democratic system. And they threatened to manipulate the press, which they control almost entirely, and without whose support a political party or government can be defeated.

Money, press, and votes determine life and death in a democracy. The Jews control all of them, and through these, the Romanian political parties turned into simple tools in the hands of the Judaic power. Thus, we who began fighting the Jews found ourselves fighting, all at once, the government, political parties, local authorities, and the army—while the Jews sit quietly on the side.

(4) Jewish arguments and attitudes

"What will foreign countries say of the Romanian anti-Semitic movement, which takes us back to barbarism? What will men of science, and civilization, say?" Our politicians repeat to us, at every step, this Jewish "argument," printed daily in all the papers. But then finally, after eight years, Germany, notwithstanding all her civilization and culture, rises up against Jewry and defeats the hydra through Adolf Hitler, and the argument is dropped.

Then they bring forth another: "You are in Germany's service, paid by the Germans to engage in anti-Semitism. Where do you get the funds?" Once again, Romanian politicians—soulless, characterless, and honorless—mimic the tune of the Jewish press: "Whence the money? You are in Germany's pay." In 1919, 1920, and 1921, the entire Jewish press assaulted the Romanian state, unleashing disorder everywhere, urging violence against the regime, the form of government, the church, Romanian order, the national idea, and patriotism. Now, as if by a miracle, the same press, controlled by the same men, changed into a defender of the state's order and laws; it now declares itself against violence. Meanwhile *we* become: "the country's enemies," "extremists of the right," "in the pay and service of Romania's enemies," etc. And in the end, we even hear this as well: that we are financed *by the Jews*.

I wonder when that day will come, when every Romanian will understand the lies and perfidious argumentations of the Jews, and reject them as something of Satanic origin? I wonder when that moment will come in which they will comprehend the perversity of this race?

Here is how three Romanian university professors, Cuza, Paulescu, and Sumuleanu, were treated in the *Israelite Courier*, official organ of the Union of Naturalized Jews, of 23 April 1922 in the editorial titled "The Ghosts":

> A clique of clowns and public offenders got together to set up a band of wrongdoers. And to the country's shame, among them one finds three professors of our universities.
>
> And these specimens, these belated ghosts, want to revive anti-Semitism... and some retrograde clowns will succeed in this, now, when official anti-Semitism is vanishing and the universal vote will also inevitably bring along the democratization of our public and social life. No! It is in vain they work! These ghosts are not going to halt mankind in its onward march, nor will it be necessary to pierce their hearts with a sharp pole; the ridiculousness of their treachery will definitively finish them...
>
> We have reported earlier the savage action originated by the so-called "National Christian Union" (composed of some five silly characters) in order to fix them once and for all in their infamous posture, and call it to the attention of Jews

that there still are wrongdoers around, against whom they should defend themselves.

So then: clique of clowns, public defenders, band of wrongdoers, specimens, belated ghosts, treachery, savage action, infamous posture—this is what Professors Cuza, Paulescu, and Sumuleanu, teachers of Romanianism, are; and what their action to save the nation is!

We have taken outrage after outrage, ridicule after ridicule, slap after slap, until we have come to see ourselves in this frightening situation: Jews are considered as defenders of Romanianism, sheltered from any unpleasantness, leading a life of peace and plenty, while we are considered enemies of our nation, with our liberty and life endangered and hunted down like rabid dogs by all the Romanian authorities. I witnessed with my own eyes these times and lived through them, and I was saddened to the depths of my soul. It is dreadful to fight for years on end for your Fatherland, your heart as pure as tears, while enduring misery and hunger—then find yourself suddenly declared an enemy of your country, persecuted by your own kind, told that you fight because you are in the pay of foreigners, and see the entire Jewry master over your land, assuming the role of defender of Romanianism and caretaker of the Romanian State, menaced by *you*, the youth of the country.

Night after night, we were troubled by these thoughts, occasionally feeling disgusted and immensely ashamed, and we were seized by sadness. Would it be better for us, we reflected, to go on our way in the world, or would it not be more suitable to seek vengeance whereby all of us would perish?—both we and the Romanian traitors, as well as the heads of the Judaic hydra.

The Congress of the Student Movement's Leaders (Iasi, 22-25 August 1923)

In a limited committee in Bucharest, it was decided that a first congress of the leaders and delegates of the student movement would be held, following one year of struggle. This congress was to take place in Cluj on 22-25 August 1923. Mota, the president of the Petru Maior student center, wrote us that local authorities informed him they were ordered to interdict this congress. We, the Iasians, replied to Cluj as well as to the other centers, that we would take on the responsibility for this congress to be held in Iasi, even if the government wished to forbid it. Our offer was accepted and we fulfilled our duty of making the arrangements for the housing of the 40 known delegates.

On the morning of August 22, we went to the railway station to meet the delegation from Cluj headed by Ion Mota, the one from Cernauti headed by Tudose Popeseu and Carsteanu, and finally the one from Bucharest led by Napoleon Cretu, Simioneseu, and Rapeanu. At 10 o'clock we headed for the Cathedral to pray and have a Requiem celebrated in memory of student war dead, one of whom was the former president of the student center, Stefan Petrovici. But to our great chagrin, we found the gates of the Cathedral chained shut and guarded by gendarmes. Meantime, old Professor Gavanescul also arrived.

Then, uncovering our heads, we kneeled in the middle of the street in front of the church, which not even the infidel Turks had closed to those wanting to pray. The priest Stiubei happened to come by, seeing us kneeling, he approached us and read a few prayers. Then, bareheaded, in silence and very saddened, we covered the distance to the University, walking down the middle of the street, with stares from the Jews being shot at us like arrows from their doorways and shop windows.

The local authorities, flanked by numerous police forces and expecting us on the University's steps, informed us that the Ministry of Internal Affairs forbade the congress. The prosecutor stopped and warned us to disperse. Irritated, I replied: "Mr. Prosecutor, I know we live in a country ruled by laws. The Constitution guarantees us the right to meet, and you, Sir, know better than I that a Minister cannot abrogate these rights guaranteed us by the Constitution. Consequently, in the name of the law that not we, but you, disobey, we call upon you to step aside."

Hardened by the sacrilege committed an hour earlier, when the church's gates were chained and we were prevented from praying; being now faced by a second unjust and humiliating provocation, of being prevented from entering our own home, the University; seeing that these measures constituted a brazen lawlessness, we attacked everything in our path and, after some fighting, forcibly occupied the University.

The 13th Regiment, arriving a bit later, surrounded the university. We barricaded ourselves in, guarding all entrances, while outside each window we could see three soldiers posted, bayonets at the ready. The congress opened in the auditorium of the School of Law at 12:00 noon, under a heavy atmosphere in this inauspicious situation. The delegates, pale with indignation, muted by the sorrow of what happened at the Cathedral and here, felt throughout the deserted halls an air of profound sadness. Everyone was worried about a possible army assault on the University and of the inevitable consequences.

We delivered no discourses. The congress fathomed the seriousness of the situation and was apprehensive of grave repercussions. I was chosen as president for the first day. We began by denouncing the day's events. Several asked for the floor to protest.

Then we began discussions regarding the movement. What attitude should we take as the new school year opens: Do we capitulate? Difficult! A whole year of struggle with no result. On the contrary, shamed, humili-ated, and beaten. Do we keep on? Again, difficult! Students are exhausted; they cannot carry on a second year of battle. Yet, Mota, Tudose Popescu, Simionescu and myself, plead for continuing our fight; plead for sacrifice, as nothing would come from capitulation but shame and humiliation. And it was impossible that, out of sacrifice, something better would not bear fruit for our nation.

By 8:00 pm, it was dark. Outside in the town, we heard commotion and noise. Constantin Pancu, the veteran fighter of 1919, surrounded by the students, remained outside. A large number of townspeople, gathered at Tufli Cafe and carrying torches, tried to advance up the hill toward the University to bring us several sacks of bread. We all jumped to the windows to look out. The demonstrators broke the cordon at Tufli Cafe and ran up the hill. A second cordon at Coroiu St. was also broken in a tough fight. We heard outbursts of cheers. Likewise, a third cordon was overcome.

We got ready to make an assault from the inside, to get out, but our people on the outside could not break through the fourth cordon. One could hear Pancu's voice, his sack of bread at his feet: "They are our children." We were crying tears of joy. It is for such people we fight, and they would not let us down.

At 9:00, negotiations began between us and the authorities through Napoleon Cretu. All the students were promised immediate freedom, pro-vided I be turned in to them. The students refused. At about 11:00, they sent word to us we could leave in groups of three, naturally intending to apprehend me as we left. We accepted. Every minute, a group of three left. At the door, they were closely scrutinized by four commissars and officers. I quickly took off my national costume, gave it to a comrade, and donned his clothes. I left with Simionescu and a third student.

As the door swung open, I dropped some coins out of my pocket. As they hit the pavement, all commissars looked downward and asked: "What did you lose, gentlemen?" We, our heads also bent, looking for the coins, answered: "Some change." Simionescu lingered behind, talking with them, searching for money by striking matches, while I escaped.

We fixed the continuation of our congress for the second day, outside of town at the Cetatuia Monastery, in the greatest secrecy. I sneaked up there disguised as a locomotive stoker and I was lucky enough to be unrecognized, even by the delegates. Ion Mota presided. With our sentries placed in strategic positions, we could detect anyone's approach a mile away. We worked in quiet and stayed there until late that day. Propositions were made, decisions taken. It was also at this meeting that December 10 was proclaimed a national holiday for the Romanian students.

On the third day deliberations continued in a small forest on the Galata Hill. By a majority vote, we decided to continue the strike. An action committee of five was elected to direct the actions of the entire student movement in all universities. The committee members were: Ion Mota in Cluj, Tudose Popescu in Cernauti, Ilie Gameata in Iasi, Simioneseu in Bucharest, and myself. By forming this committee, the old student leadership in Bucharest, insufficiently informed and indecisive, collapsed for good. It continued in name but no longer led.

For the first time, it was officially decided to give the movement a new orientation: on one hand, to fight the political parties, considered by us to be estranged from our nation; and on the other, to strengthen the faith in our new Romanian movement, the League of Christian National Defense. The congress concluded its work on the fourth day.

In the evening, everyone left for his university and I left for Campul-Lung to organize the League congress in Bucovina in which Professor Cuza and all movement leaders were to participate. I had a hard time getting there, for an arrest warrant had been issued for me. As I was traveling, I rejoiced over all the decisions made by the congress that were in the spirit of our views, but especially because we gained for our side a man: Ion Mota, president of the Petru Maior center in Cluj.

The League Congress at Campul-Lung

The congress at Campul-Lung took place on 17 September 1923. We held it only after a tough battle, because the government had forbidden it, and to enforce its edict, sent in troops from Cernauti under the command of a colonel. Strong troop cordons were set up at each entrance to the town. We concentrated all our forces at the west entrance into town. There we broke cordons, thanks to the archers from Vatra-Dornei and Candreni, giving us a whole hour to get the entire convoy of several hundred wagons through.

The congress convened in the town's churchyard. The speakers were: Professor Cuza, my father, Dr. Catalin, Tudose Popescu; then the brothers Octav and Valerian Danieleanu, who had enthusiastically organized this imposing congress with the help of Dr. Catalin. Those proud mountain peasants, with their long locks, dressed in white shirts and thick-woven coats, upon hearing the sound of the long mountain horn, gathered in their town—numerous and stormy. They believed that the hour had come, awaited for centuries, for the Romanian to trample underfoot the hydra that had been sucking him dry; thus he emerged to assume his rights as master of his country, his mountains, his rivers, and his towns. They carried the burden of the war. Their sacrifice of blood on all fronts created Greater Romania.

But to their great chagrin and disappointment, Greater Romania did not meet their expectations. This was because Greater Romania refused to break the chains of Jewish enslavement that had been torturing them for so long. Greater Romania abandoned them to further Jewish exploitation and brought down upon their heads the whiplashes of politicians who would send them to prison when they tried to reclaim their stolen historical rights.

All forests in Bucovina, all those mountains laden with firs belonging to the Orthodox Church, which was now infused with politics, and estranged, were given to the Jew Anhauh for exploitation of firewood at the unheard-of price of 10 lei per cubic yard, while the Romanian peasant had to pay 350 lei. The mountain's forests fell under the merciless Jewish axe. Poverty and sorrow spread over the Romanian villages, and mountains became barren rock, while Anhauh and his kin tirelessly carried their gold-laden coffers over the border. The partner-in-crime of the Jew in exploiting the misery of thousands of peasants was the Romanian politician, who gorged himself on his portion of this fabulous profit.

The rally delegated 30 leading peasants to go to Bucharest under the leadership of Dr. Catalin and Valer Danieleanu, to see the Prime Minister. They were to ask him to take steps against the devastation of their mountains by revoking the Anhauh-Church contract. Also, to show their love for and gratitude to the young people who had aroused them to battle, they were to beg him to put *numerus clausus* in the schools.[15]

Tudose Popescu and I were also chosen by the rally to accompany the 30 peasants to Bucharest. I left for Bucharest ahead of them in order to see to it that these peasants, who came to the capital of their country for the first time, were well-received by the students. These peasants came to Bucharest with such purity of heart, with so much pain and so many expectations, to

---

[15] That is, to implement quotas against Jewish students.

plead our cause as well as theirs. The expense of their trip was disproportionately great compared to their poor means.

Upon their arrival in Bucharest, the students received them royally—these kings of all times of the Romanian people—and they got off the train in their sacred capital with eyes full of tears. But behind the railway station there waited Prosecutor Rascanu, police commissars, and cordons of gendarmes that prevented their going through.

The gendarmes and police commissars were then ordered to strike us. Rifle butts and sticks rained blows upon the white heads of the peasants and on their serene faces. The furious students then, placing the older peasants in the middle of their group, charged, and broke the first cordon, hastening toward the Polytechnical School where they broke the second one, then a third, and escaped into Matache Macelaru Square. The peasants wept.

The next day, we all went to the Ministerial presidency to be received by the Prime Minister. We were put off until the following day; finally, we were told we would be received on the third day. We came. We entered a hall and waited about an hour, quietly, talking in whispers and walking tiptoe. An office chief showed up. "Gentlemen, go home, the Prime Minister cannot receive you. He is entering the Council of Ministers." "But we came from afar," we tried to say. The door was closed in our faces.

I thought: each man spent 1,000 lei on his fare alone. Shall we go back home, accomplishing nothing? They cannot stay in Bucharest any longer. I grabbed the door with both hands and began to shake it with all my might, shouting at the top of my voice: "Let us in or else I'll break down the door and enter forcibly." I kicked at the door with my foot. The peasants raised a clamor and put their shoulders to the door.

The door opened and about ten frightened individuals appeared, their hair on end, their faces yellow. I think they were newspapermen: "What is it you want, gentlemen?" they asked. "Tell the Prime Minister, if he does not let us in, we'll break everything here and force our way in."

Several minutes later, the doors were opened wide before us and we entered. We climbed a flight of stairs. There in a hall, standing tall and straight as a pole, stood Ion Bratianu[16]; behind him, Ministers Angelescu, Florescu, Constantinescu, Vintila Bratianu, and others. "What do you want, good men?" he asked. The two of us, young students, were still full of indignation and we would have liked to appear fiercer, thus imparting

---

[16] Bratianu was prime minister, off and on, for most of the period between 1909 and 1927.

the true note of the group's state of spirit; but the peasants, having trod with their country shoes on marble stairs and plush carpets, softened us up.

"Your Highness, Sir Prime Minister, we kiss your hands and keep ourselves respectfully at your feet. What do we want? We want justice, for the Jews have invaded us. They take out our timber by the hundreds of train flatcars while it rains in our homes through leaks in the roof, for we even lack shingles with which to cover them. We cannot keep our children in schools any longer. The Jews also filled our schools, and our children will become their hired hands."

Then other peasants spoke. Bratianu listened, making no mention of our ruckus in the antechamber. The peasants added: "We also ask for the university students, our children, that *numerus clausus* be implemented as they have requested." Bratianu responded: "Go home and have patience, because I will have the forest question looked into; regarding *numerus clausus*, it cannot be done. Show me but one single State in Europe that introduced this measure and I, too, will introduce it."

But Europe would wake up only ten years later, introducing *numerus clausus* and thus recognizing our just cause. However, Bratianu would not live long enough to keep his promise, and his successors would be only low-level servants of Judaism—men who would raise their fists to strike us and kill us on order of their alien masters.

We all left, holding no hope. Nothing is going to be done. As an immediate consequence of the audience, several hours later, Dr. Catalin, who headed the delegation, and Valer Danieleanu were arrested. A group of students that evening staged a hostile demonstration before the house of the Minister of the Interior. The student Vladimir Frimu was arrested and incarcerated in the Vacaresti prison. The rest of us then left for Campul-Lung.

The October 1923 Student Plot

Mota came along to Campul-Lung to join me in, going to Petru Rares's hermitage on Rarau Mountain—a mountain I particularly love. As we climbed it, Mota shared with me his inner turmoil:

"The students can no longer carry on next fall. Rather than all of us accepting shameful capitulation following a year of struggle, it would be better to urge them to resume classes and we, who have led them, end the movement nobly by sacrificing ourselves and taking down with us all those we find most guilty of having betrayed the Romanian interests. Let's acquire some handguns and fire on them, giving a terrifying example to be long remembered throughout Romanian history. What will become of us after that, whether we shall die or whether we shall spend the rest of our days in prison, would no longer matter."

I agreed that the final act of our fight be, at the price of our downfall, an act of punishment for the pygmies who, deserting the posts of great responsibility they held, humiliated the Romanian nation and exposed it to untold dangers. We felt in that moment, boiling in our veins, the blood that demanded vengeance for all the injustices and the long chain of humiliations to which our people had been subjected.

Shortly after this, we gathered together Ion Mota, Corneliu Georgescu and Vernichescu from Cluj; Ilie Gameata, Radu Mironovici, Leonida Bandac, and myself from Iasi; and Tudose Popeseu from Cernauti.

The first problem we faced was to decide who were the principal guilty parties; who were most responsible for the state of misery that seized the whole country: Romanians or Jews? We unanimously agreed that the first and greatest culprits were the treacherous Romanians who, for Judas's silver pieces, betrayed their people. The Jews are our enemies and, as such, they hate, poison, and exterminate us. Romanian leaders who cross into their camp are worse than enemies: *they are traitors*. The first and fiercest punishment ought to fall first on the traitor, second on the enemy. If I had but one bullet and I were faced by both an enemy and a traitor, I would let the traitor have it.

We agreed on the names of several individuals who had betrayed their country—namely, six cabinet ministers, George Marzescu heading the list.[17] At last, the hour was striking for those scoundrels who never imagined they would have to account for their deeds in a country in which they considered themselves the absolute masters over a people incapable of any reaction—the hour in which they would have to answer with their lives. This time, the nation was sending its avengers through the invisible ties of the soul.

Then we took up the second category: the Jews. Which ones should we choose, from the two million? We pondered, discussed, and finally concluded that the real chiefs of the Judaic attack on Romania are the rabbis—all rabbis in all market towns and cities. They lead the entire Jewish mass to attack, and wherever a Romanian falls, he does not fall by chance. He falls because he was marked by a rabbi. Behind every politician who sold out, there is the brains of a rabbi who laid the groundwork and ordered the Qahal or the Jewish banker to close the deal and pay him off. Behind every Jewish newspaper to inspire slander, lies, or instigation, there is a

---

[17] Marzescu (1876-1926) was a journalist, lawyer, and politician.

rabbi. But there were only a few of us, so we chose only "the big cats" in Bucharest. Had we had the numerical strength, we would have taken absolutely all of them.

Then we picked the bankers: Aristide and Mauriciu Blank, who corrupted all parties and all Romanian politicians by putting them on boards of directors and showering them with money[18]; and Bercovici, who financed the Liberal Party.[19]

Then we looked over the Jews of the press. The most insolent ones, the poisoners of souls: Rosenthal, Filderman, Honigmann (Fagure), directors of the papers *The Morning, The Truth, The Fight*—all these, enemies of Romanianism.

We left for Bucharest in groups, saying goodbye to Iasi forever. I left a letter for the students in which I explained the justification for our gesture, bade them farewell, and urged them to go back to classes, but fully to keep the faith until final victory. We all wrote to our parents and comrades-in-arms.

In Bucharest, we met again at Danulescu's house. We had known him for some time now, and he had made a good impression on us. He was not included in this team, but he gladly put us up. We left his place that evening at 8:00 to go to Dragos' house, where we were to clarify details and determine when our action should begin. We were hardly gathered together when a pale Dragos came into the room, saying: "Brothers, the police have surrounded the house."

This was on the evening of 8 October 1923, at about 9:00 pm—a moment of confusion in which we had no time to even talk. We just directed our searching looks to one another. Then I stepped out into the foyer, where I could see the figure of Gen. Nicoleanu and his commissars who were forcing open the door. The door gave way and the house was filled with commissars.

Gen. Nicoleanu shouted: "Hands up!" But we had no time, as we were each grabbed by two commissars and placed in line: myself in the right flank, then Mota, Corneliu Georgescu, Tudose Popescu, Radu Mironovici, Vernichescu, Dragos. "Turn over your revolvers!" "We do not have any," we answered. Except Mota and Vernichescu each had a Browning 6.35. Then they took us out of the house one at a time, each with his

---

[18] Mauriciu (1848-1929) and Aristide (1883-1960) Blank were Jewish father-and-son bankers.
[19] The details of this individual are unknown.

arms gripped by two commissars, and put us individually into waiting cars. Behind us in the house, Dragos' old mother was crying.

The cars started. Where were they taking us, we wondered? We did not utter one word. We asked no questions of those who held us prisoner, and who, themselves, also kept silent. After riding through a few streets, we reached Police Headquarters. They had us get out and go into a room where they searched our pockets. They took away everything we had on us, including collar and tie. This frisking, this stripping of our collars, this treatment as if we were pickpockets, was most humiliating.

But we were only at the beginning of this road of humiliation. With faces to the wall, not allowed to turn our heads, and kept in this position for some time, we were thinking: "Free men several hours earlier, proud and determined to break the chains of our people, look what we have become—some poor, powerless unfortunates, stiffly facing a wall by orders of some miserable police agents, frisked like robbers, stripped of our personal effects."

It was with this humiliation that our great suffering began, which, little by little, would rend our hearts. I think there is no greater suffering for a fighter who lives in dignity and honor than being disarmed, and then humiliated. Death is always sweeter than this.

Next, we were taken to a room and seated five yards apart on benches, with the agents at our side, forbidden to look at one another. We sat there like that for hours until we were called for interrogation. Participating in these long, burdensome hours were, besides myself, Mota, Tudose Popescu, Radu Mironovici, Corneliu Georgescu, Vernichescu, and Dragos. After a while, one by one, we were called to be questioned, in a large room with the prosecutor, the investigating judge, Gen. Nicoleanu, and some government representatives there.

My turn came towards morning. There they placed before me some of my letters and two baskets containing all our revolvers that were hidden in a supposedly safe place. I could not figure out how they got there. I could understand that we were caught, but who told them where the handguns were hidden?

My questioning began. I had no idea what the others had declared and we had no previous understanding among ourselves as to what to say, for we had not dreamed we would find ourselves in such a predicament. That's why I weighed the situation and took the decision I considered best.

A minute at the crossroads. When the first question was put to me, though three minutes had elapsed since coming into the room, I had not yet sized up the situation enough to take a decision. I felt overwhelmed by weariness and was profoundly shaken. And when I was asked to reply, I said: "Gentlemen! Please grant me a minute of reflection before I reply."

The question put to me was—to deny or not to deny? That minute I strained all the powers of my mind and soul, and decided to deny nothing. To tell the truth. And not timidly or remorsefully, but courageously: "Yes, these handguns are ours. We wanted to shoot the ministers, rabbis, and the big Jewish bankers." They asked me for their names. When I started giving them their names, beginning with Alexandru Constantinescu and ending with the Jews Blank, Filderman, Bercovici, Honigmann, all those present stared in astonishment, more and more terrified. From this, I suspected that my comrades, questioned before me, had denied everything.

"But why kill them?" "The former because they betrayed their country. The latter as enemies and corrupters." "And do you not regret it now?" "No, we regret nothing. Though we have fallen, it does not matter. Behind us, there are tens of thousands who think likewise!"

Saying this, I felt freed from the boulder of humility under which I would have further sunk, had I denied everything. Now I was standing on my faith that brought me here, proudly facing both my fate and those who seemed to hold the right of life or death over me. Had I denied everything, I would have had to stay on the defensive against the accusation lodged against me, begging indulgence, gaining the good will of my inquisitors. At the trial to follow, and on the basis of written proof in their possession, we would have had to experience a painful and shameful test, denying our own writing and our own beliefs, denying the truth—which went counter to our conscience and the honor of our movement.

As representatives of a great student movement, should we lack the courage of taking responsibility for our deeds and faith? In this case, the country and our comrades on the outside would not have learned our intentions. And indeed, the only goal of our suffering—no matter how long it might be—was exactly that the country be enlightened so it could at least know its enemies better.

Then they demanded that I put these declarations down on paper in my own handwriting. I did so. In the end, I added: "The date of the attack had not been decided upon. They caught us while discussing this. I proposed to do it in one or two weeks." At this point, the interrogators stopped me, insisting more and more that I not put down these particulars.

It was only later that I realized their reasons for this insistence— because my last phrase destroyed the judicial value of the entire accusation. A 'conspiracy' requires four elements: 1. An association of individuals with one aim in mind. 2. The designation of victims. 3. The acquisition of weapons. 4. A date established for the action. But since we had not yet decided upon a date for putting the plan into action, we were still in the discussion phase. The fixing of the date was of capital importance, for in two weeks we could have gotten ill, the victims could have died, the government could have fallen or given in, etc. Our entire defense rested on this point.

Following my testimony, officers led me into a cellar where I was placed in a cell alone. The door was padlocked on the outside. I guessed my comrades were occupying the adjoining cells. I beat on the wall with my fist, asking who else was there. I received an answer: "Mota." I then lay down on the boards to get some sleep, for I was dead tired; but not having a heavy coat, I trembled from the cold. Then lice began biting me. They swarmed over me by the thousands. I turned the boards on the other side, but the lice came on top. I repeated this operation several times until I thought it must be daylight.

Then I heard a noise at the door. It was opened, and those of the others, and we were all taken out; then placed in cars, each accompanied by two gendarmes and two commissars. The cars then left, one after the other. And the same question crossed our minds. "Where to?"

(1) In Vacaresti Prison

We passed through several unfamiliar streets on which the curious passersby stared at us. We left the capital behind and the cars stopped in front of some large gates, above which was written "Vacaresti Prison." We got out of the cars, flanked by soldiers with bayonets, spaced ten yards apart. A creaking of locks and chains was heard and the big gates were opened. One by one, we crossed ourselves and, stepping inside, were led upstairs to the prison offices where our arrest warrants were handed to us. We learned that we were arrested for conspiracy against State Security, with forced labor as the specified punishment.

We were then taken to another yard, where a tall church stood in the center. All around there were walls, and along them, cells. I was put into a cell way in back, one yard wide, two deep, then it was locked on the outside. There was only one plank-bed inside, and near the door, a small iron-grilled window. I wondered where my comrades were. Then I laid my head on the boards and fell asleep.

I woke up after two hours, shaking. It was cold and no sun's rays penetrated into the cell. Dazedly I looked around and could hardly believe where I was. I saw the misery of the cell. I told myself: "Difficult situation." A wave of pain ripped my heart. But I consoled myself: "It is for our people." Then I began gymnastic movements with my arms, to warm my-self up.

At about 11:00 am, I heard footsteps. A guard opened the door. I looked at him. 'Perhaps I had met him at some time,' I hoped. But he was a stranger, and a surly man. He looked at me with mean eyes. He gave me a loaf of bread and a dish of soup. I asked him: "Mister Guard, might you happen to have a cigarette?" "No! I do not!" He locked me up again and left. I broke the black bread and swallowed a few spoonfuls of soup.

Then I placed them down on the cement floor and began to collect my thoughts. I could not comprehend how they discovered us. Could it be that one of us was careless enough to speak about our project to someone? Did someone betray us? How did they find our revolvers?

Again I heard footsteps. I looked through the window. A priest and several men were nearing my cell. They said: "Well, gentlemen, is it pos-sible that you, educated youth, could do such a thing?" I replied, "If it is possible for this Romanian people to perish, invaded by Jewry and by be-ing overwhelmed by the sell-out, licentiousness, and ridicule of its leaders, then what we did is possible too." "But you have so many legal means!" "We have followed all legal paths until now. If even one had been opened to us, it may be that we would not have landed in these cells." "And now, is it good? You will have to suffer for your deeds!" "Perhaps from our suf-fering, something better will emerge for this people." They left.

At about 4:00, a guard came, bringing me a worn-out blanket and a large sack full of straw in lieu of a mattress. I evened-up the sack as well as I could. Then I ate a little more bread and lay down. I meditated on the discussion I had had with the priest, and thought: "A people never gained anything out of the partying and easy living of its sons. It was always the suffering that resulted in real gains for it." I succeeded in finding a purpose for our suffering and, at the same time, some moral support for these sad hours. Then I got up, knelt, and prayed: "Lord! We take upon ourselves all the sins of this nation. Receive this, our suffering now. See that a better day for this people be forthcoming through this suffering."

Then I thought about my mother and those at home who may have heard of my fate and might be thinking of me. I prayed for them, and then I lay down to sleep. Although I was dressed and covered with the blanket, I was cold, and I slept poorly on that straw mattress. I was awakened at 8:00, when a guard opened the door and asked me if I wanted to go out for sev-eral minutes. I got out and did some gymnastics to warm up.

The row of cells that included mine was somewhat higher than the rest, so I could see the entire courtyard. All at once, I saw someone wearing national dress walking among the inmates. It was *my father*. But I couldn't believe it. What was he doing here? Was he also arrested? I made a few signs and he saw me. The guard stopped me: "Sir! You are not allowed to signal." "He is my father," I answered. "That may be, but you are not allowed to signal." I looked at him and said: "Comrade, leave us alone in God's care with the suffering He gave us; don't you add more to it." And I went back into my cell.

After lunch, they took me out again. They flanked me between bayonets and led me out of the prison, where, on the road, all of us were placed in a single file at 10 yards apart, each between two bayonets. My father was leading the column between two soldiers, bayonets at the ready. There were some new arrestees; Traian Breazu from Cluj, Leonida Bandac from Iasi, and Danulescu. We were not permitted to turn our heads or to signal one another. For just a second, I got a glimpse of the sunken faces of my poor comrades-in-suffering.

But what gnawed at my heart was the injustice to which my father was being subjected. He was guilty of nothing. A lifetime fighter for this nation, a professor in secondary schools, a major, former battalion commander on the front line all during the war, several times a member of Parliament—and not an obscure one at that—he was now paraded on the streets of Bucharest between bayonets.

We left thus in a column, trudging toward the Tribunal. Romanians looked at us with indifference. But when we reached the Jewish quarter, all the Jews came out to their doors and windows. Some threw outrageous looks at us and laughed; others commented loudly, others spat. We bent our heads and walked thus, the whole way, our hearts full of pain.

At the Tribunal, our arrest warrants were confirmed. We were defended by the attorney Paul Iliescu, who was the first lawyer to offer to plead our case. We were then sent back in the same formation, on the same route. We could see on newsstands the headlines of *The Morning* and other Jewish papers: "Student Conspiracy. The Arrest of the Plotters."

Once again, I got to my cell. For two weeks, I stayed there in the cold, with no further knowledge of the others or any news from outside. After two weeks seeming like two centuries, we were taken out of our cells and placed in heated rooms, in threes. We were permitted to cook and eat together. When we saw each other again, it was like a true holiday. I was to share a room with Dragos and Danulescu. Meantime, Garneata, the president of the Association of Christian Students, turned himself in, so that our number grew to 13: My father, free of any guilt; Mota, Garneata, Tudose Popescu, Corneliu Georgescu, Radu Mironovici, Leonida Bandac,

Vernichescu, Traian Breazu, and myself, charged with conspiracy; Dragos and Danulescu, detained for having sheltered us. In addition to these, there was Vladimir Frimu, who was arrested when we demonstrated in front of the Minister of Interior's home.

We obtained a primus stove on which we cooked the food sent from the outside by relatives and friends. The regular prison food was something frightful, and the misery in which the inmates lived, indescribable. My father got permission from the prison administration for us to go each morning at 7:00 into the church in the courtyard to pray. We all knelt before the altar, saying the "Our Father," and Tudose Popescu sang "Most Blessed Virgin Mary." There, we found solace for our sad prison life, and hope for tomorrow.

Each of us set up a work schedule for himself. Mota busied himself with matters related to the forthcoming trial; Danulescu studied for his exams in medicine. I was working on plans for the organizing of the youth in the national struggle: organizing the student centers, the youth in villages, and the students in secondary schools. I worked this out down to the smallest detail, until Christmas time, so that if we got out of prison, we could put it into practice; if not, we decided to find someone on the outside to implement it. This was to be done within the framework of the League which was to be the political arm, while our section would be for educating the youth and for fighting.

On November 8, the feast of Saints Archangels Michael and Gabriel, we were discussing the possible name for this new youth organization. I said: "Let it be 'Michael the Archangel'." My father said: "There is in the church, on the left-hand door of the altar, an icon of St. Michael." "Let's go see it!" Mota, Garneata, Corneliu Georgescu, Radu Mironovici, Tudose, and I went to look at it and we were truly amazed. The icon appeared to us of unsurpassed beauty. Previously, I was never attracted by the appearance of any icon. But now, I felt bound to this one with all my soul and I had the feeling the Archangel was alive. Since then, I have come to love that icon. Any time we found the church open, we entered and prayed before that icon. Our hearts were filled with peace and joy.

The torture of our trips to the Tribunal was resumed. On foot, between bayonets, through mud, with our worn-out shoes and our feet wet. Some Jewish crooks who defrauded the State of several hundred million lei were driven to the Tribunal in cars, while we walked. Many times, our trips were made unnecessarily, only to harass us. I was called to the Tribunal 25 times, to be interrogated by the investigating judge only twice. We changed no part of our early depositions.

One thought preoccupied us constantly: "Who betrayed us?" Night after night, we sought to solve this enigma. We reached the stage where we were suspicious of each other. One morning, I went to church to pray before the icon, to reveal the traitor to us.

That evening, as we sat down to dinner, I spoke to my comrades: "I am compelled to bring you sad news. The betrayer has been identified. He is in our midst, sitting at the table with us." Everyone was looking at everyone else. Mota and I followed everyone's face, hoping for an indication. I put my hand into my breast pocket saying: "Now I will show you the proof." At that moment, Vernichescu stood up, hesitated for an instant, gave Bandae the key to the food box, and said: "I am leaving." We were puzzled by his departure, but resumed our discussion regarding the proof I refused to produce, for I had none.

When we left the table, we found Vernichescu alone. He addressed us, "Codreanu suspects me." I told him I suspected no one; thus we were reconciled.

Weeks and weeks passed, and our prison life was dragging on. We marked in pencil on the wall every passing day. Life in prison was difficult—exhausting for the man who was born free, who lived in dignity. It was horrible to feel in chains, within high unfriendly walls, far from your loved ones of whom you hear nothing. And not even here can you move around much, for three-fourths of the time, we were kept locked in our cells. Every evening, the sinister noise of bolts being drawn at your door plunged one into a mood of sadness. The enemies of this nation were free outside, enjoying respect and the good life, while we, in addition to moral indignities, often times went to bed hungry and shivering from the cold the whole night, on plank-beds and straw.

But finally, joyous days came our way. After two months of imprisonment, we received the news that the order for my father's and Danulescu's release had been received. For us, indeed, great joy. We helped them pack and shortly they were taken away. We watched as they left until they passed through the main gate. I asked my father to tell mother and the others not to worry at all. Anyone's liberation is an occasion of great joy for those left behind. Everyone is glad. Perhaps, by one's liberation, each grows stronger in the hope of obtaining his own freedom. After a short while, Dragos, Bandac, Breazu, and Vernichescu left, having been taken out of the case, as were my father and Danulescu.

Only six of us were left, charged with "conspiracy against State security." Several days later, Dragos sent the news that it was indeed Vernichescu who betrayed us; he also made copies of the latter's testimony, which was on file. We received this news with hearts full of bitterness. Our nation had always had her share of traitors.

(2) Outside

In all the universities, students returned to classes. It seemed there was a moment of disorientation. For two months, they had been living under the terror of the Jewish press, which incessantly exaggerated the gravity of our attempt at revenge and its "disastrous" consequences for the country. It shouted that we had lost the confidence of the "civilized world," that we were a Balkan state. They constantly asked: "What will Berlin say?" "Vienna?" "Paris?"

And so, transformed into the defenders of the "permanent interest of the State," Jews daily urged the country's leaders to take radical measures against a nationalist movement that must be suppressed "with the utmost violence." But just a year earlier, when Max Goldstein planted a bomb in the Senate building and the police were rounding up communist Jews, the same press was yelling:

> A state cannot maintain itself against popular will by the use of violence. Where is the Constitution? Where are the laws? Where are the constitutionally guaranteed freedoms? What are foreign countries going to say when a state takes such restrictive steps? A state cannot survive through arrests, prisons, bayonets, terror. For this violence the state uses will be returned by the multitude or isolated individuals. Force will be answered by force. Terror, with terror. And they will not be guilty, but the State that provoked them.

And now, with a shamelessness that only the blindfolded fail to see, the same press wrote:

> It is not enough that these terrorists be arrested. They must be condemned in such a manner as to make them an example. Even this is not enough: all those who propagate such anti-Semitic 'ideas' that cause so much damage to our country, ought to be arrested. This anti-Semitic weed ought to be pulled out, root and all. And this question must be dealt with mercilessly and without clemency.

To this torrent of hostility, the nationalist press opposed a fierce resistance. In addition to *The Universe*, which always expressed a correct attitude regarding the manifestations of national conscience, the nationalist movement had the support of the following newspapers:

- *The Student Voice*, put out by the Bucharest students, which only recently came under the editorship of our indefatigable comrades who were free: Simionescu, Rapeanu, Fanica Anastasescu, Danulescu, and others whose names escape me.

- *New Dacia*, organ of the students in Cluj, directed by Suiaga, Mocanu, and Iustin Iliesu, the poet and author of "The Students Hymn."

- *The Word of Iasi*, organ of the Iasi students.

- *Awake, Ye Romanian*, organ of the Cernauti students, recently moved to Campul-Lung, directed by Dr. Catalin and Danieleanu.

- *The National Defense*, official organ of the League, Bucharest, with the unsurpassed articles of Professor Paulescu, from which we reproduce the following lines:

  > The same constraint through cold, hunger and terror, successfully used by Bolshevik Jews, was used on the students.
  >   Who could ever imagine that the time would come when our children, the flower of the Romanian nation, would be compelled to celebrate the holiday of the unification of all Romanians locked up in the cellars of some prison or chased into the cold, without shelter, without food?
  >   Probably you did not realize that you were waging war against the entire Romanian nation.

- *The Union*, organ of the League, Iasi, directed by Professor Cuza, containing articles of immortal logic.

- *The Nationalist*, popular organ of the League in Iasi.

- *Freedom*, popular newspaper in Orastie, belonging to Father Mota, who revealed our gesture in its true light, being thus the first to unhesitatingly cut the curtain of silence that surrounded us during those very first moments.

The student body understood our sacrifice. That's why the student movement rallied more and more around these walls of the Vacaresti prison, in which each student center had its imprisoned representatives. Peasants, too, began showing concern for our lot. They sent us money, and had masses said for us in churches, particularly in Bucovina's mountains and Transylvania where *Freedom* penetrated. Here is a small example:

The Might of the Moti for the Students in Vacaresti
(No. 7, Year II, 4 March 1924)

Among the gifts of money received by the students locked up in Vacaresti prison from the peasants from all regions, there is one more brilliant and more precious than all the others: It is that sent by the Moti of the Apuseni Mountains. Scraping the bottom of their leather belt pockets or a corner of their kerchiefs, they gathered their 2, 3, or 5 lei to send down their valleys, on paths trod by *Iancu*, their defender of old, and sent them along with their hearts, over the long, long way to Vacaresti across the mountains, where they had heard their sons were imprisoned for wanting to save them from want and injustice, from poverty and chagrin. These contributions were sent from the poorest corner of our country, of which the song says, with so much bitterness and sorrow, "Gold lies in our mountains' core, while we beg from door to door."

The most precious gift was sent to the students in Vacaresti: a handful of change and a fragment of a beggar's soul, "hungry and naked, without lodging," a soul that hides beneath a rag, its greatest treasure, moral health, that inexhaustible source of strength, from which in times of great tribulation springs the salvation of the people!

The Moti think of the students! Their soul begins to understand, to stir, to forge a new ideal. This is the best and most eloquent sign! Listen to some of their names, from the town of Risca: Nicolae Oprea, 2 lei; Nicolae Florea, 3 lei,. N. Haragus, Aron Grecu, Tigan Adam, A. Hentiu, N. Bulg, Ion Asileu, Al. Vlad, N. Borza, N. Leucian, Antonie Florea, A. Leucian, each 5 lei; N. Ciscut, A. Riscuta, Ion Ancu, Saliu Faur, each 10; N. Florea, priest and N. Rusu, each 15 lei; N. Baia, notary public and Dutu Riscuta, each 20 lei. Total 210 lei.

The peasants will soon understand, and they will come to our side with their strong and long-enduring soul, in the expectation of the hour of justice.

(3) Thoughts of a new life

Christmas holiday is here. There in the Vacaresti prison, we thought constantly of our families back home and, especially during the long sleepless nights, we were relentlessly worried. When will our side win, we wondered? When will we get out of here? If we are sentenced to 10 or 15 years, will we be able to weather the imprisonment or will our suffering and worries sap our health day by day, until we perish?

We floated in the unknown. This state of uncertainty consumed us. We wanted to have the trial date set once and for all, in order to know sooner the fate awaiting us. The suffering and common fate we had in store bound us together more and more, and discussions over the innumerable questions raised led us to the same conclusion, little by little shaping a uniform pattern of thinking. The smallest questions regarding the national movement preoccupied us for hours and days. That was where we learned to think deeply and pursue a problem in all its ramifications, down to the finest detail.

We resumed the study of the Jewish problem and its causes, its chances for solution. We established organization and action plans. After a while, discussions were finished and we passed on to laws, to indisputable truths and axioms. We watched Romanians on the outside of our group, gropingly delving into our nationalist problem and giving birth either to a newspaper or a parody of an organization. We could see they were reaching false conclusions in matters of doctrine, were uncertain in matters of organization, and totally lacked original ideas in matters of action.

We realized then, better as a result of more profound reflection, that:

1. The Jewish problem is no mirage, but a grave life-and-death problem for the Romanian nation, with the country's leaders grouped by political parties becoming more and more like toys in the hands of the Judaic manipulators.

2. This present political system—through its concept of life, its immorality, and the democratic set-up from which it springs—constitutes a real curse upon the Romanian people.

3. The Romanian people will not be able to solve the Jewish problem unless it first solves the problem of its political parties. The first aim to be reached by the Romanian people on its way to topple the Judaic power that oppresses and strangles it, will have to be the toppling of this political system. A country has only the Jews and the leaders it deserves, just as mosquitoes can settle and thrive only in swamps. In a similar way, Jews can only thrive in the swamps of our Romanian sins. In other words, in order to defeat them, we will first have to extirpate our own defects.

The problem is even deeper than Professor Cuza had shown it to us to be. The mission of this fight had been entrusted to the Romanian youth which, if it wants to take up the challenge of this historical mission, if it wants to go on living, to continue having a country, must prepare and gather all its forces to carry on the fight and win. We decided that, should we get out of prison, by God's help, we not part ways, but stay united to dedicate our lives to this one aim.

But before busying ourselves with our people's defects, we began by looking at our own sins. We held long meetings in which each of us mentioned the defects he observed in the rest. And we tried to correct them. This was a delicate matter; no one takes lightly a critique of his own defects. Each believes, or wants to show, he is perfect. But we say: first we should know and correct our sins, and then we shall see whether we have the right or not to engage in improving upon others.

This is how the holidays passed, and then the winter. Spring arrived. We knew as yet nothing regarding our future fate—only that a great popular current in our favor was born on the outside, supporting our cause in spite of all desperate endeavors of the Jewish press to stem it. This current was steadily growing among students, townspeople, and peasants, uniformly strong in Transylvania, Bessarabia, Bucovina, and the Old Kingdom. We received letters of support and encouragement from all parts.

Spring finally brought us a great joy. Trial was set for March 29 before the Court of Ilfov. We began to get ready. But what kind of preparation could we make? We admitted to everything. We said all we had to say. Lawyers who signed up to defend us came to visit. They called to our attention the gravity of our position in view of our testimony, suggesting we change it—as well as our whole attitude. They thought it would be more prudent to deny. We categorically refused and asked them to defend us within the framework of our testimony, that we did not intend to alter it the least bit, no matter what the outcome of the trial might be.

If by any chance we were to be acquitted, how could we do without the icon that we prayed to each morning? We searched among all the inmates until we found a painter. We asked him to make us a copy, and in three weeks' time, he made an exact replica, six feet high, and a small one for me to carry on my person, and a third of medium size for my mother. Mota also had one made for his parents. Then we figured that, on the basis of our testimony, we would most certainly receive at least five years. And we knelt before the icon: "Lord Almighty! We consider these five years lost to ourselves. If we are acquitted, we pledge to consecrate them to the cause of our nation."

We decided that all of us would move to Iasi in case we were acquitted, to establish there our center of activities. From there, following the plans we had readied, we would begin organizing the country's entire youth, beginning with high school boys and girls and even younger students; those in the normal schools, trade schools, seminaries, commercial schools, and finally, youth in the villages. After that, the university centers would be revamped. All these young people, we hoped, would grow in the spirit of the faith that animated us, so that, as young adults, they would enter the political arena, where the fate of our struggle was to be determined, and, being further augmented by new graduates year after year, would become like endless waves of assault.

(4) The isolation of politicians

The political system has infected our national life. Organization of the youth is needed, as is emphasis on the necessity for their further self-education, to protect and separate them from the infection of the political system. Permitting the infection of the Romanian youth to continue means annihilation for us, and a definitive victory for Israel.

Moreover, our organizing of this youth will take care of the very problem of our political system, which, by lack of young recruits, will starve to death. The slogan of the entire younger generation must be: *No youth must ever enter the gates of a political party; he who does so is a traitor to his generation and his nation.* For in effect, by his presence, name, money, and work, he strengthens the power of the politicians. Such a person is a traitor, just as he is a traitor who leaves the side of his brothers and goes over into the enemy camp. Though he may not shoot back with a weapon, if he only carries water for those who do shoot, he is an accomplice to the killing of those falling among his betrayed comrades, and consequently a traitor to his cause.

The theory urging us to all join political parties in order to improve them—if we presume they are bad—is false and perfidious. As it has been from the beginning of the world, only fresh water has flowed into the Black Sea from thousands of rivers, but this never resulted in freshening the sea's salty water; rather the opposite. And likewise with us: by entering the cesspool of political parties, not only will we not improve them, they will corrupt us.

These were the thoughts and resolutions uppermost in our minds to implement when we would be acquitted. Our organizational set-up was ready. Our plan of action was established, down to the minutest detail. Everyone's part was set. A new newspaper was to be published, to be named *The New Generation*, and our organization as a whole was to be named "The Archangel Michael." All our flags would have to carry the image of St. Michael the Archangel from the church in Vacaresti prison. This organization, as we saw it, of the entire youth generation, was to be the youth section of the political organization of the League, having as its aim the education of this youth.

For us, this program, conceived within the Vacaresti prison walls, was a beginning of a new life. It represented something complete in inspiration, organization, and plan of action, different from anything else we had thought of earlier. It was the beginning of a new world, a foundation on which we could build for years to come. Upon leaving the prison, we were to go to all university centers and share with the students our decisions, showing them that street demonstrations and clashes no longer need occur, in view of our new plan. We would still embrace our past expressions, not denying them as ours, and would not be ashamed of them. But their time is gone. We must all engage now in a great organizing task that will bring us victory.

(5) Avenging the betrayal, and the trial

Mota was pensive. He was constantly telling us that, once out, we would not be able to make any headway unless we punished the betrayer. It always was betrayal that sapped the nation's strength, but we Romanians had never turned our weapons on the traitors; that's why treason took root and traitors multiplied in all walks of life; that's why Romanian public life was nothing now but a permanent betrayal of the people. If we did not solve this problem of treason, our work would be compromised.

We were very excited the night before our trial began. At last, our fate was to be decided. In the morning, we were taken to the office to see our families. Shortly, Vernichescu came in. Mota took him by the arm as if he wanted to tell him something, and both went into a nearby room. Several minutes later, we heard seven gunshots and shouts. We stepped out into the hall. Mota had shot Vernichescu to punish him for his betrayal. I jumped to Mota's side to defend him, for he was surrounded by police officers and functionaries threatening him.

When the commotion subsided, we were immediately taken away and put in separate cells. Through little windows, we could see Vernichescu carried out of the infirmary on a stretcher on the way to a hospital. In our cells, we all began whistling "Christian Students of Greater Romania," our fighting hymn, to accompany him thus, until he disappeared through the prison gates.

Two hours later, the investigating Judge Papadopol arrived. He had us brought upstairs, one by one, to appear before him. We all made common cause with Mota.

The next day, following a night spent sleeping on cement floors, we were taken to the Tribunal. Our situation was now very grave, yet we, in the basement of the Court House, sang our fighting songs the whole time. The trial was to begin at 1:00 pm. From around 10:00 am, thousands of students and citizens had been gathering around the Tribunal. At around noon, all the capital's regiments had been called up to control the crowds.

At 1 pm, we were led into the Court of Assizes. Presiding was Mr. Davidoglu and prosecutor was Mr. Racoviccanu. On the defense bench sat Professor Paulescu, Paul Iliescu, Nelu Ionescu, Teodorescu, Donca Manea, Tache Policrat, Naum, etc. After the jurors were drawn, the definitive writ was read, amid great silence. We listened. We realized that our fate was being decided. Then it came our turn to speak. The interrogation began. We admitted everything with the exception of having reached a final decision. We did not determine the date, but we showed the motives pushing us into this action. We showed the menace of the Jewish problem and accused the politicians of corrupting and betraying the nation. In spite of many interruptions by the presiding officer, we continued our testimony to the end.

There followed a severe and often times unjust and insinuating indictment delivered by the prosecutor. We felt the balance tipping in his favor. But the prosecution's success was short-lived. Professor Paulescu read his declaration in the church-like silence imposed by his great prestige and saintly figure. It was a short declaration—and for the prosecutor, who seemed to embarrassedly sink into his chair, a devastating one.

A recess was taken; it was now 8 pm. Outside, the crowd waited in increasing numbers. Nelu Ionescu, Tache Policrat, and others, and at the end, Paul Iliescu, spoke brilliantly. By this time, it was 5:00 am. The prosecutor, through a new indictment, tried to regain his position and win over the Court. Our lawyers answered him. At 6:00 am, we had our last word. Then we were taken out. The jurors began their deliberation.

We waited over half an hour, which seemed an eternity to us. Shortly thereafter, we heard cheers. An officer brought us the news: "You are acquitted!" We were then taken back into the courtroom, where the acquittal verdict was read to us. Outside, people were still waiting. Upon learning we were acquitted, they broke into great cheers and singing.

We were loaded in a car that took us through unfamiliar streets back to Vacaresti for the completion of customary discharge formalities. We gathered up our belongings and icons, ready to leave that grave, with its long nights of turmoil and its sufferings. But poor Mota had to stay on— who knew for how long, to suffer henceforth all alone. We took leave of him. We embraced him, tears in our eyes, and parted from him in profound pain. We left to be free; he entered his cell anew, in solitary. Oh, how many more weeks he would have to lie there alone on that cement!

As soon as we were out, the first thing we did was to go to Danuleseu and Dragos to ask forgiveness of their families for the trouble we caused them, and to thank them for their concern for us during our imprisonment. Then we left for our homes, where our mothers and the whole family were waiting, rejoicing with eyes full of tears.

At Iasi

At Iasi, I was eagerly awaited by the younger comrades. I found none of my classmates there; since last fall, they had all scattered to their home towns. I took my icon to St. Spiridon Church, where I placed it within the altar. One after another, I met all my friends and we rejoiced to see each other again.

But our joy did not last long. As I was strolling on Lapusneanu St. with my two sisters and about ten students, the police jumped on us out of the blue, striking us over the head with their rubber clubs and hitting us with their rifle butts. We were stunned: provoked in this manner and struck for no reason, in the very Iasi in which we had seen so many battles? In the Iasi in which we beat Judeo-Communism at the University in 1919, 1920, and 1922? In the Iasi in which the overwhelming Jewry and its press were knocked down and held at bay for years? Struck in my own house?

Then I turned to deliver a riposte. Anger gave me the strength of a lion, and I would have been able to take on the whole police force. But my student friends grabbed hold of me. I received several additional blows with rifle butts. Passers-by began booing the police and shouting.

Eventually the police withdrew, and I left for home, dejected, furious at my friends. But they told me, "They have orders to provoke you, and if you retaliate, to shoot you and get rid of you."

In the afternoon, I went to a student dormitory where the student leaders were gathered in a large room. They told us how, for the six months I was away, they had fought, and how much they had taken; how they went back to classes; how they handled the situation so as not to be humiliated; and how, on November 1, a religious service was held in the auditorium before all the students and professors. One of the students, Lazarescu, spoke on that occasion: "We will go back to classes, but not right away. First we will address a memorandum to our professors and the University Senate, expecting a satisfactory reply." Then he related to us how this memorandum was presented and how university professors, headed by Pro-rector Bacaloglu, granted most of the memorandum's points.

On November 6, the students resumed classes. The professors knew how to avoid an unjust humiliation of the students who fought a whole year for their beliefs.

They went on telling us how Marzescu, the Interior Minister, brought his own man in as Police Prefect, giving him free rein to crush the student movement and nationalist movement in Iasi. They explained how this man, with the help of his entire police force, engaged in this work. But because the students had gone back to classes and quiet was reestablished, he was at a loss as to how to win his laurels and earn his pay. Thus he began to provoke them.

They further related to us how, on December 10, several women students going to the Cathedral were met by intoxicated police, who beat them with their rubber truncheons, grabbed them by the hair—right in view of the professors—and dragged them through mud on the street; how, one by one, the students were beaten; how the student Gheorghe Manoliu, the choir conductor, was beaten on his ankles with sticks, then arrested; and how he, detained by the police in a state of great misery, contracted jaundice and died in the hospital. The students in Iasi clearly went through tough times in those six months.

We, in our turn, told them of our tribulations, reminding them that it was our duty to get Mota out of prison. In the end, we gave them an account of our plans for the future: How we must organize our entire generation, raise it and educate it in an heroic spirit; how we would have to isolate the political system so that no youth would ever enter its ranks, and how the system could be defeated and replaced by Cuza's League. We told them how, only through a nationalist government, expressing our Romanian conscience, force, and health, could the Jewish problem be solved, by taking legal measures to protect the Romanian element and putting brakes on the Jewish invasion. We explained how our generation has the great and sacred mission to revive this conscience, this force, and this vitality. We stated that we, the "Vacarestians," have decided that all of us are to come to Iasi and establish here the center of this action, which we would place under the protection of St. Michael the Archangel. Our comrades listened and received our plans for the future with much joy.

After the meeting, we paid visits to Professors Cuza, Gavanescul, and Sumuleanu, sharing our thoughts with them as well.

CHAPTER 3

A YEAR OF GREAT TRIALS: MAY 1924 TO MAY 1925

The Christian Cultural Home

In light of the plan we were trying to follow, our meetings were held with difficulty because we did not have a meeting place of our own. All of us being poor, we could not afford the rent for at least two rooms, in order to begin organizing the youth. We met in a wooden barracks left since the war in Mrs. Ghica's yard.

One day we decided to build ourselves a building of several rooms. But how should we go about it? On 6 May 1924, I gathered together some 60 youngsters, all university and high school students. I said:

> "Dear comrades, how long are we going to sweat it out by holding our meetings in this barracks? Up to now, Romanian students had the right to meet in their own university build-ings. But we were chased out. Until yesterday, we had the right to meet in our dormitories. We were chased out of here too. Today we meet in run-down barracks in which we get rained on. In all cities, students receive help in their noble pursuits.
>
> "Here, there is no one to help us, because the popula-tion around us is composed of enemy Jewish crowds and of politicians devoid of feeling. Our Romanians are pushed out to the periphery of towns, where they live in dark misery. We are alone. The power to carve for ourselves another des-tiny, now as tomorrow, can be found only in ourselves. We must get used to this idea, that between God and us, there is no one to help us.
>
> "That's why there is no other solution but to build the structure we need with our own hands. Granted, none of us has ever built houses or made bricks. I can understand that we need, in the first place, the courage to break down the mentali-ty in which we have grown up—the mentality that makes the young intellectual who, the second day after becoming a

student, is ashamed to carry a package on the street. We need
the courage and the will to start from scratch, the will to up-
root obstacles and overcome difficulties."

Olimpiu Lascar, a small building contractor with a big heart, who owned a
house in Ungheni on the Pruth River, encouraged me in my idea, telling us:
"Gentlemen, I suggest you come make the bricks in Ungheni, where I have
some land I will let you have. I also place my house at your disposal." We
accepted his proposition. But we had no money to pay our fare to Ungheni.
We needed about 300 lei for about 20 persons. This money, too, was given
to us by Lascar.

(1) The first work camp

On 8 May 1924, we left for Ungheni, some by train, some on foot. There
were 26 of us. We had nothing: neither shovels nor any kind of tool, nor
money, nor food. Lascar, who was expecting us, took us in. "Welcome
gentlemen! The market town Ungheni is full of Jews, like a hive. Perhaps,
seeing you, they will act less impertinently. We Christians, only a handful,
are terrorized by them." Eventually, we formed some delegations to go to
the homes of Christians, trying to borrow shovels, spades, and other needed tools.

The next day, we went to the plot of land on the shore of the Pruth
River. The local priest said a prayer for us. We worked for over a week to
get down to the good soil, for it was our bad luck that, for about 50 years,
townspeople had dumped their trash there, forming in some spots a layer
six feet thick. Helped by several professional brickmakers, we began working the clay and making bricks. We were divided into teams of five, each
making 500 bricks daily, thus attaining a total of 3,000 per day. Later,
when our numbers grew, we made even more, working from 4:00 am until
the evening.

The biggest problem was food. At first, it was the Ungheni people
who helped us; later, groceries were also sent to us from Iasi.

Our old professors, Cuza and Sumuleanu, looked somewhat skepti-
cally upon our endeavor. They found it childish, thinking we would not be
successful. A while later though, they began to appreciate our efforts and
even helped us. When Corneliu Georgescu left the University in Cluj,
where he had completed a year of pharmacy, and came to Iasi, in common
agreement with the others, we gave to the brickyard the 17,000 lei donated

to us while we were imprisoned at Vacaresti, and which Georgescu had kept for us.

Yet, as the food problem was serious, Mrs. Ghica lent us a two-acre garden plot, which was planted by other student teams, to grow the vegetables needed at Ungheni. Our work was now in two places: one group of students working at Ungheni, another at Iasi in the garden, interchanging every three or four days.

Our first work camp had the effect of generating a revolution in the thinking of the day. Everyone from all around—peasants, workingmen, and even the intellectuals—came to watch us, full of curiosity. These people had been used to seeing the students promenading, elegantly dressed, on Lapusneanu St. or singing songs of joy around tables in beer halls in their free hours. Now they saw them working clay with their feet, muddy up to the waist; carrying river water in pails from the Pruth River; bending over the shovel in the heat of the sun. These folk witnessed the crumbling of an up-to-then dominating concept, i.e., that it is shameful for an intellectual to work with his hands, particularly at heavy labor—something formerly allotted to slaves or lowly classes.

The first ones to appreciate the camp's value, from this point of view, were precisely the members of the humble classes. Peasants and workers, socially separated from the other categories, and shy, because their labor was not appreciated, showed their delight on their faces, seeing in this a sign of appreciation for their exhausting labor and of esteem for them. They felt honored and perhaps envisioned better days in the future for themselves and their children. That's why, out of the little they possessed, they brought us food daily.

Student life passed quietly. There were no longer street demonstrations and incidents. We worked full of joy, hopes, thinking we would soon have: our own home.

(2) A new blow

One day, my father went to Iasi; I met him there. At about 10:00 pm, I was heading back to my place. At Union Square, I heard some commotion at a restaurant and I stopped to see what was going on. Two students—the brothers Tutoveanu—were having an altercation with Professor Constantinescu. The Prefect of police arrived on the scene, handcuffed the students, and took them away toward police headquarters, beating them. I, saying nothing, just watched this scene sorrowfully.

Then I noticed that Commissar Clos, accompanied by three or four police officers, was coming toward me. Two paces from me, he shouted: "What are you doing on the street at this hour, you good-for-nothing?" Bewildered, I just looked at him. Because he had known me for so many years, I couldn't imagine that he would ever address me like that. I thought he took me for someone else. But I felt myself grabbed by the neck and shoved back. Then again: "You stare at me, still? Vagabond... Crook!" I said nothing, but I stood my ground, looking at them. Then under blow after blow, pushed by the four policemen, I was "walked" more than 30 yards to the corner at Smimov. Here, I tipped my hat, saluted them, and said: "I thank you, gentlemen."

Deeply hurt, crushed by grief and shame, I went home to spend that night in torment. It was the second time in my life that I was struck, both within the month. I controlled myself. But you, oppressors in the entire world, do not count on the power of one's self control. He who controls himself, will one day explode, terrifyingly.

The following day, I told my father what happened. "Leave Clos in peace" he said. "Don't do anything. Two slaps on the face of such a person just dirties your palms. The time of his justice will come, rest assured. They are probably ordered to provoke you. But you must control yourself and try not to go out alone anymore."

I accepted his advice. But it seems to me that a man who is beaten and does not retaliate is no longer a man. He feels ashamed and dishonored. I carried this dishonor like a large boulder on my heart. But worse was yet to come, several days later.

(3) Overwhelmed by blows at the garden

The garden was all spaded. We came from Ungheni to put in tomatoes. At 5:00 am on 31 May, 50 students were ready to start work. While still in formation, as we finished the roll call, I noticed several soldiers at the back of the garden. Then suddenly, over 200 of them burst into the yard, loading their weapons. They surrounded us. I told the boys: "Everyone stay put. Don't react."

At the same moment, I saw, like a black cloud, a group of about 40 men around the gate, running in step, revolvers at the ready, shouting and swearing. It was Manciu the Prefect and his police.

They were beside us in no time. Two commissars and the chief of police placed three revolver barrels against my forehead. They looked at me with bloodshot eyes, cursing. Manciu shouted: "Tie his hands behind his back!" He struck me. Two others lunged at me, pulled out my belt, and tightly tied my hands in back with it. Then a blow from behind hit me on my right jaw. Another man, Vasiliu Voinea, came near and whispered in my ear: "You'll be dead before evening! You won't live to chase out the Jews!" He cursed and kicked me; then blows rained down on my face, while others spat at me.

Our entire front, trapped between rifles and revolvers, stood immobilized, watching, helpless to come to my aid. Mrs. Ghica ran downstairs, demanding: "What is the meaning of this, Mister Prefect?" And he replied: "I'll arrest you too!" Off to the side, I spotted Prosecutor Buzea, witnessing the scene.

Revolvers in hand, those in custody were then searched. Whoever moved was struck and thrown to the ground.

After that, flanked by eight gendarmes with fixed bayonets, they placed me 10 yards out front; the others were likewise flanked by 200 gendarmes. And they marched us off. I was ahead, hands tied behind my back, my face spat upon, followed by the others. We were escorted thus all along Carol St., before the University, on Lapusneanu St., Union Square, on Cuza-Voda, to the Police Prefecture.

The Prefect and his policemen walked on the sidewalks, rubbing their hands. The Jews, jubilating in front of their stores, respectfully greeted them. Saddened, I could hardly see in front of my eyes; I felt that, from now on, everything is finished.

Several high school students passing by me, stopped and tipped their caps to me. They were immediately apprehended, manhandled, and put with the rest of us.

After being paraded like this for more than a mile through the middle of town before the Jewish population, in this state of utter humiliation, we were taken into the Police Prefecture. They threw me, tied as I was, into a filthy hovel; the others were kept in the yard.

(4) Upstairs, in the Prefect's office

One by one, the young prisoners were taken upstairs into the Prefect's office for interrogation. The Prefect sat at his desk, and the other interrogators, over 30 of them, were on chairs around him. "What did Codreanu tell you?" he demanded. "He did not tell us anything, Mister Prefect," answered the student or young high schooler. "Now you will declare everything he told you!"

The person's shoes were taken off and his ankles chained together. A weapon was introduced between these, and he was lifted upside down, the weapon being held on their shoulders by two soldiers. Manciu, his coat off, began beating the soles of the victim's feet with an ox whip. Poor fellows: hung upside down, thus beaten on their feet, unable to stand the pain, began to scream. Realizing they faced these henchmen—brute commissars who sneered with gusto at the frightening situation in which the nation's children were being tortured by some enemy-paid scoundrels, far from any soul that could weep for them and intervene on their behalf—they cried for help.

Then the Commissar Vasiliu had their heads lowered into pails of water to stifle their cries of pain and despair.

When finally, the pain became unbearable and they felt their bodies could no longer take it, they shouted that they would admit everything. The Prefect went to his desk in the expectation of their confession, while the victims, their legs freed, looked around dazed. Then they burst out crying, falling to their knees: "Forgive us, Sir, but we don't know what to declare." "No? Get him up again!" he ordered his commissars and gendarmes. And each poor fellow, his heart frozen, watched as the preparations for his agony recommenced.

Again lifted upside down on the weapon, again beaten on the feet. Again they felt, one by one, the Prefect's blows falling on their feet. Their feet became bloody, ebony-black, so swollen that they could not put their shoes back on. Among those thus tortured were: the son of the present prosecutor of Ilfov County, Dimitriu; and the son of Maj. Ambrozie, his eardrum broken, and who in later life became a commissar at the same police prefecture.

Beaten in this manner, they were then carried into a separate, secret room. At around 9:00, I was called in. My hands still tied, and numbed, two gendarmes escorted me into the Prefect's office. There, he sat behind a desk, and around him sat the more than 30 men—commissars, commissar-aides, and officers. I looked into their eyes, thinking I might find one compassionate heart. But I found nothing but general satisfaction; they were all smiling: Botez, the Chief of Security, Dimitriu, the Director of the Prefecture, Commissar Vasiliu, Clos, and the rest.

The Prefect took out a sheet of paper. Then: "What exactly is your name?" "I am Corneliu Codreanu, candidate for a juridic doctorate and attorney in the same bar as you." "Put him down!" Three men, servile scoundrels, lunged at me and knocked me down in front of his desk. "Take off his shoes!" They took them off, one man for each shoe. "Put chains on him!" They chained my feet. I told them: "Mister Prefect, you are now the stronger, master over life and death; but tomorrow, when I leave here, I will take revenge."

At this moment, I heard some noise and voices in the hall. Professor Cuza arrived with Professor Sumuleanu and parents of the children: Col. Nadejde, Maj. Dumitriu, Butnariu, Maj. Ambrozie, and others, accompanied by the prosecutor and medical examiner, Professor Bogdan. The Prefect and the others jumped off their chairs and went out into the hall. I heard the Prefect saying. "What do you want here? I ask you to get out!" Then Professor Cuza's voice: "Who do you think you are talking to? Do you think we came here, just so that you could throw us out? We have come, accompanied by the prosecutor, as complainants against you." "Gendarmes, throw them out!" ordered the Prefect. Professor Sumuleanu posted himself at the door of the room in which the victims were locked, saying, "Mister Prosecutor, we will not leave here until this room is opened for us." Several commissars: "There is no one in this room. It is empty." Professor Sumuleanu: "Open the room now!"

Upon the prosecutor's intervention, the room was opened and six youngsters were helped out by their parents and brought into the Prefect's office. The medical examiner, Professor Bogdan, examined all of them, issuing medical certificates. Several hours later, all those in the yard were freed. I was kept in for two more days, after which I was sent to the examining magistrate. He let me go. I told him: "Your Honor, if I am not given justice, I am going to get it myself."

I went home. Professor Cuza, with Liviu Sadoveanu, came there to see me. "We heard that you said you wanted to take the law into your own hands. Don't do anything of the sort. We will report this to the Ministry of the Interior, demanding an investigation. We are sure to receive satisfaction."

(5) On Rarau Mountain

I was morally crushed. All my plans collapsed. I left both the brickyard and the garden to fate and boarded the first train to Campul-Lung in Bucovina. There, on the green paths, I slowly climbed up the mountain, carrying in my soul the burdens and the humiliation of yesterday, as well as puzzling torments regarding the future. It seemed I had no friend in the world except the mountain—the Rarau, with its hermitage.

When I was about 4,500 feet up, I stopped. I looked over mountains and hills for hundreds of miles, but no scene could replace the picture of infamy and humiliation to which I and my comrades had been exposed; I could still hear their sobbing, and it hurt.

It was getting dark. Not a living soul around—only trees with vultures shrieking around the barren cliffs. I only had with me my heavy coat and a loaf of bread. I ate some bread and drank some water springing from among the rocks. I gathered pieces of wood to make myself a shelter, a hut. I lived here for a month and a half. The little food I needed was brought to me by shepherds from old man Piticaru's sheepfold. I was brooding, ashamed to go down among people. I wondered, What sins have I committed, that God sent this misfortune upon my head now, just as I was ready to launch such a grand and beautiful plan?

I wrote to Mota: "I don't know what ails me; it seems I am not myself! Good fortune abandoned me. Misfortune has been following me for some time, step by step; in anything I start, I fail. And when fortune no longer serves you in battle, all those around you begin to desert you. You bring them together at the cost of 30 victories, and one defeat is enough for them to leave you."

My soul was ravaged by doubts. I was at a crossroad. We were fighting for the good of the country and were treated like enemies of the people. We were mercilessly hit by the government, police, gendarmes, army. Should we also use force? They are the State—by tens of thousands, hundreds of thousands. We, a mere handful of youngsters, exhausted in body by hardships, hunger, cold, and prison. What force do we represent, to expect at least a small chance of victory? If we tried, we would be crushed. And in the end, the country, dazed by the Jewish press, would say we were some madmen.

Shall we not use force and violence, as they do? They provoke, torture your men, scatter them, and kill you. Shall we permit ourselves to be killed? But at our age, we have not yet written anything down and it would not even be known why they killed us; better for all of us to leave the country. To leave and to curse; to wander throughout the whole world. Better for us to beg, in country after country, than be so humiliated here in our own land.

Or shall I descend from this mountain, weapon in hand, and do justice, that I may do away with the beast blocking the road and stifling the life of our nation. But what about our plans afterwards? I will die in my endeavor or die in prison; I cannot bear a prison regimen. I love liberty. If I do not have it, I die.

But what about Mota? Such a move means both my martyrdom and Mota's, whose chances for acquittal will vanish completely. Our entire group will be crushed. All our well-meant thoughts, all our plans for organizing, will have been in vain—all would have ended here.

For six weeks, there on top of the mountain, I was tormented by these thoughts, failing to find a solution. Under the weight of my worries and anguish, my chest began hurting and I felt my powers waning. I had been an impetuous man who never gave in to anyone. I was sure of myself and confident in my powers. Wherever I went, I won. This time, difficulties crushed me!

I descended from the mountain. I left everything to fate; I could not find any solutions. But from then on, I carried with me a revolver that I intended to use at the first, slightest provocation; no one was going to budge me from that resolve.

I went to the brickyard. There, Grigore Ghica, left in charge of the work, had responsibly carried on. The number of bricks in storage increased considerably. Two new ovens, each with a capacity of 40,000 bricks, were built. This was around July 15. The fellows received me affectionately. Nothing unusual happened in the yard.

In Iasi though, I found changes. Police commissars, who earlier hardly had shoes on their feet, were now newly outfitted from top to bottom by the Jews, who felt like absolute masters. The Police Prefecture had an automobile at their disposal given by the Jews. They exhibited an impertinence we had not encountered since 1919 during the communist movements, when they imagined themselves to be on the eve of revolution and when every little Jew, in Iasi or over the Pruth, assumed the airs of a people's commissar.

(6) Efforts to destroy our bloc

The Judeo-Liberal power had heard of our group and of our vow taken at Vacaresti, realizing that the students would rally around us as one. Nothing frightens Jews more than a perfect unity in others—the unity of feeling in a movement, in a people.

That's why they will always be for "democracy," which has but one advantage—and that, for the nation's enemy. Democracy breaks up the unity and the spirit of a people. Faced with the perfect unity and solidarity of Judaism in Romania and the rest of the entire world, a people, divided into democratic parties and thus fragmented, will be defeated.

This was also true of the student movement. Since we had no perfect unity, Jews found factions or leaders whom they could convince, masonic-fashion, suggesting to them all sorts of ideas that had no other purpose but to break up our unity. But now, since our group this time presented an unshakeable oneness with possibilities of rallying the entire student movement, we were confronted with an interminable series of carefully-woven lies and intrigues, aiming to split Mota away from me, and the others from one another. Jews found weak elements among the students who could be used as unwitting tools. Pretending that they were sharing great secrets with them, Jews launched intrigues that caught on even among students' parents—some of whom became the fiercest advocates for breaking the ties of their sons with this group.

How were we able to resist? Only through the foresight of our plans made in Vacaresti. We realized from the very first moment that this classic attack used by Masonry and Judaism would be aimed at us. We were ready. So that, the moment it started, we resisted even our closest relatives. And as soon as we detected an intriguer at work, we got together and informed the whole group.

Here is some advice for all organizations, as I call their attention to a system commonly used everywhere. In order to parry the attack: 1. Never believe tendentious information, no matter where it comes from. 2. Immediately report attempted intrigue or subterfuge to the group in question, to the involved persons, and to the leaders. In this way, an attack may be repelled.

(7) My betrothal

On 10 August 1924, at the Ungheni brickyard, surrounded by my comrades and my parents, I celebrated my betrothal to Miss Elena Ilinoiu, the daughter of Mr. Constantin Ilinoiu, a train conductor. He was a man of great goodness and great tenderness of soul. After that, I moved into their home, where I was received with open arms, even though they had a family of five children. This family was a constant support in the fight I was waging. Their care for me and their love sustained me.

On September 13, I went home to Husi, where I celebrated my birthday in my parents' home. I had just turned 25.

The Mota-Vlad Trial

The trial of Mota, and of the student Leonida Vlad who procured the revolver, was set for 26 September 1924. Vlad turned himself in several days after the shooting, and was kept in prison with Mota all the time. I left for Bucharest, where deliberations opened before the Court of Assizes.

Mota energetically defended his thesis that treason must be punished. Public opinion, fed up with traitors, followed the unfolding of the trial with lively interest and enthusiasm. People saw in Mota's gesture the beginning of action against traitors and proof of moral health. His deed burst like a light on the dark side of Romanian life where, century after century, fighters for the good of the people had been felled through treason. All the students at all universities held huge demonstrations for his acquittal. Around the Tribunal in Bucharest, again, thousands of people were massed who wanted a new life for their country and demanded Mota's freedom.

At daybreak, popular justice brought a verdict of acquittal. This was enthusiastically received throughout the whole country. Mota, after seeing his parents, left Cluj for Iasi, where he settled down, in accordance with our vow.

On What Happened in the Garden

The humiliation and dishonor to which we were subjected during the lawlessness of May 31st had crushed us morally; it became an open wound that deepened more and more, consuming our life and seemingly drawing us closer to the grave. The humiliation you feel when both you and yours are dishonored gives you a feeling of profound pain, making you shun people, ashamed to be seen. It would seem you feel this world despises you, laughing in your face because you are incapable of defending your honor; that you endanger society proper, letting it be believed through your cowardice that an oppressor can, unpunished, dishonor it and hurt it according to his whims. These pains grew proportionately as our attempts to obtain legal redress were rejected with a cynicism that led us to desperation. Victims who sued for legal satisfaction risked being beaten again by the police, this time within the very walls of the praetorium of justice and even before the judges.

In the end, however, it was the complainants who were condemned. What happened on May 31st did not remain without its repercussions. Below, I reproduce newspaper stories on this event, along with attempts to get satisfaction for the outrage. On 8 June 1924, *The Universe* published the following story:

The Iasi Police:
Students were Beaten by the Police Prefect Himself

"We imagine Mr. Manciu, the prefect of the Iasi police, as being like one of the most notorious policemen of the last century, exemplified by violence and brutality. Manciu, though a policeman of only a year's experience in a university town like Iasi, inaugurated his system of anachronistic police violence last year at the congress of university professors. He was able to stop a congress of university teachers because that is what his police impulses dictated to him.

The protests that followed, against the indignities heaped upon this most distinguished group of intellectuals, remained fruitless, for Mr. Prefect of the Iasi police had political backing for doing what he did.

And since then, Mr. Manciu has assiduously continued his police methods, which he particularly exhibited these past days, when he beat, he zealously struck, he maliciously bled the students, then ordered his subalterns to imitate him with the same brutal zeal.

No matter what the students of Iasi had done, had they even been assassins, they should not have been beaten. First, an investigation should have been made, the public prosecutor's office should have been informed, they should have been arrested, possibly put in chains, but not beaten to a pulp.

Manciu is certainly obliged in the course of his duties also to apply certain regulations regarding 'the protection of animals.' We even believe he enforces them. In other words, he sees to it that horses are not beaten, that pigs are not tortured. And yet Mr. Manciu who, as a student, must have studied penal law and must have read something of the penal literature that perhaps was recommended to him by our distinguished penalist Mr. Iulian Teodoreanu himself, a man who has been preaching the abolition of brutal sanctions in prisons, personally beat the students, tortured them, covered them with blood.

But, what if the beaten students are not guilty of any of the absurdities of which they are accused? Then what? Should he in turn be thrashed? Certainly a judicial investigation is needed. But a sanction is also needed to make it impossible for Mr. Manciu to strengthen his muscles on the heads of students.

The paper continues on 9 June 1924:

The Students of Iasi were Maltreated

They were Provoked by the Police. Tortured for no reason. A Brutal Police Prefect. Manciu Must be Fired.

We wrote in an earlier issue on the banditry committed by Mr. Manciu, the Police Prefect of Iasi, against the students. Today we shall reproduce several passages from the memorandum the students forwarded to the Ministry of the Interior. In the memorandum, they say:

"Christian students of Iasi University decided one month ago to build, through our own labor, a cultural home… Hardly gathered, we found ourselves surrounded by a gendarme company and the entire police apparatus headed by Prefect Manciu. While all of us stood very quiet, their weapons extended, they lunged at us, started swearing and struck us in the most barbarous possible manner. We were searched, as they thought they would find weapons on us, but nothing was found on any of us. During the search they tried to put into the pockets of our colleague Corneliu Zelea Codreanu, a revolver and some papers, which he protested. Because of this he was beaten by the Policeman Manciu, Inspector Clos, Commissar Vasiliu and, together with the rest of the agents, he was tied as if he were the worst of thieves. The same thing happened to a large number of those of us who were there.

"We were arrested, surrounded by military cordons, taken to the Police Prefecture. We met on our way several students of various high schools, who were going toward the sports park to practice, as they were directed by their principals to do. All of them were arrested and taken along with us to police headquarters, naturally after they were beaten by Policeman Manciu himself and the other policemen, for everybody to watch. They too, were kept at police headquarters the whole day. Some of us were beaten until we fainted, then were freed; others gave declarations under duress while some were freed with no declarations being taken.

"The above-mentioned deeds cannot go unpunished. The Prefect of police Manciu, proved to be an agent provocateur and guilty of torturing students and high scbool boys in Iasi, must receive punishment for such lawlessness."

Iasi Under the Terror of the Police Prefect

Transported to the police dungeons, these students were subjected to the most terrifying tortures. Some of them were hung upside-down, beaten on the soles of their feet with the ox sinew. The student Corneliu Codreanu was bound, then slapped and tortured by the police prefect himself. His health was shaken. The other arrested students show serious body lesions.

Three hundred students have reported the above-mentioned facts to the general prosecutor, demanding that the medical examiner look into the condition of their tortured colleagues.

(1) The word of professor A. C. Cuza

In a special issue of the newspaper *The Union*, of 1 June 1924, Professor A. C. Cuza published a judicious article, as follows:

But in the face of these constant brutalities and innumerable abuses, groundless—specially committed so that they would terrorize the Romanian students—some questions strongly pose themselves: What does the government want, that keeps such a policeman at the head of such a city as Iasi? What does the policeman himself want? Do they want to cause thoughtless reactions, as a result of this continuous frustration that seems to be provoked daily?

This provocation is all the more undignified and the more irritating because, at the same time, policeman Manciu frequents the meetings of the Jewish association *Macabi* and ostentatiously leads these sport-minded Maccabees in excursions, behind their white and blue flag. And one sees him lounging in his car every day—not the one he traveled in the other day to Ciurea—but in the new car that apparently was bought for him by the Iasi Israelite community through a public subscription. This is the same Qahal that encourages him in the press and at every opportunity, in his aggressive attitude toward the Christian students.

We protest with utmost indignation against this action of continuous provocation. We demand that the superior authorities intervene, in order to put an end to an undignified and dangerous state of affairs, that neither Iasi nor Christian students can tolerate any longer.

— A. C. Cuza

(2) Protest meetings against Manciu

The following telegrams were sent:

> TO HIS MAJESTY THE KING: "Wishing to meet, in order to protest the lawlessness of Policeman Manciu against our students and children who were daily beaten and insulted, we were prevented by police and gendarmes, even though the prosecutor authorized our meeting. We respectfully submit to Your Majesty our complaint and ask to be protected." (There follow 1200 names).

> TO THE MINISTRY OF THE INTERIOR: "Our children were picked off the streets, savagely maltreated by police Prefect Manciu. We demand immediate investigation, followed by severe sanctions. Hurt in our parental feelings, losing all patience, we expect justice without delay.
> — Maj. I. Dumitriu, Maj. Ambrozie, D. Butnaru, Elena Olanescu, Capt. Oarza, Gheorghiu, etc.

In it issue 15 November 1924 issue, *Romanian Action* published the following under the signature of the renowned writer Dr. Ion Istrate:

> An impressive meeting of public protest was held on 8 June 1924 in the Bejan Hall, under the honor presidency of Gen, Tamoschi. Manciu's conduct was condemned by: University Professor A.C. Cuza, student Grigorescu representing Christian students, craftsman Artur Rus, metallurgist C. Pancu. University Professor C. Sumuleanu from the School of Medicine gave an impressive description of what he saw at the police station: broken eardrums, swollen cars, bloody eyes, broken arms and legs bruised by the ox sinews of Manciu's savages. He declared that, had he had a son so tortured by the barbarian heading the police force, 'he would not have hesitated for an instant to blow the rascal's brains out.'
>   Then spoke Maj. I. Dumitriu, who concluded by saying: 'I trust the country's justice will give us satisfaction. If not, I swear here before you and I shall know how to respect my oath—that I will take justice into my own hands.'

Attorney Bacaloglu also spoke, then craftsman Cristea, attorney Nelu Ionescu and Professor Ion Zelea Codreanu. At the end a protest motion was voted upon in which the Ministry of justice was asked for satisfaction on the one hand, and the government was asked to fire Manciu on the other.

In *Our Country* (No. 24, 15 June 1924), the well-known writer A. O. Teodoreanu published an article, from which I reproduce the last passages:

Justice, called upon to speak up, declares all the 'arrested 168 students' innocent and decides that they must be freed immediately. The student Zelea Codreanu is kept under arrest despite this, put on trial by Policeman Manciu who is a lawyer besides, for conspiracy. The most elementary law manuals and common sense tell us that in marriage, duel or conspiracy, one person alone cannot figure. In order to place such a label on a person as above, one who issues it must be in a particular state of inebriation which would make him see at least double.

In other words, one cannot talk with him. But, in the name of the entire slandered Romanian population, from which we gladly exclude, with no loss to anyone, its timid representatives in Parliament and the press, we ask of the government whether it considers it best to leave the (inevitable) punishment of Manciu up to his victims, or more opportune to prevent it. Fortified by the decisive word of justice we do not hesitate to label 'the conspiracy' of Iasi as a treacherous frame-up...

— A.O. Teodoreanu

(3) An administrative investigation is ordered

As a result of the numerous protests stemming from this event, the Administrative Inspector Vararu was sent out to investigate the case. Here is the memorandum forwarded to him by Maj. Ambrozie:

MEMORANDUM

Mr. Inspector, Definitely wishing to establish the whole truth as to our telegraphic report on the torture of our sons, the

Minister of the Interior has sent you to investigate; as we believe you wish to give full exposure to this case, we have put together this memorandum containing a narration of the facts. The event happened as follows: It was known in Iasi both by school principals and by the students' parents, that students were making bricks in Ungheni to build a home of their own in Iasi, and that they worked a garden placed at their disposal by Mrs. Ghica on Carol St. Some of the students and high school boys met once a week under the leadership of the student Corneliu Z. Codreanu, when work 169 assignments were made, namely: 40 students were sent to Ungheni to make bricks, and 20-25 high school boys were sent to water the vegetable garden.

The police prefect was aware of this; but he figured he might as well concoct something sensational, like a 'conspiracy,' particularly when newspapers in Iasi are practically owned by him and consequently would fall in with his game. Said and done. On 31 May 1924, between 4:30 and 5:00 in the morning, when he knew some 65 students had come to work in Mrs. Ghica's yard, his entire police force and many armed troops made a sudden charge against them because of the gravity of the contrived 'conspiracy.' The human mind refuses to comprehend what happened when students and high school boys were surrounded like ordinary criminals and were barbarously struck on the spot by agents, the military, and even by Policeman Manciu himself.

A half hour later, all of them, headed by Corneliu Zelea Codreanu and under heavy escort, were headed down the main street toward police headquarters; on their way they met another group of high school students who by order of their professors were going to Copou to play 'oina'. These, because they permitted themselves the luxury of greeting those in chains, were immediately arrested, beaten and taken to police quarters, as accomplices of the former.

Arrived there, the prefect, not bothering to inform the public prosecutor's office of the gravity of the situation, began a 'sui generis' interrogation all by himself; namely, he beat, manhandled and tortured these students and high school boys to force from them declarations that they were a part of the conspiracy, to make them tell what they knew.

But what were they to tell, when they knew nothing of the sort? Almost all of them were beaten, but the most seriously hurt were:

1. My son, Cezar Ambrozie, senior at the Pedagogic Seminary, who was personally whipped by the prefect over the head with an ox sinew, and in the end, because he did not produce the expected answer, was given a blow of the fist on the left ear, which broke his eardrum.

2. High school student Dumitriu Sprinti, Maj. Durnitriu's son; his feet were chained together and he was turned upside down being hung on a rifle held by Sgt. Cojocaru and Cpl. Teodoroiu. He was beaten on his feet with the ox sinew by the prefect personally until he passed out.

3. High school boy Gh. Gurguta had his hands and feet tied. Then he was placed on the floor face down and beaten with the ox sinew, and in order to stifle his screams, a pan of water was placed under his face and an agent Posted there pushed his face down in to the water when he screamed louder.

During all this torture, two gendarme officers were also present: Capt. Velciu and Lieut. Tomida, whose soldierly dignity, we hope, will not prevent them from revealing the truth, since it was not dignified of them to witness such treatment; to use troops in the torturing as well as using a military weapon as a tool of torture, when it is well known what its use ought to be. According to what students and high school boys related, while Policeman Manciu was engaged in such operations, Prosecutors Culianu and Buzea passed through his office. I believe they will tell the truth.

The beatings and tortures stopped altogether only later, when First-Prosecutor Catichi came to police headquarters, as demanded by a committee composed of; Professors Cuza and Sumuleanu, attorney Bacaloglu, Col. Nadejde and Medical Examiner Bogdan who examined the children and legally established, there in the police prefecture, the wounds enumerated in the medical certificates attached to this report.

As you can see, Mr. Inspector, we have followed legal procedures up to today, namely:

1. We had asked the first-prosecutor and the medical examiner to come to the prefecture for them to verify the wounds of the students.

2. We brought suit against the torturers before the Court of District II.

3. We informed the public prosecutor's office, where the medical examiner's report was also sent, the case being referred to investigating Magistrate Iesanu.

4. As officers and men of honor we could have demanded from Mr. Manciu satisfaction by means of weapons, but he had disqualified himself when he refused meeting Capt. Ciulei in a duel.

Honestly, this is the truth. We beg you to be good enough to consider that, among the offended parents, two of us are high ranking officers who, for having proceeded legally, are exposed for no one has yet given us satisfaction to this day. Our belief is that the Minister of the Interior will give us complete satisfaction, bringing Prefect Manciu before the bar of justice for his misdeeds, and will intervene to the Ministry of War for Manciu, though a reserve inferior officer, knowingly tortured the children of his superior comrades.

— Maj, (ss) Ambrozie

The result of the investigation was as follows:

1) Prefect Manciu was *decorated* with "Romania's Star" and with the rank of commander.
2) All police commissars who tortured us were *promoted*.

Encouraged by these measures, the police unleashed further persecution against us, this time extending it over the whole of Moldavia. Any commissar, to increase his sources of revenue from the Jews or to get promoted, grabbed a student by the throat, beat him to a pulp in the street or at police headquarters. He had to answer to no one for his deeds.

The Fatal Day

This being the situation, on 23 October 1924, I presented myself at the Court House of District 11 of Iasi as a lawyer, together with my colleague Dumbrava, to represent the student Comarzan who was tortured by Manciu.

The prefect showed up with the whole staff; and there, in full court session, before the lawyers and the presiding judge Spiridoneanu, he rushed at us.

Under these circumstances, risking everything, about to be crushed by the 20 armed policemen, I pulled out my handgun and fired.

I aimed at whoever came closest. The first to fall was Manciu. The second, Inspector Clos. The third, a man much less guilty, Commissar Husanu. The rest vanished.

In no time at all, in front of the Court House, several thousand Jews had gathered, their hands high in the air, their fingers like talons crooked in hatred, waiting for my departure in order to rip me apart. Holding the gun in my right hand, in which I still had five rounds, I grabbed Victor Climescu, a lawyer in Iasi, by the arm, asking him to accompany me to the Tribunal. We stepped out and walked thus through the howling mob of Jews— which had the common sense, upon seeing the handgun, to step aside.

I was caught by the gendarmes on the way, separated from Mr. Climescu, and taken into the Police Prefecture. Here the commissars jumped on me to disarm me of the gun—the only friend I had in the midst of this misfortune. I gathered all my strength, resisting them for about five minutes. In the end, I was overpowered. They then chained my wrists behind my back and placed me between four soldiers with bayonets at the ready.

After a while, they took me out of that office and far back in the courtyard, placing me in front of a tall fence. The gendarmes retreated, leaving me there alone. I suspected they wanted to shoot me. I stood there for several hours, until late in the evening, waiting to be shot. I remained unphased.

The news of this tragic vengeance spread with truly lightning speed. When it reached student dormitories, it caused a real outburst. From all mess halls and dormitories, students started running down the streets toward Union Square. There they demonstrated at length, singing; then they tried to head for the Police Prefecture. But the army, by now on the scene, succeeded in stopping them.

Though chained, I was glad to hear their singing, for that meant they had been freed of their tyrant. Late in the day, I was taken upstairs into the same office of torture, where Iesanu, the investigation judge, now sat behind the desk—the same man to whom I complained four months earlier, demanding justice. He interrogated me summarily, after which he issued the warrant for my arrest.

I was then thrown into a paddy-wagon and transported to Galata prison up on the hill above Iasi, near the monastery built by Petre Schiopul, ruler of Moldavia. There, I was put into a room with ten other prisoners, where my chains were taken off. My cellmates gave me a cup of tea. Then I lay down to sleep.

The next day, I was placed in solitary in a room with cement floor, one bed of boards, no blanket or pillow; the door was padlocked. The room had two windows, whose panes were whitewashed on the outside. I could see nothing. One wall was so damp that water ran down it. The first day in that room, a guard—old Matei—brought me a loaf of black bread. He opened the door a crack, thrust his hand in with the loaf, for he was not permitted to enter. But I was not at all hungry.

At night, I stretched out on the boards and covered myself with my coat. I had nothing to put under my head. I shivered. They took me out in the morning for two minutes, and then I was locked up again. A student, Miluta Popovici, who was also under arrest, was able to get near my window during the day, wiping the pane clean about the size of a fingertip, so that I could see outside. Then he walked away, and when about 60 feet away, carefully signaled to me with his fingers. I understood he was using the Morse code. Thus I learned that all Vacarestians were re-arrested: Mota, Garneata, Tudose Popescu, Radu Miromovici—all except Corneliu Georgescu, whom they could not apprehend. They too were brought to the same prison and put together in one room. I learned that my father was also brought there.

The second night was much worse. I was very cold and couldn't sleep at all. Almost the whole night, I paced the cell. In the morning, again, I was taken out for two minutes, then locked back in; old Matei gave me another loaf of bread.

At noon I was handcuffed, put into a paddy-wagon and taken to the Tribunal for the confirmation of my arrest warrant. Following this formality, I was brought back to Galata into the same dark room.

Outside, the weather was getting worse. With no heat, I was beginning to shiver. I tried to get some sleep on the boards but I was able to doze off only for about half an hour at a time, for my bones ached. Because of the cold coming up from the cement floor, my kidneys began to ache. Realizing I was losing my strength, I appealed to my will and to gymnastics. Throughout the night, every hour on the hour, I got up to exercise for ten minutes, obstinately trying to keep my strength.

The following day I felt ill. My strength was visibly waning, despite my determination and will power. The night that followed, the cold was even worse, and my will no longer functioned; I felt broken, I saw black before my eyes, and I collapsed. As long as my will lasted, I hadn't worried.

But now I realized I was in bad shape. I was shaking all over and could not stop. How difficult were those seemingly endless nights!

The prosecutor came in the next day to see me. I tried to hide the shape I was in. "How are things here?" "Very good, Sir." "Have you got nothing to report?" "No, nothing." I spent 13 days like this; then they made a little fire for me. They gave me bed linen, blankets, and some matting that was hung on the walls. I was permitted to be outdoors one hour each day.

One day, I got a glimpse of Mota and Tudose deep in the back of the yard and I signaled to them. It was then that I learned that my father had been freed; likewise Liviu Sadoveanu, Ion Sava, and another student who had been arrested.

(1) Two articles regarding the Manciu case

The next day following the events at Targul-Cucului, *The Word of Iasi* of 27 October 1924 published an article signed by Nelu Ionescu, lawyer, former president of the Association of Law Students, from which I quote:

> Comments made by the Jewish liberal press concerning the death of C. Manciu are slanted and in bad faith; they start with a gross falsification of facts—facts which were only the inevitable consequence of a regime of abuses and injustice— in order to turn into a hero, at any price, the man who was but an instrument, and to heap the blame on some imagined fascistic anti-Semitic conspiracy.
>
> The students were forcibly prevented from entering the Cathedral to pray; were prevented from eating in common in a restaurant; were brutalized and prevented from walking the streets; were prevented from holding meetings in their own university and at their association's offices; were prevented from working their own garden for their own use; were beaten on the street, in police cellars and in public squares by the entire police force, from the lowliest cop all the way up to the one who was but yesterday the police prefect of this city.
>
> Students, showing a self-mastery worthy of admiration and a trust in justice that honors them, initiated a series of suits against Prefect Manciu and his subalterns, for severe cruelty and abuse of power and individual liberty.
>
> This gesture of the students was not understood. And re- gretfully we must say that Justice did not meet the expecta-

tions that an entire generation, animated by the purest sentiment of legality and order, placed in it.

The female student Silvia Teodorescu, kicked in the back
by Manciu in broad daylight on 11 December 1923 on Carol
St. in front of Col. Velsa's house—a fact stated and attested
to in having numerous eyewitnesses—not only did not succeed in having Manciu convicted before the Court of Urban
District I, but she as plaintiff ended up convicted of slander.
At the trial, it was learned that during the kicking she addressed to Manciu the words: 'this is savagery.'

On the evening of 14 December 1923, the law student,
Lefter, from Galati, as he was entering Hotel Bejan where he
resided, was with no reason surrounded by a band of policemen and gendarmes. Together with Manciu and by his orders, they beat him with bludgeons, canes, rifle, butts, kicks
and fists, until he fell to the ground unconscious, following
which he was dragged into a side street, dumped and left
there without any assistance.

Though Lefter sued, Manciu was exonerated, not having
to bring any witnesses to his defense.

But what is one to say of the barbarity and savagery of
last summer, perpetrated on the students working in the garden of the Ghica residence?! Twenty-five students, beaten on
the soles of their feet like thieves for a full day, a fact that
was verified by the first prosecutor and by the pathologist,
for an imaginary conspiracy so insignificant that it did not
even warrant an investigation.

And not only this but when, upon the students' demands
for an administrative investigation, one was conducted last
summer by Mr. Vararu, he was profoundly shocked by the
abuses he himself confirmed. However, Vararu's report to
the appropriate Ministry resulted in Manciu being decorated
with Romania's Star.

This then is the man who died; one speaks only well of
the dead, but this does not prevent us from telling the truth.

Manciu suspended meetings; Manciu stopped those
wanting to enter the Cathedral; Manciu beat students on the
streets, at the police and in public squares; insulted those
who complained and threatened their defenders. Manciu,
protected by cordons of police of icers and gendarmes, beat

the students, tied and foot, who could throw back at them through the rain of spittle and blows of his demented subalterns, only looks of contempt and temporary resignation. Behold the man of duty and behold the kind of order this man was dispensing!

Public opinion is on Corneliu Codreanu's side. It likes his manly gesture and, appreciating the superior motive of this gesture warning a regime and serving an idea, absolves him of the customary incrimination for such a deed, justifying him completely and in fact, public opinion approves of him.

Personally, I salute Corneliu Codreanu's heroic gesture, who once again remains intransigent in matters of honor and determined when dignity is involved.

Several days later, the newspaper *The Union* published Professor Cuza's article:

Prefect Manciu's Death —
The Fatal System and its Consequences

For a full year now, the police of Iasi have experienced a real tragedy, whose last act is known by all. Due to the fatal evolution of events the following victims fell: Prefect Manciu, Inspector Clos, Sub-commissar Husanu, and no less, the doctoral candidate Corneliu Zelea Codreanu. Prefect Manciu died; Sub-commissar Husanu fights death; Inspector Clos sustained a deep wound; Corneliu Zelea Codreanu lingers in jail. What is this tragedy that fells so many victims? In what manner can we speak of the fatal evolution of these events? Who are the guilty parties?

Manciu was Mr. Marzescu's police prefect in Iasi. It was in this capacity alone that he was brought here and was maintained until the end—all the excesses of which he was guilty notwithstanding. Which makes it abundantly clear that his actions were approved. The abundant proof that he was approved, that he worked according to a preestablished plan at the direct inspiration of Mr. G. G. Marzescu who supported him, are the distinctions accorded him-his 'merits' in office and the promotion of his personnel.

The fatal system inspired by Manciu was the terrorization of Christian students: to give the Jews satisfaction and to prove that 'order' can be maintained 'by energetic means'. The unfortunate Manciu, who had no special talents, put the fatal system into operation with an unusual brutality even when it came to university professors: commencing his career on the occasion of the general meeting of the Association of University Professors of Romania, held in Iasi on Sept. 23-25, 1923 under the presidency of our eminent colleague Professor I. Gavanescul. Prefect Manciu insulted the universities, brutalized and arrested innocent students, thus compelling their professors to protest and seek satisfaction. ...

Having received an imperative mandate to terrorize students, Manciu operated in conformity with its aims and according to the established plan-treading on the path of fatalism. ...

Not only was Prefect Manciu retained in his post, but he was rewarded for his attitude and encouraged to pursue his fatal system further. The Jewish press eulogized him daily, proclaiming him a savior of law and order and a superior being. The government, having at Iasi as its representative G. G. Marzescu, instead of accepting the findings of Inspector Vararu, pinned on Manciu's chest Romania's Star and promoted the personnel he had used to commit his lawlessness. For instance, Commissar Clos, one of the guiltiest, was promoted to police inspector. The Department of Justice, headed by the same G.G. Marzescu, Manciu's supporter, in lieu of energetically and promptly stepping in against the perpetrated abuses, condemned the victims.

The Jews of Iasi, well-pleased, presented Manciu with the gift of an automobile, which he accepted, scandalizing all Romanians and inducing greater resentment—particularly among the students, who could see Manciu's defiant insolence as he proudly drove the Jews' car through town. Upheld in his position, supported and encouraged in this manner, Prefect Manciu, by his impulsive temperament, lacking any self-control, imagined that he reached a pinnacle of glory by the application of his system.

It is this sequence of events that brought Prefect Manciu to the last act of this tragedy. Corneliu Zelea Codreanu acted in legitimate defense. The responsibility of Prefect Manciu's death rests first of all with him who placed Manciu at the head of the police department and supported him, namely the

Minister of Justice, G. G. Marzescu. The responsibility rests
with the Jewish press and all those who urged him on and encouraged him, congratulating him for applying his fatal system.

(2) Hunger strike

About ten days before Christmas, Mota, Garneata, Tudose, and Radu
Mironovici, who had been arrested 60 days earlier, and innocent of any
wrongdoing, went on a hunger and thirst strike. They said: either our freedom, or death. Endeavors on the part of various authorities to talk to them
failed, for they barricaded themselves in their cell, permitting no one to
enter. These youth had long since become an image of all Romanian students; a true symbol.

When news of their strike was heard, students and everyone else understood the gravity of their act, in view of their well-known strength of
resolve. Should these youth die within the walls of Galata? In Iasi and
Cluj, spirits became so agitated that a mass vengeance would have ensued
on those whom the people would have considered to be responsible. Not
only students, but also old folks, well-established in society, were loudly
demanding: "If these children all die there, we will start shooting."

The government began to fathom that it was facing a general determination and tension; that this nation began to show her will and dignity.
My father issued a manifesto, from which I reproduce the following passage:

AN APPEAL
Romanian Brothers: The students: Ion I. Mota, Ilie Garneata,
Tudose Popescu, and Radu Mironovici, detained for two
months in the Galata prison, declared a hunger and thirst
strike at 1:00 pm on Tuesday. They have taken this difficult
step because they are completely innocent, because they
were imprisoned at Vacaresti, and because they came to realize that certain politicians wish to gradually ruin their health
and life through imprisonment.

These young heroes, the choicest flower of the country's
future, were endowed by God, among other qualities, with
wills of steel. Consequently, their determination to die of
hunger and thirst—in order to protest the injustice whose
victims they are and the enslavement of our nation by Jews,
through the aid of certain politicians—is not a joke, but a
grave decision.

EITHER LIBERTY OR DEATH!

Romanian Brothers: Will we wait to see, two or three days from now, the four coffins holding the bodies of these heroes, being borne down the street? Old and young alike, think; one does not speak of the corpses of the four students, but of the death of our children, of all of us.

It is our duty to take quick measures of peaceful and legal protest, but energetic and determined, against this government, and thus prevent this iniquity, to stop the assassination of our sons.

At Christmas, following eleven days of hunger and thirst strike, they were freed. But they were so emaciated that they were taken out of the prison on stretchers directly to the hospital. Some had left a period of imprisonment only several months prior to this last detention—and Mota, only one month earlier, having finished an uninterrupted one year, so that their strength was sapped. The consequences of this strike are felt even today by some of them, ten years later, while poor Tudose took them with him to the grave.

(3) Alone at Galata

In the same damp and dark cell, sitting on the hard edge of my bed, arms crossed over my chest, head bent under the weight of my thoughts, time passes slowly, minute after minute. How terrifying solitude is! With regrets, I remember the verses: "*Gaudeamus igitur, Juvenes dum sumus.*" (Let us therefore rejoice, while we are young!) These are verses that have warmed, cheered, crowned with the crown of joy the youth of all student generations. To be joyful, to have a good time, is a right of youth, before that age comes when man's life is weighed down by hardships and worries, ever increasing, ever greater.

I was not granted this right. I had no time for enjoyment. Student life, during which everyone enjoys himself and sings, for me had ended. I did not even realize when it had passed. Over my youth had come worries, difficulties, and blows too soon, and all these tore it to pieces. Whatever is left of it is further obliterated by these gloomy cold walls. Now they deprive me even of the sun.

Many weeks have passed since I linger in this darkness and I can enjoy the sun only for an hour a day. My knees are constantly frozen. I feel the coldness of the cement floor creeping up through my bones. The hours pass slowly; very slowly. I take a few bites at noon and in the evening. I cannot eat more. But it is particularly at night that the real torment commences; it is about 2:00 or 3:00 in the morning when I fall asleep.

Outside is stormy weather. Here, on top of the hill, the wind is stronger. The snow is pushed by the wind through the cracks in the door until it covers a fourth of the cell area. By morning, I always find a layer quite thick. The heavy quiet of the night is interrupted only by the hooting owls that live in the church towers; and, from time to time, by the voices of the guards who shout as loud as they can. "Number one! OK! Number two! OK!"

I was pondering, wondering, worrying, yet unable to clear the puzzle: A month? Two months? A year? How much? A lifetime? The rest of my life? Yes, my arrest warrant threatened for me forced labor for life.

Will a trial be held? Certainly; but it is going to be a difficult trial. There are three forces that are coalesced against me: (1) The government, which is going to try to make an example of my punishment, particularly in view of the fact that this is the first time in Romania when anyone has faced, gun in hand, the oppressor who trampled underfoot his dignity, offended his honor, and ripped off his flesh in the name of the principle of the power of state authority. (2) The Jewish power within Romania, which would do anything to keep me in its clutches. (3) The Jewish power from abroad, with its money, its loans, and its pressures. All of these three forces are interested in preventing my ever leaving here. Against them are poised the students and the Romanian nationalist movement. Which will win?

I realize that my trial is more a test of forces. No matter how right I was, if enemy forces were only a little bit stronger than our camp, they would not hesitate for one moment to destroy me. It has been so many years since they waited to catch me, for I placed myself across all their plans. They will make all efforts so that I will not be able to escape them. At home, my mother, having heard so much terrifying news year in and year out, her home raided at night by prosecutors and searched by brutal commissars, was receiving blow after blow.

Reflecting upon my life coming to such a sad fate, she sent me the Akathist of Virgin Mary, urging me to read it at midnight for 42 consecutive nights.[1] I had done so, and it seemed that as I neared my goal, our side was gaining strength while the enemy retreated and the dangers subsided.

---

[1] A devotional poem composed by St. Romanos circa 550 AD.

(4) The trial is transferred to Focsani

I was informed in January that the trial had been moved to Focsani. Focsani, at that time, was the biggest liberal stronghold in the country. Three cabinet members hailed from that town: Gen. Vaitoianu, N. Saveanu, and Chirculescu. It was the only town in the whole country where the nationalist movement did not catch on. Our efforts to accomplish something there had failed. There, we had no one, except Mrs. Tita Pavelescu, a veteran patriot with her paper *The Sentinel*, which preached but to the wind.

The students in Iasi, upon learning about this transfer, became very worried. Numerous groups waited in the railway stations around Iasi to accompany me to Focsani, for it was rumored that my escort would try to shoot me on the occasion of this transfer, under the pretext that I tried to escape.

Some two weeks later, Botez, the Chief of Security, came with several agents, put me into a car that was escorted by a second car. We drove out of Iasi through the Pacurari barrier to the Cucuteni depot. There, I found a group of students, and on the train that pulled in there was another group. But I could not talk to any of them.

While the police got me into the prisoners' railcar, they demonstrated in my support. We traveled almost the whole night.

I approached Focsani certain of my condemnation. Local police and the prison warden were expecting me at the station. I was immediately whisked away and incarcerated.

At first, the regimen was stricter than at Iasi. Gavrilescu, the county prefect, who seemed to be a mean man, without any justification—no prefect has the right to interfere in the prison's regimen—wanted to impose a severe regimen on me. He even came into my cell where we had an altogether unpleasant discussion. The miracle, that neither I nor particularly those who brought me to Focsani expected, was that, three days after my arrival, the entire populace, irrespective of political party and in spite of all efforts on the part of the authorities to turn it against me, spontaneously came over to my side. Liberal politicians were abandoned not only by their own supporters but by their families as well.

For example, the Chirculescu high school girls sent me food, and they sewed for me a regional national shirt. I even heard they refused to sit at the table for meals with their father. It was then that I met several people: Gen. Dr. Macridescu, the most venerable figure in Focsani; Hristache Solomon, a moderately rich property owner, but a man of great moral authority, to whom even his enemies tipped the hat; Mr. Georgica Niculescu; Col. Blezu, who sent me food; Vasilache, Stefan, and Nicusor Graur; and others. All these, and many others, from whom I received their more-than-paternal care.

Yet my health was not in good shape. My kidneys, chest, and knees ached. Trial date was set for 14 March 1925. With that in mind, thousands of flyers were printed in all university centers as well as in other towns. In Cluj, Capt. Beleuta printed, and distributed throughout the whole country, tens of thousands of such flyers. His home, open day and night to nationalist fighters, was changed into a veritable headquarters. In Orastie, at Father Mota's printing shop, scores of thousands of popular poetry brochures and hundreds of thousands of flyers were printed. My comrades had some of my letters written by me in the Vacaresti prison printed as a brochure, titled: *Letters of an imprisoned student.*

The government came out with opposing material, to be spread near and far. But they had no effect whatsoever, for the wave of national feeling grew imposingly and irresistibly.

Two days before the trial was to begin, hundreds of people and students from throughout the country began arriving at Focsani. From Iasi alone, over 300 came, taking up a whole train. I was transported by the authorities in a carriage to the National Theater, where the trial was to take place. But this was ordered postponed, though the jury was drawn. They took me back to the prison.

But outside, the unjustified postponement of the trial produced a general indignation that quickly changed into an enormous street demonstration—one that lasted throughout the afternoon and late into the night. The efforts of the army to quell the spirited crowd got nowhere. The demonstration was directed against the Jews and the government. Jews then realized that all their pressures in the case would backfire. This demonstration was overwhelmingly important for the outcome of my trial. It put Jewry out of the fight, because they realized that my being sentenced could have disastrous repercussions against them. Although Jewry did not beat a total retreat, it lessened its pressure on the authorities.

Meanwhile I received suggestions to petition to be freed and assurances that I would be freed, but I refused to do it. Easter arrived. I celebrated the Resurrection alone in my cell. When the bells of all the churches in town began pealing, I knelt and prayed for my fiancée and myself, for my mother at home, for the souls of the dead, and for those fighting outside—that God may bless them, fortify them, and grant them victory over all enemies.

(5) At Turnul-Severin

At about 2:00 am one night, I woke up as someone tried to open the pad-lock. Prison officials came to fetch me; my trial was unexpectedly trans-ferred to Turnul-Severin, at the other end of Romania. I hastily gathered my few belongings. Then, surrounded by guards, I was placed in a truck that took us to the edge of town near a rail line. Shortly thereafter, a train stopped and I was put into the Black Maria railcar. So I was leaving this town of Focsani, which, at the opportune moment, bravely faced the tre-mendous pressures of officialdom, and whose citizens broke their party ties, and sometimes family ties, to appear in a superb and impregnable unanimity of sentiment.

As I traveled, I wondered what kind of people I would find in Tumul-Severin. I had never been there, I knew no one in that town. Wherever the train stopped, I heard people talking, laughing, descending, or boarding the train, but I was unable to see anything because the car I was in had no win-dows. It was only one inch of wall that separated me from the rest of the world, from freedom. Perhaps among those who crossed the tracks out there in those railway stations, there were many who either knew me or were my friends. But they were unaware I was inside that car.

Everyone is headed somewhere. Only I was unaware of where I was headed. All walk lightly and gaily, while I carry on my soul, heavier than a millstone, the burden of this immense unknown that awaits me. Shall I be sentenced for life? For less? Shall I ever leave the ugly and black walls of prison, or will it be my fate to die there?

I realize full well that my trial is not a matter of justice, it is a ques-tion of force; whichever of these two forces is the stronger will win. Will our nationalist current be stronger or the Judeo-governmental pressure? But it cannot be like this! Whoever is right shall be stronger and conse-quently will inevitably win.

And as the train kept rolling, I felt my pain more poignantly. My heart was seemingly attached to every stone in Moldavia, and as I was leaving everything further and further behind, I felt as if bits of it were gradually being chipped off. All day I traveled like this, locked alone in a jail car.

We reached Balota, I believe, toward evening. A gendarme officer accompanied by agents came in and asked me to step out. They led me behind the station, where we got in a car and drove off. They seemed to be very good men, trying to strike up a conversation with me, to crack a joke.

But I, borne down by other thoughts and needs, was not inclined to converse. I answered them with good will, but briefly.

We entered Turnul-Severin. Driving along several streets, I experienced real joy in my heart, and delight, for my eyes again saw people walking the streets. We stopped at the prison gate. Once again, the padlocked gates opened, to again close behind me. The warden and personnel received me like an honored guest. The good room they assigned to me had a wooden floor, not cement like earlier ones. Here too, detainees approached me as they had in the other prisons, with affection; and I helped them later in their unending material and moral misery.

The next day I stepped out into the courtyard. From there I could see out in the street. Around noon, I noticed, massed before the prison gates, over 200 small children between 6 and 7 years of age; upon seeing me pass by, they began waving their tiny hands at me, some using handkerchiefs, some caps. They were school children who heard I had come to Turnul-Severin and was there in prison. Those children would be there daily from then on, to show me their sympathy. They waited for me to pass, to wave their tiny hands.

At the Tribunal, President Varlam, a man of great goodness, treated me very courteously. Less so Prosecutor Constantineseu, of whom it was rumored he took it upon himself that, together with Prefect Marius Vorvoreanu, he would obtain my conviction, but I did not believe it. They were at first rather severe, behind which I detected some meanness.

But little by little, they were softened up by the wave of public opinion, by the enthusiasm emanating from small children to old folks. At that time, everyone was feeling Romanian and saw in our fight a sacred struggle for the future of this country. They were aware of my misfortunes and saw my act as a revolt for human dignity, a gesture that any free man would have made. These people, descendants of Iancu Jianu and Capt. Tudor Vladimirescu, whose pistols had been brandished in the defense of the nation's honor against the humiliation of centuries, understood readily what happened at Iasi. No argument could budge them.

It was in vain that the prosecutor and the prefect shouted—I was surrounded by the affection and care of all the families in town, even of those who played an official role, like that of Mayor Corneliu Radulescu, for whom I developed a great admiration.

But especially was I surrounded, as nowhere else, by the children's love and understanding for my tribulations. They were the first ones to demonstrate on my behalf in Turnul-Severin. I remember with tenderness how small tots from the suburbs also began to come—they who hardly knew how to walk. I watched them assemble from all parts, at a given time, as if following a program. All of them were quiet and well behaved. They did not play or sing. They just watched, waiting to see me pass by an opening so they could wave at me; then they left for home. They understood that there is something sad in this prison, and their common sense told them there was nothing to laugh about here.

Then the gendarmes started chasing them away. The following day, I no longer saw them. Sentinels were posted to stop them from coming.

The Trial

The date of the trial was set for May 20th. The Tribunal's president received 19,300 signatures of lawyers wishing to defend me, from all over the country. Two days before the trial, trainloads of students began to arrive. Just as at Focsani, the students from Iasi came, 300 strong. Likewise the students from Bucharest, Cluj, and Cernauti, came in large numbers. Among those who came, there was a Focsani delegation headed by the former jury foreman, Mihail Caras, who now signed up as defender representing the jury from Focsani. Prosecution witnesses also arrived: the policemen of Iasi.

Proceedings began in the National Theater, Counselor Variam presiding. By my side, on the bench of the accused, were: Mota, Tudose Popescu, Garneata, Corneliu Georgescu, and Radu Mironovici. On the defense bench sat: Professor Cuza, Professor Gavanescul, Paul Iliescu, Professor Sumuleanu, Vasiliu-Cluj, Nicusor Graur, and the entire Turnul-Severin bar, etc. The theater was full to capacity, and around it outside, over 10,000 people were waiting. The jurors were picked. They took the oath and gravely sat in their places.

The indictment was read. The interrogation followed. I told things as they had happened. The other five replied to their questioning likewise, telling the truth, namely that they were not at all involved in the case being judged. The prosecution witnesses were one Jew and the policemen from Iasi. During the proceedings, they denied everything. Nothing was true. All beatings, all torturing, pure inventions. They even denied the medical certificates issued by Professor Bogdan, the pathologist. Their attitude, considering they took an oath upon the cross to tell the truth and only the truth, provoked the indignation of the entire courtroom.

One of the witnesses, Commissar Vasiliu Spanchiu, whom I now saw metamorphosed into the most tenderhearted being, saw nothing, did nothing. Standing up, with the presiding judge's permission, I asked him loudly, full of indignation: "Are you not the one who struck me in the face with your fist, in Mrs. Ghica's garden?" "I am not." "Are you not the one who dipped the students' heads into pails of water while they, hung head down, had the soles of their feet whipped?" "I was not there at the time. I was downtown." On his face, in all his gestures, by his whole behavior, one could see he was lying; though he swore on the cross, he lied. The entire crowd in the theater was seething with indignation.

Suddenly, as if the collective fury of the crowd willed it, a man in the audience jumped up, lifted the commissar up in his arms and bodily carried him out. It was Mr. Tilica Ioanid. We heard him shout as he pushed the commissar down the back steps: "Get out of here, scoundrel, for we do not guarantee your life!"

Returning, he told the other commissars from Iasi: "With your own hands you have savagely tortured these children. Had you done something like this here in Turnul-Severin, people would have slaughtered you. Your presence in this town stains it; leave on the first train, otherwise misfortune will befall you."

As a matter of fact, this gesture was welcome, for people were upset. It relaxed the whole tense atmosphere. The torturers were humiliated, and now as they walked, they greeted people by bowing to the ground, begging for the minutest sign of attention from the humblest carrier of the tricolor band. "As if we are not good Romanians! What were we to do? We received orders." "No! Scoundrels! You had not the heart of a parent, nor the heart of a Romanian. You had no honor, nor respect for the law. You say you had orders? No! You had traitors' hearts." This is how people told them off on the streets.

Then for about two days followed depositions of defense witnesses, among whom was the elderly Professor Ion Gavanescul of the University of Iasi, himself manhandled by Prefect Manciu at the Congress of the University Professors; also officers of the Military Lycee and School of Infantry, my former superiors and teachers. Then victims and parents testified, reenacting before the judges, and almost in tears, the painful scenes of humiliation to which they had been subjected. The civilian observer was Mr. Costa-Foru, the head of a masonic lodge in the capital. Defense lawyers and others spoke.

I took the floor last. I said: "Gentlemen of the jury. Everything we have fought for was out of faith and love for our country and the Romanian people. We assume the obligation to fight to the end. This is my last word." This was in the sixth day of my trial, 26 May 1925.

All six of us were taken to a room, there to await the verdict. We were not overly excited, but somewhat so, just the same.

Several minutes later, we heard thunderous applause, shouting and hurrahs, coming from the large hall. We had no time to reflect upon this, for the doors opened and the crowd took us into the meeting hall. When we appeared, carried on their shoulders, everyone stood in acclaim and fluttered their handkerchiefs. Presiding Judge Varlam too, was seized by the wave of enthusiasm he could not resist. The jurors were all at their places, this time wearing tricolor lapel ribbons with swastikas.

As soon as the verdict of acquittal was read to us, I was carried on shoulders outside, where there were over ten thousand people assembled. They all fell into a column, carrying us on their shoulders along the streets, while people on the sidewalks showered us with flowers. When we reached Mr. Tilica Ioanid's home, I addressed the people from his balcony in a few words, expressing my gratitude to the Romanians of Tumul-Severin for the great love they showed me during the trial.

Returning to Iasi

After I thanked several families in Turnul-Severin by visiting them, for the manner they adopted toward me, I boarded the next day a special train for Iasi. The special train was not for me, but for the over 300 Iasians who came to the trial, to which were hooked up the cars of the Focsanians, Barladians, and Vasluians. Thousands of people came to the station to see us off and to decorate our train with flowers. The train left. Behind, the multitude fluttered handkerchiefs expressing its love and wish to continue the fight by "hurrahs" that made the air reverberate. From my window, I watched that large crowd of people, none of whom I had known before, but that now parted from us with tears in their eyes as if they had known us for years. Inwardly I prayed, thanking the Lord for the victory He gave us.

It was only now, as I passed from car to car, that I could see my comrades from Iasi again, talking to each and rejoicing together that God made us victorious, saving us from the threat from that all our enemies thought I would not be able to escape. In one compartment, I encountered Professor Cuza, and Professor and Mrs. Sumuleanu. They were contented, being surrounded by our love. All the compartments were beautifully bedecked with flowers and greenery.

And at the first stop out of Tumul-Severin, a new mountain of flowers was brought—to our great surprise—by peasants with their priests, and by teachers with their school children, all of them dressed in national costumes.

There were many people in each railway station awaiting the arrival of the train. These were not like the cold, official receptions. It was neither duty, nor fear, nor self-interest that brought those people out. I saw old folks at the edges of some crowds who cried. I wondered why. They knew no one on the train. It seemed that an unknown force compelled them to come, mysteriously whispering to them: "Go to the depot, for among all the trains that pass by, there is one that goes on the line of Romanian destiny. All the rest run for the interests of those riding them, save this one that runs on the people's course, for the people."

Crowds sometimes establish contact with the soul of the people. A moment of vision. Multitudes see the nation, with its dead and all its past; feel all its glorious moments as well as those of defeat. They can feel the future seething. This touch with the whole immortal and collective soul of the nation is feverish, full of trembling. When this happens, crowds cry. This perhaps is the national mystique that some criticize because they do not know what it is and which others cannot define because they cannot experience it. If Christian mystique aiming at ecstasy is man's contact with God, through a "jump from human nature into the divine one" (Crainic), national mystique is nothing more than man's contact, or that of the multitude, with the soul of their people, through a jump outside of personal preoccupations into the eternal life of the people. Not intellectually, for this could be done by any historian, but living, with their souls.

When the train, all decked out with flags and greenery, stopped at Craiova, the station's platform was crowded by more than 10,000 people. We were carried on shoulders behind the depot, where we were welcomed by one of the townsmen. Professor Cuza spoke. And then myself, briefly. We were received this way at all the stations, large and small, but especially in the towns of Piatra-Olt, Slatina, and Pitesti. Though there were no nationalist organizations in most of these towns along the railway, and no one put out any flyers to call out people to the stations, the platforms were all full of thousands of people to greet us.

It was about 8:00 in the evening when we arrived in Bucharest. Again, I was lifted up, triumphantly carried on shoulders through the station to the front, where the whole square was a sea of heads that extended along Grivita Way, far beyond the Polytechnical School. There must have been over 50,000 people, showing an enthusiasm that could not be dampened by anything. Professor Cuza addressed them. Then I.

As a matter of fact, throughout the entire country, there prevailed such a powerful patriotic current that it could have led the League into power then and there. But these propitious, tactical, politically great moments, which this movement would never see again, were not seized upon. Professor Cuza did not know how to take advantage of a great tactical opportunity that is so rarely encountered by political movements. In the eyes of any objective observer familiar with political clashes, the League's fate was sealed at that moment.

We left. All night people met us at stops. There were over 1,000 in Focsani at 3:00 in the morning, who had been waiting since 4:00 pm the previous afternoon. They wanted us to stop there for one day. But we kept on going. A delegation made up of Hristache Solomon, Aristotel Gheorghiu, Georgica Niculescu and others, boarded the train. They told me: "Since we did not have the good fortune to host your trial in our town, you must have your wedding in Focsani. On June 14, early in the morning, you must be in Focsani. Everything will be taken care of." The delegation left the train at Marasesti after I promised that I'd be in Focsani as planned.

We arrived at Iasi in the morning, exceedingly tired. Students and townspeople were at the station. They carried us on their shoulders through the city to the university. There we were met by cordons of gendarmes. The crowd broke through and entered the university, taking us into the amphitheater. There, Professor Cuza spoke, after which people dispersed peacefully. I revisited the little house on Flowers Street that I had left eight months earlier.

The next day, I left for Husi, where my mother was expecting me, crying in the doorway.

CHAPTER 4

JUNE 1925 TO JUNE 1926

My Wedding

Accompanied by my mother, father, brothers, and sisters, the bride and in-laws, I left on June 13 for Focsani. There, we were guests in Gen. Macridescu's home. That evening, we were visited by the wedding's organization committee. They informed us that everything was ready and that already over 30,000 people had arrived from other towns, who were all quartered, with more coming that night; and further, that all inhabitants of Focsani received these guests with joy and happily put them up.

A horse was brought to me the next morning, according to our old popular tradition, and after I rode by the bride's house, I led a column to the Crang Grove outside of town. On both sides of the road there were people, with children even in the trees. Following behind me were the godparents, riding in ornate carriages. The bride's wagon came next, drawn by six oxen and bedecked with flowers, followed by the wagons of the guests. In all, there were a total of 2,300 wagons, carriages, and cars, all embellished with flowers, and the people were dressed in national costumes.

Codreanu and his wife, Elena (undated)

I reached the Crang, more than four miles from Focsani, and the tail end of the column had not yet left Focsani. The wedding ceremony took place on a platform specially built for that purpose. There were between 80,000 to 100,000 people present. After the religious ceremony, we danced the hora and other national dances, and the celebration continued with a banquet on the grass. The inhabitants of Focsani brought provisions for themselves and also for the out-of-town guests.

The entire festivity was filmed. Several weeks later, it was shown in movie houses in Bucharest—but only twice, because the Ministry of Internal Affairs confiscated the film and the one copy, and burned them.

The celebration ended toward evening in a general feeling of brotherhood. Together with my wife and a few comrades, I left for Baile Herculane that night, where we spent two weeks with a family of old friends. Mota, for his part, went to Iasi to commence digging the foundation of the Christian Cultural Home on the lot donated by engineer Grigore Bejan.

After One Year, Work Resumes

I returned to Iasi to work by the side of my comrades to build our home. We pursued the old plan of construction, as well as that of organizing the youth, which had been interrupted by fate for nearly one whole year. Donations began to come in. Peasants from the remotest villages in Transylvania, Bucovina, and Bessarabia sent in some from their meager means to the "House in Iasi," as they affectionately called it.

All these contributions poured in by virtue of the sympathy our movement enjoyed at that time in all social strata. Pictures showing how students and coeds were building their own home stirred a particularly great enthusiasm. This was something totally new, which had not been seen before either in our country or abroad. This activity generated so much sympathy in Iasi that when office workers left at the end of the day, they came to the building site, took off their coats, and grabbed a shovel, pick axe, or cement wheelbarrow. Students from Cluj, Bessarabia, Bucovina, and Bucharest met there for this kind of work. Brotherhoods of the Cross had by now been organized in many cities under Mota's supervision, so that young high school students were coming there from all over to work, returning home educated in our spirit.

Two years of student struggle, of agitation, and suffering, common to all the youth of Romania, brought about a great miracle: a reestablishment of the nation's spiritual unity—something that had been threatened by the incapacity of the older generation to fuse and join with the great national community. Now the youth, gathered from all parts of the country, were consolidating and sanctifying this unity of soul through their common efforts, in the 'school of work,' for our country.

Dangers that Threaten a Political Movement

There was now a formidable current flowing throughout the whole country. I do not believe that anything as unanimous as this had yet existed in the country. The League, however, was not doing well, for lack of organization and lack of a plan of action.

As a result of this great current, there also existed a threat that some compromising and dangerous elements might infiltrate the movement. A movement never dies under the blows of the enemy without, but because of the enemies within, like any human organism. Normally, only about one person in a million dies of external causes (run over by a train or a car, shot to death, drowning, etc.); man usually succumbs to internal toxins, and he dies poisoned.

As it was, in the wake of the Vacaresti, Focsani, and Turnul-Severin trials, anyone who wished could join our ranks. Some joined to engage in swindling: collecting subscriptions, sales of brochures, loans, etc. and no matter where these characters appeared, they invariably compromised the movement. Others, who joined as political climbers, began fighting and telling on each other, each vying for the leadership position or for a seat in Parliament, etc. Others were of good faith but lacked discipline, refusing to obey orders from their superiors; these people interminably haggled over each directive, each acting on his own. Others, again having joined our ranks in good faith, were simply incapable of integrating themselves into our spirit.

There are many very good individuals possessed of such a moral structure that they just cannot merge into an organization like ours and therefore endanger its very existence from the inside. Some are intriguers by birth; whatever they join, they destroy. Certain others have a fixed idea; they honestly believe they have found the key to all solutions, seeking to convince you of their worth. Others are ill, afflicted with the malady of journalism. They wish, at any price, to be newspaper directors or to see their name printed at the end of some article. There are others who act in such a way that, no matter where they go, they succeed in compromising the whole fight and in eroding the trust the organization enjoyed there. Finally, there are some who are specifically paid to engage in intrigue, in espionage, and will compromise any noble endeavor of a nationalist movement.

How much care, how much circumspection, then, must be exercised by the head of a movement with respect to those wanting to come under his leadership! How much he must do to educate them, and how much untiring supervision he must exercise over them! Without these precautions, a movement is irremediably compromised. Regretfully, Professor Cuza was totally unaware of these imperatives. His slogan was: "Anyone can join the League, but only he who is able stays in." This attitude brought a real disaster. In fact, several months later, the League became a cauldron of intrigues, a real hell.

My belief at that time, which I still hold today, was that an organization must not permit "whoever wishes" to come in, but only whoever "deserves to join." And it must allow to remain only those who are—and only for as long as they are—correct, hard-working, disciplined, and faithful.

If signs of gangrene, such as those mentioned above, appear in an organization, they must be immediately isolated, then eradicated most energetically. If not, the infection spreads like a cancer throughout the entire organism of the movement, and the cause is lost. Its mission and future being compromised, it will either die, or drag out its days between life and death, incapable of accomplishing anything. Our efforts to move Professor Cuza to remedy this situation failed, because, on the one hand, he was totally unaware of these elementary principles of leading a movement, and on the other, because the intrigues succeeded in isolating us, too, from him, and consequently began to paralyze any influence we might have had with him.

We, the Vacarestians—realizing this, and seeing the desperate assaults, the waves of intrigue battering us, aimed at splitting us from Professor Cuza—went to his home, again swearing allegiance to him and asking him to trust us that we would do everything in our power to redress the state of affairs within the movement. Our attempt proved futile; he noticed that we saw things in an entirely different light, both with respect to organization and to a plan of action, and even with respect to the fundamental doctrine of our movement. We started from the idea of man's moral worth, not as a numerical, electoral, or democratic digit. But he was convinced that we only held such an idea because we were the victims of some intriguers.

A Critique of the Leader

Who is responsible for this state of affairs? The leader, of course. Such a movement has to have a great leader, not a brilliant doctrinaire who remains oblivious to the waves of the movement down below; it needs an imposing leader, to dominate and control the movement.

Not everyone can fill this function. A professional is needed, a man possessing inborn qualities, a connoisseur not only of principles of organization but also of development and fighting. It is not enough to be a renowned university professor to be in command of such a movement. Here is needed a good helmsman, an accomplished skipper to lead us over the waves, a man to know the law and to be familiar with the secret of such leadership; one who would know the winds and the depths of the sea, who should be familiar with dangerous reefs, who finally would hold the helm with a firm hand.

It is not enough that a man proving that Transylvania belongs to the Romanians is entitled therefore to assume command of the troops setting out to conquer it. So too is the fact that he can theoretically demonstrate the existence of a Jewish peril is not sufficient for him to be entitled to take command of a popular political movement that proposes to solve this problem. There are two levels of activity here, totally differing, levels demanding aptitudes and qualifications that are totally opposite in the involved individuals.

We can picture the first level: The domain of theory, the abstract field of laws. There, the theoretician engages in researching truth and its theoretical formulation. He begins at the bottom from concrete realities, from the ground up, climbing to formulate laws there in his creative domain.

The other level is down on the Earth. Here, the man who is endowed with leadership qualities engages in the art of imposing truth by the play of forces. He reaches for the heights in order to be in harmony with the laws, but his place of accomplishment is down here on the battlefield, in the area of strategy and tactics.

The former man creates ideals and delineates objectives; the latter realizes and fulfils them.

By virtue of the natural principle of the division of labor, the cases in which the qualities of these two functions are found in a single individual are extremely rare.

Professor Cuza is, above all else, a theoretician. On the theoretical plane he shines like the sun. His work is the following:

a) Research and formulation of the truth of the law of nationality.
b) Discovery and perfect identification of the enemy of nationality: the Jew.
c) Postulating solutions to the Jewish problem.

That is all! However, this is a colossal accomplishment! For, though all scientific evidence is on his side, all men of science are against him, striking at him from all directions and trying to topple his findings. But he resists.

This first level does not require the use of men, of human forces; on the contrary, the man on the first plane shuns people. But the second plane demands, first of all, people. Just any people? Certainly not! But people whom the leader must change into human forces. This means:

1.   Knowing how to organize them according to certain rigid principles.
2.   Giving them a technical and heroic education in order to augment their power, namely, to change men into human power.
3.   Leading these forces, now organized and educated, onto the strategic and tactical battlefield to fight other human forces, or nature itself, in order to attain a useful aim.

If the doctrinaire is expected to master the science of researching and formulating truth, the leader of a political movement is expected to master the science and art of organization, education, and leadership of men. Professor Cuza, excelling and unsurpassed on the first plane, when brought down on the practical one, showed himself ignorant, awkward, and naive as a child; he is incapable either of organizing or of technically and heroically educating his followers—incapable, in other words, of leading human forces.

A man who is illustrious on the theoretical plane will never be able to score a victory on the second plane. He will be vanquished or, at best, he will be content with small successes obtained for him by those around him.

What are the characteristic spiritual traits that the leader of a political movement must possess? In my opinion, they are:

1. An inner power of attraction. There are no independent, free people in the world. Just as in the solar system, each star follows its own orbit on which it turns around a greater power of attraction. Likewise, people, particularly in the field of political action, gravitate around some attracting personalities. It is the same in the realm of thought. On the outside remain those who want neither to show an interest nor to think.

A leader must have such a power of attraction. Some have it over ten people, being thus leaders for them only; others over a whole village, a county; others over an entire province or country; and some even outside the boundaries of a single country. The individual's capacity to lead is limited by the extent of his inner power of attraction. It is sort of a magnetic force which, if not possessed by a man, renders him incapable of leading.

2. Capacity for love. A leader must love all his comrades-in-arms. His love must penetrate to the edges of a movement's community.

3. Knowledge and sense of organizing. People attracted within the orbit of a movement must be organized.

4. Knowledge of people. While organizing, one must take into account the principle of the division of labor, using each in his place, according to his aptitudes, and refusing to accept anyone lacking them.

5. The power to educate and to inspire heroism.

6. Mastering the laws of leadership. When a chief has an organized and educated troop, he must know how to lead it into the political battlefield to compete with other forces.

7. A sense of timing. A chief must have a special sense to indicate to him when to wage a battle. An inner intuition must tell him: Now! This minute, neither later nor sooner.

8. Courage. When a leader hears that inner command, he must have the courage to draw out his sword.

9. The conscience of just and moral objectives to be pursued by honest means. This is in addition to all the virtues of a soldier that a leader must possess: spirit of sacrifice, resistance, devotion, etc. He must be animated by a spirit of high morality, for there is no lasting victory if it is not based on justice and legality.

A Case of Conscience

In fact, Professor Cuza was not responsible for the chaotic situation in which the League floundered. When he opposed our efforts to organize, he had, I believe, a clear awareness of his theoretical competence and of his lack of power on the political plane. It was *we* who were responsible, and especially myself, for we forced him against his will to engage in an action in which he was weak. As a matter of fact, he was absent from all important events that took place during those two years of struggle. All the fights that shook the whole country and roused the Romanian masses, were initiated without the help of Professor Cuza. In each of them he was of great help, certainly, but always in the end, they did not belong to him.

I erred; and as there is no mistake that does not soon turn against those who committed it, my mistake too, will bear upon us as on the movement. And this will happen when Professor Cuza, incapable of understanding us, works alone, without our support.

This year was a difficult one for him too. After 30 years of dedication at the University of Iasi, the government committed the unheard-of inequity of deposing him from his chair. When he was accused of instigating the students, Cuza replied: "I am an instigator of the national energies." A lifetime of fighting and of illustrious teaching in the service of the Romanian nation was ended by such a reward on the part of the people led by the Judeo-politicians.

This low blow was followed by an incident in which he was provoked and struck in the face by a Jew. When such an outrageous act became known, students went into all the pubs and struck every Jew they met. On the occasion of that demonstration, ten students were arrested—Mota and Iulian Sarbu included, who were sentenced to one month in jail. They served it in Galata. Urziceanu, a student, took several shots at the individual suspected of being the moral instigator of the insulting act of violence.

At School in France

On 23 September 1925 we laid the cornerstone of our student home. The walls were about three feet high when, considering that I gave to our nationalist movement all that I could at my age, I thought it opportune to go abroad again in order to complete my education—the more so as my health was not in very good shape as a result of my difficult trials. I was prodded towards this decision also by the fact that I felt somewhat isolated in my opinions regarding the League's organization and plans of combat. I told myself, "It is possible that I am wrong, and it would be better for me not to hinder the development of a viewpoint that might, after all, prove to be a good one." This was especially true in light of the fact that lately the League had acquired new strength by (1) uniting with "Romanian Action," led by Professor Catuneanu, which brought to our side such eminent intellectuals as Valer Pop and Father Titus Malai; and (2) by joining forces with "The National Fascia," a smaller but healthy organization.

Hopefully, the innocent shortcomings of the League's leadership would now be remedied by the presence of so many elite men, among whom one could count: our lawyer Paul Iliescu from Bucharest (with his own following of intellectuals); Gen. Macridescu, heading another elite group from Focsani; the distinguished professor of sociology from the University of Cernauti, and an old nationalist, Traian Braileanu; and the illustrious professor of pedagogy Ion Gavanescul from the University of Iasi, who up to now had not joined our movement, though he too was preaching the national idea for a lifetime from his chair of pedagogy. Also with us now was the erudite professor of physiology Nicolae Paulescu at the University of Bucharest, a connoisseur without equal of Judeo-masonic manipulations, who illumined the national movement in the capital.

In addition to these personalities who honored our movement and imparted to it an unsurpassed prestige, we enlisted the precious aid of *Liberty*, the most widely read and appreciated Romanian popular newspaper, edited by Father Mota.

My comrade Mota—Father Mota's son—who was expelled from the University of Cluj, only a sophomore, decided to go abroad with me to finish his law studies. We both agreed to go to one of the smaller towns in France. We chose Grenoble. I had 60,000 lei from the sales of my pamphlet, *Letters of an Imprisoned Student*, and from wedding presents; Mota had monthly aid from home.

After saying goodbye to our families at home, we paid our respects to Professor Cuza and to our comrades. Then we went up Rarau Mountain to the hermitage to pray, and began our trip. My wife and I left first. Mota followed two weeks later.

After a long journey through Czechoslovakia and Germany, followed by several days' stay in Berlin and Jena, we entered France and stopped at Strasbourg. What surprised me most was the fact that this city, contrary to all my expectations, had changed into a real wasps' nest of Jewish infection. Stepping off the train, I expected to see people of the Gallic race that, with its unequalled bravery, had marked history's centuries. Instead, I saw the Jew with his aquiline nose, thirsty for profit, who pulled me by the sleeve to enter either his store or his restaurant—the majority of restaurants around the railway station were run by them. In the France of the assimilated Jew, everything was kosher. We entered restaurant after restaurant in order to find a Christian one, but in each we saw the sign in Yiddish: "Kosher food." Finally we found a French restaurant, where we ate. We found no difference between the Iasian Jews and those of Strasbourg; the same figure, the same manners and jargon; the same Satanic eyes in which one read and discovered, under a polite appearance, the urge to swindle.

(1) At Grenoble

One more night of traveling and we arrived at Grenoble in the morning. What wonders opened to our eyes! What scenery! A city situated for ages of time at the foot of the Alps. A huge rock advanced toward the center of the city, as if to cut it in two. Gray, rugged, and bold, it dominated the houses, which, though many-storied, seemed like little anthills by contrast. Further away, but also near the city, there was another mountain full of old fortifications, trenches, and parapets, that had been transformed into one immense fortress. Far away in the background, above all these, white as honor, the snow shone year-round over the imposing massive Alps.

Awed by what we saw, and walking as through an enchanted castle in some tale, I told myself: "This is a city of bravery." And sure enough, as I continued to walk, I was certain I was right, for, stopping before a statue, I read: "*Bayard, chevalier sans peur etsans reproche*" (Bayard, knight without fear or reproach). Bayard was a great epic warrior in the fifteenth century, who, after a lifetime of battles, was mortally wounded and lay dying, holding his sword—whose handle now was transformed into a cross, from which the brave old man received in the hour of his death, a last benediction.

We rented a room in old Grenoble. There is also a new, modern Grenoble, but we liked the old section better. Mota arrived a little later.

We registered at the university—he, for his bachelor of law degree; I, as a candidate for the doctoral degree in economy. I began auditing freshman and sophomore courses, but I understood absolutely nothing. These were the first lessons. I could make out only isolated words. However, doggedly continuing to audit these courses, by Christmas I began to understand the lectures quite well. There were only eight doctoral candidates and that is why these classes developed a familiar character of close bond between student and professor. The professors, extremely conscientious, did only teaching, not politicking too.

Meals for all three of us were prepared by my wife. On holidays, I began to make small excursions around the city. I was impressed by castle ruins and old towers. Who lived in these fortresses of old? They must have been forgotten by everyone. Let me go pay them a visit. I entered such ruins and stood there for hours in undisturbed quiet, talking with the dead. I visited a little old church on the edge of town dating back to the fourth century, St. Lawrence Church—and to my astonishment, I saw more than 50 swastikas on its blue-tinted ceiling.

In the city, on the Prefecture Building, the Palace of Justice, and other institutions, one could see the Masonic star, the symbol of the absolute control of this Jewish hydra over France. That's why I retreated into the quarter of old Grenoble, where the churches with their crosses were darkened by age and forgetfulness. I turned my back on modern movie houses, theaters, and cafes, finding enjoyment among ruins where I suspected Bayard may have lived. I sank myself into the past where, to my great happiness, I lived in the historic France, in Christian France, in nationalist France—not in the Judeo-Masonic, atheistic, and cosmopolitan France but in that of Bayard! Not in Leon Blum's France![1] The square *Marche des Puces* (Flea market), as Frenchmen called it, was full of Jews, which accounted for its name. In fact, the university too was overwhelmed by them. There were 50 Jewish students from Romania alone studying here, in addition to the five Romanians.

I also visited the ancient monastery *Grande Chartreuse*, whose 1,000 monks were chased out by the atheistic government. On various icons I could still see the marks of the stones thrown by the mob during the French Revolution (1789), when they mutilated the image of God.

It was not too long before material worries came over us. My money was getting low and I did not expect any from back home. In spite of all the severe economizing, we could not manage on what Mota alone received. We spent many hours thinking how we could earn some money without disrupting the schedules of our course work. Realizing that needlework is appreciated and well paid in France, we decided to learn embroidering from my wife and then try to sell these Romanian embroideries. We learned this trade in the course of several weeks. We embroidered in our free time, had our products exhibited in a store window and, adding the little we thus earned to what Mota received from home, we managed to live very modestly.

(2) General elections back home (May 1926)

Around Easter time, letters and newspapers that we regularly received from home brought news of the fall of the Liberals from power and the advent of Gen. Averescu. New general elections were to take place around the middle of May. For the League, this was the first opportunity to engage in a great battle. I told myself: "I must go home to take part in this fight. And then come back to my studies."

---

[1] Blum was the Jewish prime minister of France.

I wrote to Professor Cuza, asking him for fare money. Receiving no reply, I then wrote to Mr. Hristache Solomon in Focsani. He sent me 10,000 lei, out of which I left a portion for my wife. With the rest, I left for home.

I arrived in Bucharest around the beginning of May, during the full electoral campaign. I went immediately to Professor Cuza, who did not appear very glad to see me there, telling me there was no need for me to come, for the movement could do well even without me. This hurt me a bit, but I did not get angry. There is no room in a political organization for a member who gets angry for being admonished by the leader. The admonishing may or may not be justified, yet one should never get angry; this is the principle that must guide a man in any organization.

Then I left for the county of Dorohoi to assist Professor Sumuleanu. From there I went on into other counties, Campul-Lung, Iasi, Braila, etc. Meanwhile, as a result of a letter I received from Professor Paulescu, and at the further insistence of Gen. Macridescu, I decided to run myself in Focsani. There I was, in the most disgusting and (for me) unwanted predicament: to go out begging for votes. Where? Among the crowds, who, right at the time when they ought to have been inspired by the most sacred sentiments—for one dealt with his country and its future—were dazed by the abundantly-offered drinks by electoral agents, and were possessed by the passions unleashed by the evil spirit of the politicians. In these moments, over the serene and clean life into villages, the flood tides of political corruption descend. This hell spreads throughout the whole country, and from it emerges the next leadership of the country for one, two, three, or four years.

It is from this heap of putrefaction that democracy—"holy" democracy—produces the leadership of a country!

I arrived at Focsani, which had been under a state of siege ever since the Ciorasti baptisms. In order to be able to go on the campaign trail, one had to have a pass for free passage, issued by the garrison commander, which I requested and received. Around 10 o'clock in the morning, accompanied by Mr. Hristache Solomon and others, we left in two cars. But 500 yards outside of town we ran into a barricade of two wagons placed across the road, with several gendarmes nearby. We stopped. The gendarmes came to us and told us we were not allowed to pass. I produced the general's order and showed it to them. They read it and then said: "Even so, you cannot pass."

I ordered my companions to open the road. Following a brief scuffle, the road was passable. The cars started moving slowly. The gendarmes, several yards behind us, knelt, aimed, and began firing. I said: "Keep moving, they are shooting in the air."

One bullet hit a fender; another passed close to us. We continued driving. But two bullets stopped us: one punctured the gas tank, the second a tire. We could not continue driving. We got out and walked home.

Again, we went to the general who had issued our free passage permit, and reported what happened, Gen. Macrisdescu also being present. He replied: "You are free to travel. I ordered no one to stop you. Perhaps it was the administrative authorities." From there we went to the Prefecture together with Gen. Macridescu. The county prefect was Nitulescu, a surly and rough man. Very calmly, we entered his office. Gen. Macridescu related the events. But the prefect, from the very first moment, treated us in a very uncivil manner. He began to deliver an interminable speech from his lofty position. "Gentlemen, the superior interests of the State demand..."

"Listen here, Mr. Prefect," I broke in, quite upset. "I see that you do not wish to be reasonable. Tomorrow morning, I shall leave on the campaign trail and if the gendarmes fire on us again, I will come back here into your office and I'll fire on you."

And without waiting for a reply, I turned around, leaving the others behind. Several hours later I was summoned to the Council of War. I went. A royal commissar interrogated me. I declared in writing exactly what happened. They arrested me. And I said: "Well gentlemen, you do nothing to those who actually fired at me, yet I, who only said I would fire, you arrest!" So, there I was again, in an incarceration room of a regiment's barracks.

Three days later I was called in by the general. An officer led me into his office. "Mr. Codreanu, you must leave the town of Focsani." "Sir, I am a candidate here. Your ordering me to leave is against the law. Certainly, I shall not oppose this measure because I cannot do so, but I ask that you give me this order in writing." "I cannot put it in writing." "Then I shall leave for Bucharest to complain about this treatment."

The general let me go free, asking for my word of honor that I would leave on the first train out. And I did leave for Bucharest on the first train.

The next day, I presented myself to Mr. Octavian Goga, the Minister of Internal Affairs, who received me well. I related to him what happened to me and demanded justice. He promised me he would send out an administrative inspector to investigate the case, and he asked me to come see him again the following day. I came. He put me off until the next day. But, as time was running out and the election day was drawing near, on the fourth day I left.

Again I took a free passage permit from the general, and again we started out driving. There were only two days left before elections. We reached the first village, where there were a few villagers gathered together as on the eve of any election, but they seemed frightened by the prevailing general terror. The gendarmes showed up: "You are permitted to talk to these people, but only for one minute. This is our order!"

I spoke for one minute and then we went on. It was the same in all the other villages—only for a minute in each. Pity justice and legality in this country! One is given the privilege of voting, one is called upon to exercise this privilege; if you don't show up to vote, you are fined, and if you do show up to vote, you are beaten. Romanian politicians, be they liberals, supporters of Averescu, or national-peasants, are only a band of tyrants who use slogans like "Legality," "Freedom," and "The rights of man" to shamelessly and fearlessly trample underfoot a whole country, with all its laws, all its freedoms, and all its rights. What possible recourse is left us, I wondered, for the future?

On election day, our delegates were beaten, covered with blood, and otherwise prevented from getting to polling places; whole villages could not get near polling stations. The result: I lost, though in the town of Focsani, I won over all the political parties. "No matter," I told myself. "Had I won, it would have disrupted my plans for continuing my studies."

Two days later, to my great joy, I heard the nationwide election results. The League totaled 120,000 votes and sent into Parliament ten deputies: Professors Cuza and Gavanescul from Iasi; Professor Sumuleanu from Dorohoi; my father from Radauti; Paul Iliescu from Campul-Lung; Professor Calan from Suceava; Dr. Haralamb Vasiliu from Botosani; Valer Pop from Satu-Mare; engineer Misu Florescu from Piatra-Neatnt; and Iuniu Lecca from Bacau. Truly an elite corps of men had been elected who honored the nationalist movement, men whom people looked upon with boundless love and lively hopes. Those 120,000 votes represented the best and purest in the Romanian nation. Voters overcame all threats, all enticements, and all obstacles in order to reach the voting booths. But those who could not reach them were very numerous—even more than those who made it. There were at least another 120,000 votes that had either been stopped or stolen from the ballot box.

I went back to France, satisfied with the results but constantly haunted by the following question: How could we win if all administrations conducted elections in such a manner, using corruption, theft, and force against the popular will?

(3) In the Alps

Arriving in France, I was too late to take my exams in the June session. I was faced with a grave problem. Mota would have to return home to fulfill his military service in the fall. How were we going to make a living when, from our embroidery work, we could provide hardly enough for one individual, let alone for two souls? I tried to find some work in the city, anything at all. Impossible. Then I thought perhaps out in the country, near town, I might be able to secure something. Together with Mota, I went in several directions in search of work; but in the evening we came back unsuccessful.

One day we took the tram to Uriage-les-Bains, some six miles from Grenoble. There, streetcars run not only in the cities but outside as far as 12 miles in all directions, for there is abundant electrical energy generated by the waterfalls in the mountains. From Uriage we followed some paths up the mountain. After about a half hour, we got to Saint Martin, quite a large village with a well-paved road through it, well cared-for stone houses, several stores, and a beautiful tall church. But we passed on. After another hour of walking, climbing constantly in heat that made us sweat, we arrived in a small hamlet, Pinet-d'Uriage.

We were at an altitude of approximately 2,700 feet. Above us the Alps offered an admirable prospect, as they were covered with snow. It seemed that the snow started but a few miles from where we were. On our left, toward the Chateau de Vizille, a beautiful valley stretched out; toward Grenoble to our right, another one; and along the valley, the paved road meandering down shone like the water of a river bathed in the sun.

On the fields we could see the people working. We wondered how there, on the slope of the mountain just a few miles from perpetual snows, wheat could grow as tall as a man; or oats and barley, as well as all kinds of vegetables. Probably because of the milder climate and a rock-free soil. In fact, their soil was of low fertility, even poor. But farmers continually used manure or fertilizer.

As we saw them working their fields, we were faced with the same problem as in the other villages: how to get into conversation with them to tell them we were looking for work. We passed them by, not daring to talk. Further up there were some more houses, five or six. We went there. We got to the last one. Beyond it, no other human habitation between us and the massive Beldona, except for tourist cabins.

Nearby an old man was mowing. We had to speak to him. We greeted him and began talking. He realized we were foreigners, consequently asked us what we were. We told him we were Romanians, that we liked it here very much and we wanted to rent a room to spend several months in the clean air. The old man was boastful, and probably thinking he found someone from whom he could learn many things, asked us to come and join him and sit at the outside table, on which he placed a bottle of black, astringent wine and three glasses, which he filled. Then he began questioning us, following our answers with great curiosity: "So you say you are Romanians?" "Yes, Romanians, Romanians from Romania." "Is Romania far from here?" "Almost 2,000 miles." "Are there also peasants in your country as there are here?" "There are many, Pere Truk," for this was his name. Finally we answered all his questions, thus making friends with him quickly.

But we did not tell him anything of what ailed us, because the old man realized that we were educated people, "gentlemen," and he would have lost all his illusions had we told him we were looking for work. We only asked him if he knew of a room for rent somewhere. He gave us an address and insisted we tell the landlord that it was he, Pere Truk, who sent us.

As we left, we expressed our thanks and promised that we would come back to help with his mowing. We found the address he gave us several houses down the slope. It was the house of M. Chenevas Paul, a pensioner about 70 years old, well dressed, a former noncommissioned officer, now retired. He was proud to be the only pensioner in the village. He owned two houses side by side which he used all for himself, for he was alone. All his relatives had died. He rented to us his smaller house, comprising two rooms below, one large and one small, and another room above (all houses there had a second story). In the downstairs room there was a stove to cook on. In the one upstairs, simply furnished, there was a bed. All this conveyed an aspect of emptiness. It was apparent that no one had lived in it for a long time.

We agreed on 400 francs until Christmas (that was for six months). In Grenoble we were paying 150 francs a month. We paid in advance for three months and said we would move there in a few days. Then we went back to the city in good spirits. I felt that now, having fulfilled my residence course work required in the doctoral program, I would study for the exams here, and would go down into Grenoble only to take them.

(4) At Pinet-d'Uriage among French peasants

Several days later, Mota, my wife, and I were climbing the same paths, belongings on our backs, to our new quarters. At last, we settled down. Mota took leave of us and left for Romania. We stayed behind with only a few francs in our pockets. A dire situation! How were we going to eat?

The next morning, rather depressed, I went to Pere Truk. I helped with the mowing and hay loading all day. He asked me to eat with him both at noon and at suppertime. Had I been able to take something to my wife also it would have been perfect, but I returned empty-handed. I went again the following morning. This time he had someone to work for him, a short man with red, unkempt hair, and shiny restless eyes in which I could not find any trace of goodness; he seemed to be a mean man. His name was Corbela. But the peasants of the region all speak *patois*, namely a peasant dialect that differs much from the official language both in pronunciation and in the structure of words. This difference is so great that a city Frenchman cannot understand a country Frenchman who speaks it. But the latter also know the official language.

The three of us were invited by a housewife, the old man's woman, to eat at her place at noon. She was an old woman just like old women back home. In France, peasants do not eat an onion with a mound of cornmeal mush at noon as do our peasants; as a rule, they have a vegetable dish, a meat course, then cheese; and regularly a glass of wine. I thanked them for inviting me to their meal but said I would not eat. Considering that I felt embarrassed, they insisted. Then I told them that, being Friday, I fasted until evening. This was an old habit for me, one that I had kept for three years, ever since I was initially imprisoned in Vacaresti prison. When Corbela heard I was fasting, he asked me gruffly: "But why do you fast?" "Because I believe in God." "How do you know there is a God? Did you see Jesus Christ?" he continued. "No, I did not see Him, but this is how I am; I do not believe you telling me He does not exist, while I believe the innumerable martyrs who, when spiked on the cross, cried out: 'You may kill us, but we saw Him.'" "Ah, the priests! The charlatans! I crush them under my heel, pushing it into the ground, like I would crush a worm."

Seeing him so aroused, I broke off the discussion.

That evening I left for home with a basketful of potatoes and a piece of bacon the old man gave me. I worked likewise that Saturday. On Sunday, I went to church. There were many people, probably the entire village. In a side pew, close to the altar, solemn as a saint, stood a man who resembled Corbela. I took another look. He followed the priest very closely. At a certain moment he approached the priest and very humbly assisted him. It was he, Corbela! Cantor, sacristan, and bell-ringer.

Later as I made friends with the villagers, I told them about my encounter with Corbela, all of us enjoying a good laugh. "We too have our fools among us," I was told. "They listen to important people who hate the

Church. But we, the French peasants, believe in God as we have learned from our parents."

The priest, a man of vast culture, a doctor in philosophy and theology, was living in great misery, receiving no salary from the atheistic state that persecuted priests as enemies. The latter live only on help received from the few villagers.

The following week I worked for someone else, harvesting potatoes, who gave me a larger quantity of potatoes, the basis of our existence for some time. I moved on to another peasant to help with sheaving wheat and threshing. In each village, people own a threshing machine in common which is used in turn by all. Yields are rich and beautiful as gold.

After about a month, the villagers began to get used to me. I was known as "*le roumain*" (The Romanian). They heard I was a doctoral student and we had talks in the evening. They were interested in questions of philosophy, politics, international relations, and in political economics, particularly in the subjects of pricing, law of supply and demand, and other laws determining prices, as well as causes of price fluctuation and the right time for marketing their products. Peasants between 25 and 40 years of age were well-oriented in these topics and one could discuss with them even higher questions; they understood them perfectly.

After a while I began studying for my exams. Mota took his exams in June successfully. I worked days, and evenings and at night I studied as much as I could. In this first year, I took four subjects: political economy, the history of economic doctrines, industrial legislation, and financial legislation. But in about two months, I was beginning to lose my strength. Our nourishment proved inadequate. Lately we had been on a diet of boiled potatoes almost exclusively. Every two or three days, a quart of milk, and meat but once weekly, occasionally cheese. This was all I could earn by working. But worse than me was my wife, who became anemic.

I took my exams in October. I flunked them, though in the main subject matter, political economy, I obtained the highest grade and in the other subjects, passing marks. In financial legislation I got a nine, the passing grade for doctorate being ten. For the moment I was disoriented. I had never been a shining element when it came to studying, but up to now I had never flunked an exam, given that I was among the average students. This was a serious blow in view of our difficult economic predicament. The difficulty was that I could only retake my exams in three months, and then, in all the subjects. I became stubborn and resolved to start all over. Farm work in the fields had ended. The ground was snow-covered. The only work available was cutting firewood in the forest. My payment for work there was a wagonload of wood.

Fortunately, we began getting financial help from back home from Father Mota, who obtained a loan in my name.

We spent the winter months and Christmas holidays amongst the peasants, mainly with the Belmain-David family. I again registered for my exams in the February session for my first year of the doctorate, and passed them all. I began studying immediately for those of the second year: administrative law, the philosophy of law, the history of French law, and civic international law. In the spring, I rented a patch of garden that I began to work on my own.

But in May 1927 I received a desperate letter from Mota and others from Focsani as well, and from students, asking me to come back home right away; the League had broken into two. Mota and Hristache Solomon also sent me money for the trip. But I had another month before the exams. I visited the Dean of the Faculty, informing him of the emergency demanding my return to Romania and requesting permission to take my exams ahead of the regular session. My petition was approved. On May 16 I took and passed my exams. On May 18 I left for Romania, after taking leave of the inhabitants of Pinet, among whom we had lived nearly a year. When we left, some of them, the old ones, cried. Others accompanied me to the Grenoble station.

I came to France with the worry that I would find an immoral, corrupt, and decayed people, such as it was reported often times throughout the world. But I reached the conclusion that the French people, whether peasant or townsman, are a people of intense morality. The immoralities belong to spoiled foreigners, the rich of all nationalities, attracted by Paris and other large cities. The leading class, in my opinion, is however irremediably compromised—thinking, living, and acting under the influence, and exclusively under the influence, of Judeo-Masonry and its bankers. Judeo-Masonry uses Paris as its world headquarters (London, with the Scottish Freemasons, is but a subsidiary). This leading class has lost contact with French history and the French nation. That is why as I left France; I was making a big differentiation between the French people and the French Masonic state. For the French people, I carried in my heart not only love but also a faith that will never be shaken in its resurrection and victory over the hydra that plagues it, darkening its reasoning, sucking its strength, and compromising both its honor and its future.

At Bucharest

I arrived in Bucharest. It was a disaster. The League had broken into two. The hopes of this nation were crumbling. A whole people who strained to gather up its exhausted strength in a difficult moment of history, and fought the greatest peril ever to threaten its existence, was now falling to the ground, all its hopes shattered. Such a disaster, to the valiant hearts of thousands of fighters, all of them seeing in a moment all their past sacrifices and all their hopes crashing down. This calamity inspired a feeling of profound pain, even in those who stood outside our movement. I had never before seen more widespread sorrow. All those waves of enthusiasm from Severin to Focsani, from Campul-Lung to Cluj, were now changed into waves of grief and despair.

I went to the Parliament to see Professor Cuza. To my great astonishment, in the midst of general grief, he was the only joyful man. I give here, with the greatest possible accuracy, our conversation. "Welcome back, dear Corneliu," he said, advancing toward me, arm outstretched. "You are a good fellow. Just keep on minding your business as you have done so far, and everything is going to be just fine." "Sir, I am depressed to the bottom of my being by the misfortune that befell us."

"But no misfortune took place. The League is stronger than ever. Look, I returned from Braila yesterday. It was something fantastic. I was received there with bands, drums, and unending hurrahs. You'll see the country's atmosphere. You do not know what it is like. The entire country is with us." We said a few more words and then left.

Dumbfounded, I wondered: "Could a leader, seeing his troop rent by grief, divided into two and possessed by despair, really enjoy such a perfect disposition and good humor? Not realize the disaster boiling under him? But perhaps he does realize it! If so, how, then, is it possible for him to be rejoicing?"

The parliamentary and extra-parliamentary activity of the League's ten deputies during their term, left quite a bit to be desired. Were they weak men? Decidedly not! Were they of bad faith? Decidedly not! They were of absolute good faith but they had small deficiencies, either as to knowledge of the Jewish problem—because they were the newer League members—or because they were a little cumbersome and slow in action and in hitting the trail, being the older ones. But such deficiencies are inherent in all men gathered into an organization, and they must be lovingly and tactfully corrected by the leader. Then, what were the real causes for this state of affairs?

In my opinion, they were:

1. The lack of coordination of their parliamentary and extra-parliamentary activity.
2. The lack of spiritual unity, a unity absolutely indispensable to such an organization that is surrounded on all sides by enemies who try to take advantage of any internal dissension.

But these two drawbacks are basically the result of the true cause: *the lack of leadership, and the leader's errors.* A leader must constantly expound his views to all the fighters around him in order to reach a unity of thinking of his following; to elaborate a plan of action; to direct the action of his men; to be a permanent servant of the movement's unity, trying by his love, observations, reprimands, to smooth out misunderstandings and inherent discord within the organization; to be a constant example to his followers of fulfilling one's duty; and to handle matters with justice, respecting the norms of leadership taken upon himself and on the basis of which he assembled his supporters.

But Professor Cuza did none of these. He did not educate his men. He did not even consult with them. "Let us have a consultation, Sir," requested some of them, "so that we can know the attitude we should take, and how we should present ourselves, in Parliament." "We need hold no consultation because we are not a political party."

He never issued any directive to anyone. One can find valuable tomes, scores of pamphlets written by Cuza, hundreds of articles. But I dare anyone to bring me ten circulars or action orders given to the most troubled political organization from 4 March 1923, its founding, to 20 May 1927, the moment of its abolition.

One will not find ten, nor five, not even three. Cuza had urged others, but he himself was not one to spur his followers to action; he punished others, but when he did so, he caused a real disaster because he did not handle the matter wisely. Meantime, certainly, in view of the situation thus presented, some of the deputies, sensing that things were not running as they should, expressed their dissatisfaction. They saw that gradually the movement was heading toward ruin, especially because, in addition to lack of directives from time to time, certain outbursts by Cuza in Parliament had a devastating and disconcerting effect upon the entire movement. For instance, when, immediately following the opening of Parliament, one of the League's deputies protested against the state of siege imposed at Focsani and the unheard-of abuses, Cuza stood up, commanding the government for having done so, even saying he would have done the same thing, because people were agitated on account of the Jews. Another time, discussing the Royal message to Parliament, answering members of the National Peasant Party (in fact they were in the opposition at the time), he declared: "The People's Party could become a governing factor through a system of rotation with the Liberal Party if Gen. Avereseu would adopt the doctrine of the League of Christian National Defense."

Such statements—thrown from the eminence of the parliamentary tribune just when thousands of men, beaten, tortured, and wronged, were anxiously awaiting, as a weak succor for their suffering, a word condemning the government—disseminated instead an atmosphere of general discouragement.

In the following I quote the *Official Monitor* regarding a passage by Cuza from the discourse just mentioned:

> There are then at the present time, in the service of the state, two mature parties, parties of order, of the present-day order, governmental parties, which complement each other and which assure the normal play of constitutional mechanism: the People's Party and the Liberal Party.
>
> They both stand on solid foundations, relying on production interests which, though differing, are nevertheless general, real, and permanent and assure their existence and the efficacy of their action. The new work of political and constitutional organization of the country is their work in which they collaborated, each to the extent of the responsibility and role they played as governing or opposition. The People's Party will continue this work by all the improvements that sincere practice and good faith shall indicate as necessary for the further consolidation of the state and the total unification of the country.
>
> The Liberal Party is the exponent of Romanian bourgeoise interests, of financial, commercial, and industrial legitimate interests, indispensable for the country's well-being.
>
> The People's Party, called to perfect the economic organization of the state, basing it on real foundations, preoccupied by everyone's needs within the superior interests of the country, relies particularly on the overall real and permanent interests of agricultural production, which is a preponderant factor of our economic life.

The People's Party, which has the deepest and most extensive roots throughout the country, within social harmony…wants to give the plowmen, masters of their soil, the role they deserve in the state's economy in accordance with their labor and their numbers.

(Official Monitor, 30 July 1926, p. 395).

This attitude on the part of the leader of a national movement is unconscionable. To present such a eulogy of the political parties that the nationalist movement denounces as a calamity fallen over Romania, and against which it has fought with grievous sacrifices in order to create a new fate for this country, differing from the one meant for it by the parties' politicians, is the same as a death sentence for your own movement.

To sing the praises of a rotational system represented by the Liberal and Averescan parties, denounced by you for a lifetime as enemies of the people, means to remove any chance for victory of the national movement you have led, at the same time proving that you yourself do not put any faith in it. What would people say of the commandant of heroic troops who fight, make supreme sacrifices, believe in their victory, live, and are ready to die for it, if he, during a discourse amidst a fight in front of thousands of wounded soldiers, would eulogize enemy troops and forecast their victory?

What would happen to the poor troop that, instead of hearing a word of encouragement of its hopes in victory, would hear its own commanding officer speak of the wonderful victorious prospects of the enemy?

What would happen? The troop would scatter, demoralized. And this is exactly what did happen. Many fighters on the front of the national movement left in despair. Owing to this strange attitude, the League's deputies began showing their unhappiness. They were wrong, I think. They had no right to express their dissatisfaction except to the president and within the limited circle of the leadership. But they went out of bounds. Under such conditions, each word haphazardly uttered means an additional misfortune over the one caused by the movement's president himself. Gradually, the mistakes of one group and then another led to coolness in their relations. Until one day, with no sufficient reason, with no advance consideration, thus without respecting the norms and laws of the organization, deputy Paul Iliescu was expelled from the League of Christian National Defense; and what's more, President Cuza informed none of the parliamentarians of his decision but purely and simply announced from his prestigious position the dismissal, demanding that the deputy be simultaneously thrown out of Parliament and his seat in Campul-Lung declared

vacant. This struck like a bolt of lightning over the heads of the poor deputies of the League.

Two days later, Professor Sumuleanu, who in the meantime had hur-
ried in from Iasi, presented a communication to the Chamber of Deputies
signed also by the other deputies, Ion Zelea-Codreanu, Valer Pop, Dr.
Iiaralamb Vasiliu, and Professor Carlan, in which they stated that Cuza's
declaration was certainly premature, because the League's statutes stipu-
late that exclusions are pronounced by the committee, which in this case
was totally in the dark. It did not know of any guilt on the part of this man,
yet it did not ask that he not be expelled, but only that he first be judged so
he could defend himself; it demanded, in other words, that the League's by-
laws be respected; that the law that everyone vowed to respect, be obeyed.

At the same time, Cuza was approached with this same request. The
result of these interventions: all signatories were expelled from the League,
Professor Sumuleanu and my father included, some of them having higher
merits of labor and sacrifice in the formation of the League than Professor
Cuza, Sumuleanu being himself the League's Vice-President. All these,
likewise, were expelled without being judged; without being told a thing;
without being approached. In my opinion, the procedure used by Cuza in
his capacity of president of the organization—whose duty it was to exercise the greatest concern for the well-being of the organization and the
greatest care in any step that might endanger its existence—was fundamentally erroneous. In fact, it was not only unjust, but totally uncalled for, particularly considering the individuals involved who represented the very
group who were leading the League. They were the creators of this organization. The measure was unreasoned, and Cuza did not foresee its consequences for the movement.

A special issue of *The National Defense*, put out immediately following their expulsion, stated that these men, with Professor Sumuleanu and
my father heading the list, had sold out to the Jews, thus spreading this
insinuation throughout the country. Sumuleanu, Professor Cuza's constant
friend for a quarter of a century, a man of exemplary correctitude, was horribly and unconscionably attacked in this special issue at the direction and
under the advice of Cuza. He walked the streets overwhelmed with grief,
having been accused of treason. Then he published a pamphlet in reply
titled: "The Treachery of Some Friends." His riposte was only one consequence of the errors committed by Cuza. In this case, Cuza, in my opinion,
had been not only unjust but was more than unjust. Those who were expelled, on their part, erred by printing flyers containing equally unjust attacks, but their error followed in the wake of Cuza's. All these attacks and

counter-attacks were unfolding to the great despair of Romanian fighters and the great satisfaction of and ridicule by Jewry. It was at this stage that I returned from France. The question as to whether the parliamentarians expelled from the League should be permitted to serve out their terms was being debated in Parliament.

I ask myself even now: "I wonder whether, when Cuza took those steps, he was not the victim of some suggestions or intrigues, or did he persuade himself that this was the right thing to do?"

Several days later, several members of the League who were petrified by Cuza's measures demanded their annulment and respect for statutes. This resulted in elimination of this group, among whom were: Gen. Macridescu, Professor Traian Braileanu, Ilristache Solomon, Professor Catuneanu, etc. At large, the rumor was systematically spread that all expellees sold out to the Jews. Among the active agents disseminating those rumors were Col. Necuicea and Liviu Sadoveanu, the right- and left-hand, respectively, of Professor Cuza.

Those expelled then formed themselves into the Statutory League of Christian National Defense, thus indicating that they stood within the League's statutes. At this time, Cuza called for a great national assembly in Iasi, in the Bejan Hall, to which about 1,000 people came. They ratified the expulsions on the false basis that the members expelled had sold out to the Jews. I shall stop here, leaving out observations on what was printed either by one side or the other, considering that as much as I have put down on paper should be enough for understanding the situation of the movement at that time. I would only like to add that time—nine years have passed since—proved Cuza to have erred, because neither Professor Sumuleanu, so grievously hurt in his honor, nor my father who received nearly mortal blows from the Judaic power—which Cuza cannot boast of having suffered—nor Gen. Macridescu, Professor Gavanescul, Professor Traian Braileanu, Professor Catuneanu, Dr. Vasiliu, Professor Carlan, Father Mota, etc.—none of these had sold out to the Jews. Years later, after this disaster had devastated the League, Cuza came to his old friend, Professor Sumuleanu, whom he had struck down so cruelly, and said: "Dear Sumuleanu, I have nothing against you. Let us make peace!" But Professor Sumuleanu turned away and as he left, said: "It is too late"—not because he did not want to forgive the cruel blow he had received, but because down there, one saw the ashes of a movement and of Romanian hopes.

My Reaction in the Face of this State of Affairs

When I arrived from France amidst this disaster that descended on the national movement, I intended to salvage what yet could be saved. I hastily convoked in Iasi the Vacaresti group and part of the leaders of student youth from the four university centers.

I hoped to localize the split, by forming a youth bloc, and thus to prevent this atmosphere of hate that was dissipating the ranks of the older generation from enveloping the youth. As it was only natural, I wanted to base this bloc first of all upon the awareness that disunity and hate among us meant death for the national movement. Once this bloc was formed, I wanted to direct our efforts toward the burning ranks of the veterans, to apply determined pressures in order to reestablish the unity, and thus save the situation. But my plan fell through. The youth was already enveloped by the consuming flames of hatred, so that in Iasi, in spite of all ties existing between the youth and myself, my proposition found no response in their hearts.

The student leadership in Iasi could have given the signal of a saving initiative, but unfortunately a series of weak elements had assumed control of it, their negative tendencies precluding the acceptance of my proposals. It was only the Vacaresti group, out of all the youth, that supported my point of view, to which I must add a few Iasian students, about 10 or 12. These were all that rallied around us, out of all the youth of the country.

I pursued my plan.

We all left for Bucharest to see both sides. We went first to see the "Statutories," asking them to make any sacrifice needed in order to reestablish the movement's unity. After several hours of discussion, they agreed conditionally, being even disposed to make sacrifices, but insisting that statutes be respected in the future. After that we went to see Professor Cuza. But he, following our pleading and argumentation, refused. It is better for me not to reveal the discussion we had on that occasion.

We left. Despondency took over our souls. All that had been built, all the movement's brightness of yesterday did not come as a gift of fortune. Everything grew out of fighting step by step, foot by foot. We had carried the burden of our grave decisions, faced innumerable perils, risks, physical and moral suffering, some more heart-rending than others. We had given the health of our bodies, the blood of our hearts; we had fought and sacrificed day in and day out. Now, all seemed turned into ashes.

CHAPTER 5
THE LEGION OF
MICHAEL THE ARCHANGEL

Faced by the situation mentioned above, I decided to go with neither side—not meaning to resign myself, but to organize the youth, assuming this responsibility according to my soul and wit, and to continue the fight, not to capitulate.

Amid these troubles and times at the crossroads, I remembered the icon that protected us in the Vacaresti prison. We decided to close our ranks and to pursue the fight under the protection of the same sacred icon. With this in mind, we brought it to our home in Iasi from the altar of the St. Spiridon Church, where it had been placed three years previously. The Vacaresti group agreed immediately to my plans. Several days later, I convoked a meeting in Iasi in my room on 20 Florilor St. for Friday, June 24, 1927, including the Vacaresti group and the few students still with us.

Several minutes before the meeting was to begin, I entered in a register the following order of the day:

> Today, Friday, 24 June 1927 (The feast of St. John the Baptist), at 10 o'clock in the evening, is founded under my leadership, 'The Legion of Michael the Archangel.' Let anyone who believes without reservation, join our ranks. Let him who has doubts remain on the sidelines. I hereby nominate Radu Mironovici as leader of the guard of the icon.
>
> Corneliu Zelea Codreanu

This first meeting lasted one minute, only long enough for me to read the above order. After this, those present left in order to ponder whether they felt sufficiently determined and courageous to join an organization like this, without a program other than the example of my life as a patriot up to then and that of my prison comrades. I even gave the Vacaresti group time for reflection and search of their conscience, for them to be sure whether they had any doubts or reservations, because once enrolled, they had to unhesitatingly keep on going for the rest of their lives.

Our intimate feelings from which the Legion was born were these: it did not interest us whether we would triumph or be conquered, or whether we would die. Our purpose was different: *to advance united*. Moving forward in a united front, with the help of God and the Romanian people's justice, no matter what destiny awaited us—that of being vanquished or that of death—it would be a blessed one and it would bear fruit for our people. Professor Nicolae Iorga once said: "There are defeats and deaths which can awaken a nation to life, just as there are triumphs of the kind which can put a nation to sleep."

During the same night, and entered into the same register, we edited a letter to Professor Cuza and one to Professor Sumuleanu. At 10 o'clock the next morning, all the Vacarestians got together and went to the house of Professor Cuza, 3 Codrescu St.

After so many years of battles and difficult trials, we were now going to see him to take our farewell, and to ask him to release us from the vows we took. Professor Cuza received us in the same room in which he had stood for me, 28 years earlier, at my baptism. He was standing behind his desk; we in front. I read him the following letter:

> Sir,
> We are coming to you for the last time to say goodbye and to ask you to release us from all the vows we took. We can no longer follow you on the road you have taken, for we no longer believe in it. To march by your side without faith is impossible, because it was faith that nourished our enthusiasm in battle. Begging you to release us from our vows, we remain to fight alone in the best way that our minds and hearts can guide us.

Professor Cuza then spoke to us in the following manner: "My dear friends, I release you from your vows and advise you that, stepping into life on your own, do not make mistakes. Because, particularly in politics, mistakes are very costly. You have as an example the political errors of Petre Carp, which had fatal consequences for him. On my part, I wish you the best in life." Then he shook hands with all of us and we left. We thought that it was correct on our part to proceed thus and that we were obliged, as dignified fighters, to take this path.

From there we went to Professor Sumuleanu on Saulescu St., reading to him the other letter written approximately in the same terms, in which we informed him and his "Statutories" that we could not go along with them either and that we would carve for ourselves from now on our own path. Leaving him, we felt in our hearts how very much alone we were, alone as in a desert, and we were going to build our road in life through our own powers.

We gathered even closer to the icon. The more difficulties that might assail us and the more our compatriots' blows might be showered heavily on our heads, the more we would seek the protection of St. Michael the Archangel and the shadow of his sword. He was no longer for us an image on an icon, but very much alive. There at the icon, we took turns keeping watch, night and day, candle burning.

Matter versus Spirit

When we gathered together in the room at our home, the five of us plus some ten freshman and sophomore students, and when we wanted to write several letters announcing our decision to Mr. Hristache Solomon and others, only then did we realize how poor we were; all of us put together lacked even the money for envelopes and postage. Up to then, any time we needed money, we went to the older veterans and asked them for it. But now we had no one to turn to. To launch a political organization totally penniless! It was both a difficult thing to do and a daring one. Especially in a century in which matter is all powerful, in which no one starts anything, however small, without first asking himself "How much money do I have?" God wanted to prove that, in the legionary struggle and victory, matter played no role. Through our daring gesture, we turned our backs on a mentality that dominated everything. We ourselves destroyed one world in order to raise another, as high as the sky. The absolute rule of matter was overthrown so that it could be replaced by the rule of the spirit, of moral values.

We were not denying and will never deny the existence, function, and necessity of matter in the world, but we did deny and forever will deny the right of its absolute domination. In other words, we were striking a blow at a mentality that placed the Golden Calf in the center and as the main purpose in life. During those first beginnings, we found the only moral strength in the unshaken faith alone, that placing ourselves in life's original harmony, *matter's subordination to the spirit*, we could subdue the adversities and be victorious over the satanic forces coalesced with the purpose of destroying us.

Another characteristic of our beginning, in addition to this lack of money, was the lack of a program. We had no program at all. And this fact will no doubt raise a big question mark. Whoever heard of a political organization lacking a program that stemmed from reason, from the mind or one or several people?

It was not those of us who *thought* alike that banded together, but those of us who *felt* alike. Not those among us who *reasoned* in the same way, but those who had the same moral-emotional-spiritual construction.

This was a signal that the statue of another Goddess—Reason—was to be smashed. Mankind had raised her against God, and we—not intending to throw away or despise her—should put her in her proper place, in the service of God and of life's meaning. If then we had neither money nor a program, we had, instead, God in our souls, and He inspired us with the invincible power of faith.

Against Treachery

Our birth was greeted with a hurricane of hate and ridicule. The two camps of the League—Cuzists and Statutories—broke relations with us. All students in Iasi left us, and the Cuzist attacks, previously directed at the Statutories, were from now on to be aimed at us, piercing like arrows into our hearts. We would not be hurt by the arrows' wounds but we were going to be terrified by what we were to discover in people.

Briefly, we would be rewarded and honored with the weightiest insults for everything we had done before, and suffer blow after blow. We would not only feel the hate but would see lack of character and incorrectitude of soul in all their nakedness. Soon we would become "exploiters of the national idea" for our personal benefit. We would not have believed that those who pounded their breasts with their fists a year earlier, claiming rewards for their pretended suffering, would now have the courage to throw into our faces the accusation just mentioned.

Soon people would learn that we had "sold out to the Jews," and even articles full of insults were going to be written, and there would be peasants who would believe it and men who would turn their backs on us. Unjustly! Insults that our enemies never dared use against us before, out of fear, were coming now at us from *our friends*, fearlessly and shamelessly.

If it be true that we who had gone through such suffering and whose bodies had endured so much abuse, would be capable of such an infamy—namely, to sell ourselves as a group to the enemy—then there would be nothing left anymore to do but set dynamite to this people and blow it up. Any people that gave birth and raised in its bosom such children deserves to live no longer.

But if it be untrue, those who invent such lies and disseminate them are scoundrels who drain away the nation's trust in its own future and destiny. For such as these, no punishment from their country is great enough.

What confidence could this people have in victory and the future if, in the midst of the tough fight it is waging, it hears that we, its children, raised in its arms, in whom it placed its most sacred hopes, betrayed it?

I leave those days only in the memory of those of us who lived them. To them, my comrades of that time, witnesses of those hours, I said: "Do not be afraid of these pygmies, for whoever has such souls, cannot ever win. Someday you will see them fall on their knees at your feet. Do not forgive them. Because they are not going to do it out of remorse for the committed transgression, but out of treachery. And now, even if hell, with all its unclean ghosts, should confront us, unmoved in our firm stand, we will vanquish them."

Up to that time, I had known the beast in man. Now I saw the scoundrel in man. Guard yourselves and the children of today and tomorrow of the Romanian people, and of any other people in the world, of this frightening plague: *treachery*. All the intelligence, all the learning, all talents, all education will be of no avail to us if we are going to be treacherous.

Teach your children not to use treachery either against a friend or against their greatest foe. Not only will they not win, but they will be more than defeated, they will be crushed. Nor should they use treachery against the treacherous person and his treacherous ways, for if they should win, only the persons change. Treachery will remain unchanged. The treachery of the victor will be substituted for that of the defeated. In essence, the same treachery will rule the world. The darkness of treachery in the world cannot be replaced by another darkness but only by the light brought by the soul of the brave, full of character and honor.

And yet, at the very beginning of this barrage of hatred and treachery, some men came to us as to a refuge giving them hope: Hristache Solomon, that man of great honor and conscience; engineer Clime; engineer Blanaru; attorney Mille Lefter; Andrei C. Ionescu; Alexandru Ventonic; Dumitru Ifrim; Cosachescu; Ion Butnaru; Ilierodeacon Isihic Antohic, etc. All these distinguished and veteran fighters in the League now gave me the impression of some shipwrecked souls, whose ship sank in the middle of the sea, and they landed, tired and troubled, on our small island on which they could find inner peace and confidence in the future.

Gen. Macridescu told us: "Though I am old, I will go with you and I will help you, only on one condition: that you not shake the hands of these people who lack honor. If you did this, it would disgust me no end and I would lose all my hopes in you." Also, Professor Ion Gavanescul began to show an interest in us and in what we were doing.

The Beginnings of Legionary Life

Four lines marked our small initial life:

1. *Faith in God.* All of us believed in God. None of us was an atheist. The more we were alone and surrounded, the more our preoccupations were directed to God and toward contact with our own dead and those of the nation. This gave us an invincible strength and a shining serenity in the face of all blows.

2. *Trust in our mission.* No one could be presented the smallest reason for our possible victory. We were so few in number, so young, so poor, so hated and detested by everyone, that all arguments not based on fact, pleaded against any chances of success. And yet we went ahead, thanks only to the confidence in our purpose, and an unlimited trust in our mission and in the destiny of our country.

3. *Our mutual love.* Some of us had known one another for some time, having formed close friendships, but others were youngsters, freshmen or sophomores in college, whom we had never met. From the very first days, an ambience of affection between us all was established, as if we were of the same family and had known each other since childhood.

The need for an inner equilibrium was obvious in order to be able to resist. Our common affection had to be of the same intensity and force to match the wave of hatred from outside. Our life in this nest was not a cold, official life, with distance between chief and soldier, with theatrics, rhetorical statements, and assumed airs of leadership. Our nest was warm. Relations between us were absolutely casual. One did not come in as into a cold barracks but as into his own house, among his own family. And one did not come here just to take orders, but one found here a ray of love, an hour of spiritual quiet, a word of encouragement, relief, help in misfortune or need. The legionary was not asked so much for discipline, in the sense of barracks discipline—as for propriety, faith, devotion, and zeal for work.

4. *The song.* Perhaps because we had not started out on the road of reason by setting up programs, contradictory discussions, philosophical argumentations, and lectures, our only possibility of expressing our inner feelings

was through singing. We sang those songs in which our feelings found satisfaction. "There, High Up on a Black Rock," Stefan the Great's song— the melody of which, it was said, had remained unchanged from his time to this, from generation to generation. It is said that, at the sound of this melody, Stefan the Great triumphantly entered his fort at Suceava 500 years ago. When we were singing it, we felt alive with those times of Romanian greatness and glory; we sank 500 years back into history and lived there for a few moments, in touch with Stefan the Great and with his soldiers and archers. "Like a Globe of Gold," the song of Michael the Brave; Avram Iancu's song; "Let the Bugle Sound Again," the march of the Military School of Infantry in 1917; "Arise Romanians" written by Iustin Iliesu and Istrate, which we proclaimed as the Legion's hymn. To be able to sing, one has to be in a certain state of spirit, an inner harmony. A person bent on robbing somebody cannot sing, nor can one who is about to commit some other wrong; nor he whose soul is consumed by envy and hate of his comrade; nor he whose soul is devoid of faith.

That is why you, legionaries of today and tomorrow, anytime you feel the need to orient yourselves in the legionary spirit, must return to these four lines of our beginning that constitute the basis of our movement. The song will be a guide to you. If you are unable to sing, you must know that a sickness gnaws at the depth of your spiritual being or that life has filled your innocent soul with sins. And if you cannot rid yourselves of these sins, you ought to step aside, leaving your place to those who can sing. Pursuing our life on the above-mentioned lines, we set out to act from the first days. I designated leaders who received and gave orders.

We did not start out by engaging in some spectacular actions. As we were faced by some problem, we set out to solve it. Our first action was fixing the room in our home in which the icon of St. Michael the Archangel was kept. We whitewashed it, we scrubbed the floor. The legionary girls began sewing curtains. Then legionaries wrote down several maxims that I collected, either from the Gospels or from other writings. They embellished our walls. Here are some of them:

"God carries us on His victorious chariot."
"Whoever wins… I shall be his God."
"He who does not have a sword, let him sell his cloak and buy one."
"Fight bravely for faith."
"Avoid carnal pleasures, for they kill the soul."
"Be vigilant."
"Do not destroy the hero that is in you."

"Brothers in fortune… as in misfortune."
"Whoever knows how to die, will never be a slave."
"I await the resurrection of my Fatherland and the destruction of the hordes of traitors," etc.

In a week's time, our headquarters was set up.

Our second action was of a different nature: it pertained to what our attitude should be toward outside attacks. We decided not to respond to them, which was extremely difficult for us all. Our moral being was being ripped apart. But this was the time of heroic endurance. Another action: No one is to try to convince anyone to become a legionary. The customary sleeve-pulling and fishing for members always displeased me. The system was and has remained contrary, even to this day, to the legionary spirit. We shall state our point of view, simply. Whoever wanted to join, would come. And he will join, if he is accepted.

But who was coming? People of the same spiritual essence as ours. Many? No. Very few. In Iasi, one year later, there were only two or three more than the first day. In the rest of the country however, there were more who joined as they learned about our existence.

All those approaching us were characterized by two distinct and clearly visible qualities:

1. A great correctitude of soul.
2. The lack of personal interest. Among us, no one could profit.

No promising prospects opened up. Here everyone had only to give soul, wealth, life, capacity for love, and trust.

Even if one who was an incorrect individual or was motivated by some personal interest joined, he could not remain with us, for he would not find a propitious setting here. He would automatically leave, in a month, a year, two or three—retreating, deserting, or betraying.

Our Program

This nest of youth was the first beginning of legionary life, the first corner-stone. It had to be laid on solid ground. That is why we did not say: "Let us go out to conquer Romania!" Nor did we go through villages and shout: "A new political organization has just been formed, come ye all and sign up!" We had written up no new political platform in addition to the ten existing ones in the country—all of them "perfect" in the eyes of their authors and supporters—and we did not send out legionaries to wave a program around in villages, calling people to adhere to it in order to save the land.

In this viewpoint, again, we differed fundamentally from all the other political organizations, the Cuzists included. All of these believed that the country was dying because of lack of good programs; consequently they put together a perfectly-jelled program with which they started out to assemble supporters. That's why everyone asks: "What is your program?"

This country is dying of lack of men, not of lack of programs; at least this is our opinion. That, in other words, it is not programs that we must have, but men, new men. For such as people are today, formed by politicians and infected by the Judaic influence, they will compromise the most brilliant political programs. This kind of compromised man is alive today in Romanian politics, we earlier met in history. Nations died under his rule and states collapsed.

The greatest wrong done to us by Jews and the political system, the greatest national danger to which they exposed us, is neither the grabbing of Romanian soil nor even the tragic annihilation of the Romanian middle class, nor the great number of Jews in our schools, professions, etc. and not even the influence they exercise over our political life—though each of these, in itself, is a mortal danger for our people. The greatest national peril is the fact that they have deformed and disfigured our Daco-Romanic racial structure,[1] giving birth to this compromised type of man, creating this human refuse, this moral failure: the politician who no longer has anything in common with the nobility of our race; who dishonors and kills us. If this species of man continues to lead this country, the Romanian people will close its eyes forever and Romania will collapse, in spite of all the brilliant programs with which the "trickery" of this degenerate creature is able to dazzle the eyes of the unfortunate multitudes. Among all the pests brought to us by the Jewish invasion, this one is the most frightening!

All peoples with whom we Romanians came into contact and fought, from the barbarian invasions until today, have attacked us on a physical, economic, or political level, leaving untouched our moral and spiritual patrimony and our conscience. From these things, sooner or later sprang forth our victory, the breaking of the foreign yoke—even when they came upon us in large numbers and took all our riches, even when they ruled us politically.

---

[1] The "Daco-Roman" theory of the origins of the Romanian people holds that they are descendants of a colony of the Roman Empire. 'Daco' refers to the Dacian people, who were the original inhabitants of the Romanian region.

Now, for the first time in our history, Romanians face a people which attack us not with the sword but with weapons that are specific to the Judaic race. With these weapons, they strike and paralyze first the moral instinct of peoples, then systematically spread all sorts of moral sickness, thus to destroy any possibilities of reacting. That is why our people feel disarmed and defeated.

As a consequence of seeing this state of affairs, the cornerstone on which the Legion stands is *mankind*, not the political program; *mankind's reform*, not that of the political programs. "The Legion of Michael the Archangel" will be, in other words, more a school and an army than a political party. In these critical times, the Romanian nation has no need of a great politician, as many wrongly believe, but of a great educator and leader who can defeat the powers of evil and crush the clique of evil-doers. But in order to do this he will first have to overcome the evil within himself and within his men. From this legionary school, a new man will have to emerge, a man with heroic qualities; a giant of our history to do battle and win over all the enemies of our Fatherland, his battle and victory having to extend even beyond the material world into the realm of invisible enemies, the powers of evil. Everything that our mind can imagine more beautiful spiritually; everything the proudest that our race can produce; greater, more just, more powerful, wiser, purer, more diligent, and more heroic— this is what the legionary school must give us! A man in whom all the possibilities of human grandeur that are implanted by God in the blood of our people be developed to the maximum.

This hero, the product of legionary education, will also know how to elaborate programs; will also know how to solve the Jewish problem; will also know how to organize the state well; will also know how to convince the other Romanians. And if not, he will know how to win, for that is why he is a hero. This hero, this legionary of bravery, labor, and justice, with the powers God implanted in his soul, will lead our Fatherland on the road of its glory.

A new political party, be it even a Cuzist one, at best can give us a new government and a new administration; a legionary school, however, can give this country a great type of Romanian. It can produce something great that we never had before, which could break in two our whole history, to lay the foundations for the beginning of a different Romanian history to which this people is entitled. For our people, by virtue of its suffering and sufferance, by virtue of its purity and gallantry of soul, has been perhaps the only people in the world which, in all its history, never committed the sin of invading and subjugating other nations.

We shall create an atmosphere, a moral medium, in which the heroic man can be born and can grow. This medium must be isolated from the rest of the world by the highest possible spiritual fortifications. It must be defended from all the dangerous winds of cowardice, corruption, licentiousness, and of all the passions that entomb nations and slay individuals. Once the legionary has developed in such a milieu, i.e. in the nest, in work camp, in the legionary organization, and in the family, he shall be sent into the world: *to live*, in order to learn how to be correct; *to fight*, in order to learn to be brave and strong; *to work*, in order to be diligent and love all those who work; *to suffer*, in order to steel himself; *to sacrifice*, in order to get accustomed to overcoming his selfish interests, serving his Fatherland.

No matter where he goes, he will create a new milieu of an identical nature. He will be an example; he will transform others into legionaries. And people, in search of better days, will follow him. The newly arrived will have to live by and respect the same norms of legionary life. All of them together, in the same army, will comprise a force that will fight and will win. This is what "The Legion of Michael the Archangel" is to be.

Aspects of Romanian Public Life

In what follows, I present the general aspect of our public life in the midst of which, and against which, "The Legion of Michael the Archangel" was just forming. The Averescu government fell about a month before. On 7 July 1927, the Liberals came to power. They staged new elections and, as usual, the government had the majority. Nevertheless, the administration had to overcome, by any means, the great popular current supporting the National-Peasant Party. The poor masses of the Romanian people ran from party to party, from promise to promise, attaching their sincerest hopes— with their centuries-long confidence—to each party in turn, but ending up cheated and dejected, all hopes shattered. And this will continue to be so until they finally understand some day that they have fallen into the hands of robber gangs set on profit and loot.

There were three large parties: Liberal, Averescan, and National-Peasant, and several smaller ones. Fundamentally there was no distinction between them, other than differences of form and personal interests—the same thing in different shapes. They did not even have the justification of differing opinions.[2]

---

[2] A striking similarity to modern-day politics in America, where the two main parties share many basic presumptions and differ only in many trivial aspects.

Their only real motivation was *the religion of personal interest*, with any desideratum and superior interests of the country left out. That is why the spectacle of political fights was disgusting. The chase after money, personal situations, wealth and pleasures, and loot gave these fights an aspect of merciless hostility. Political parties appeared as real organized bands that hated and fought each other for the booty.

Only a struggle for the Fatherland or for an ideal that surpasses personal interests, egoism, and lust, is calm, decent, noble, and without blind unleashing of passions. One can put enthusiasm into it, but not base and blind passion.

The hatred and baseness involved in these fights is sufficient proof that they were not waged in the realm of lofty and sacred ideals or based on principles, but in the sorry depth of the most shameless personal interests. The politician's world unfolds in luxury and scandalous partying, in the most disgusting immorality, riding on the back of an increasingly demoralized country. Who is to devote any attention to its needs?

These politicians, with their families and their agents, need money for partying and entertaining their political clientele, for purchasing votes and human consciences. One by one, they, in bands, descend upon the country to despoil her. This, in the last analysis, is what their governing amounts to. They drain dry the budgets of the state, the prefectures, the city halls. They attach themselves like ticks to the boards of directors of all enterprises, from which they will receive, without effort, salaries in the millions from the sweat and blood of the exhausted worker. They are included in the councils of the Jewish bankers, from whom they collect honoraria of more millions as the price for betraying their country.

They originate scandalous business deals that stun their countrymen. Corruption spreads in public life like a plague, from the humblest servant up to cabinet ministers. They sell themselves to any and all; anyone with money can buy off these monsters, and through them the whole country. That is why, when the squeezed country can no longer give them money, they yield up to consortia of foreign bankers, one by one, the riches of our land, and thus give away our national independence. A real glut of men of business spreads over the whole of Romania, who do not work or produce anything, but suck the sap of the country.

Such are the exploits of the politicians. Misery, demoralization, and despair spread among the lower level. Scores of thousands of children die, mowed down by illness and hunger, weakening thus the people's power of resistance in the fight it wages against the organized Jews and which is supported by the alienated politicians and defended by the entire state apparatus. The few honest politicians, several score perhaps, maybe even party leaders, are not able to do anything anymore. They are like some poor puppets in the hand of the Jewish press, of the Jewish or foreign bankers, and of their own fellow politicians.

This mess, this demoralization, this infection, is sustained step by step by the whole phalanx of Jews, interested in our destruction, in order to re-place us in this country and thus steal our riches completely. Through their press, which usurped the role of our Romanian press, through hundreds of filthy broadsheets, through an immoral and atheistic literature, through movie houses and theaters which spread licentiousness, and through banks, the Jews have become masters of our country. Who could oppose them? Today, when they are the promoters of disaster and their appearance is the signal of our national death, who shall confront them?[3]

The national movement lies prostrate on the ground. In these last elections, the League came out 70,000 votes fewer, totaling less than 50,000, or under two percent nationwide. From the ten parliamentarians it had yesterday, today it has none. There must come a day when the legion-ary will know how to face this monster and how to tackle him in a life-or-death battle. He, alone.

Our Apprehensions Facing this World

Our small number compared to the giant force of this all-powerful might made us oftentimes pose questions such as these: What if we are outlawed? If these hydrae realize what we plan, they will raise before us every possible obstacle and try to crush us. Their eyes are fixed upon us. They can provoke us. They did it once to us, when, quietly and peacefully, we started work at Ungheni; then they took us to the brink of the abyss with all our plans. What are we going to do if they provoke us? Shall we again pull out our pistols and fire, so that our bones may rot in prisons and our plans may fail?

Faced with glimpses of such perspectives, the idea of retreating into the mountains sprouted in our minds—there, where the Romanian willing-ly fought all enemy hordes. The mountain has been close to us for a long time, to our life. It knows us. Rather than letting our bodies dry up and our blood dry out in our veins in the bleak and ugly prisons, better to end our life dying to the last man up in the mountains, for our faith. We thus reject the humiliation of finding ourselves again in chains. We will attack from there, by incursions down into all the Jewish wasp nests.

---

[3] Again, the parallels to most Western nations today are remarkable.

Up above, we will defend the life of the trees and the mountains from further devastation. Down below, we will spread death and mercy. We will be sought out, to be caught and killed. We will escape, hide; we will fight back; and in the end, certainly, we will be downed. For there will be but few of us, sought by Romanian battalions and regiments. Then we will receive death. The blood of all of us will flow. This moment will be our greatest discourse addressed to the Romanian people, and the final one.

I called Mota, Garneata, Corneliu Georgescu, and Radu Mironovici and shared these thoughts of mine with them. We had to think both about good and bad days ahead. We had to have solutions and be prepared for anything. Nothing ought to surprise us. We will follow the path of the national laws, not provoking anyone, avoiding all provocations, not answering any provocation. But when we are no longer able to suffer, or when insurmountable obstacles are placed before us, our road must be toward the mountains.

It is not advisable to try a rebellion of the masses, because in these days they would be decimated by cannon, resulting in spreading only misfortune and sorrow. On the contrary we must work alone, in limited numbers, and only on our own responsibility. They all agreed.

"It cannot be," they said, "that our blood, the blood of 20 youth, would not redeem the sins of this nation. It cannot be that this sacrifice of ours will not be understood by Romanians, that it would not make their souls and consciences tremble, and that this will not constitute a starting point, a point of resurrection for Romanians." Our death, in this fashion, could eventually bring this people more good than all the frustrated endeavors of our lifetime. Nor will the politicians who will kill us go unpunished.

There are others among our ranks who will avenge us. Not being able to win while alive, we will win dying. After that, we lived with the thought and determination of dying. We had a sure solution for victory, come what may. It gave us peace of mind and strength. It will make us smile in the face of any enemy and any attempt to destroy us.

Stages of the Legion's Development: *The Ancestral Land*

We were born on 24 June 1927. Several days later, we occupied our headquarters. Now we felt we should have our own publication in order to enlarge our field of influence, formulate in it the norms of our life, and direct the movement through it. What should we call it? "The New Generation" was suggested; I did not like it. It sounded like a definition; it distinguished us from another generation, which will not do. *Pamantul Stramosesc*: "The Ancestral Land." Let this be its name. This title keeps us tied to our country's earth in which our ancestors rest; the land that must be defended. It plunges us deep into undefined realms. It will be more than a name; it will be a constant call to battle, the appeal to bravery, the stirring up of the warlike qualities of our race. Moreover, in addition to those qualities I mentioned earlier, this title underscores another structural trait of the legionary's soul: *bravery*, without which a man is incomplete. For if a man is only just, correct, devoted, faithful, diligent, etc., but lacks the heroic qualities that would enable him to fight unscrupulous, dishonest, and incorrect enemies, he will perish at their hands.

Here we were now with the axis of our movement already fixed; one end rooted in the earth of our Fatherland, the other in the heavens: "The Ancestral Land" and Michael the Archangel. But a paper costs money, of which we had none. What are we going to do? We decided to write Father Mota, asking him to print it for us on credit, in the old printing shop of *The Liberty* in Orastie. He accepted; he would print our paper and we would pay him from subscriptions and sales. *The Ancestral Land*, issue No. 1 was published on 1 August 1927 in a magazine format as a bimonthly, having in the center of the cover the icon of St. Michael the Archangel. On the icon's left, we reproduced the following words from St. Michael the Archangel's icon in the Church of the Coronation in Alba-Iulia: "Towards the unclean hearts who come into the purest House of the Lord, I mercilessly point my sword." And on its right, a stanza from Cosbuc's poem "Decebal to his People:" "Though we were descended from the Gods, we still owe the debt of death; whether one dies young or a stooped old man is just the same, but it is not the same to die a lion or a dog in chains!"

Underneath, a map of Romania that showed in darkened spots the extent of the Jewish invasion.

The Ancestral Land (1927, number 9)

Contents of the First Issue

The leading article, entitled "The Ancestral Land," delves into the situation of the national movement following the conflict within the League and endeavors to explain our position. It ends with the entreaty "Face to the enemy!" It is signed by Corneliu Z. Codreanu, Ion Mota, Ilie Garneata, Corneliu Georgeseu, and Radu Mironovici. The second article is signed by me, "It is Your Hour, Come"—a continuation of the same line of thought covered in the first article. The third one was signed by Ion Sava, a young and talented fighter who took part in many battles of the student movement, who attached himself to us, but did not become a legionary. Its title: "The Results of the Elections."

There follows a brief panegyric on the occasion of King Ferdinand's death, who had passed away a few days before.[4] Above his picture, bordered in black, appeared the title "Our King Has Died."

Then followed Mota's article, which includes this passage:

By the Icon

It is from the Icon and the Altar that we started, then we wandered for a while, carried away by human waves, and we reached no shores, despite the purity of our impulses. Now, with heavy hearts, dispersed, torn, we gather in the shelter, to our only warmth and consolation, strength and comfort, giver of power, at the feet of Jesus Christ, on the threshold of the heavens' blinding brilliancy, at the Icon. We have not been engaged in politics, not even one single day in our lives, ever. We have a religion, we are the slaves of a faith. We consume ourselves in its fire and, totally subjected to it, serve it to the limit of our strength. There is no defeat and disarming for ourselves, for the power whose tools we want to be, is eternally invincible.

We cannot, for the time being, discuss in detail the causes of the old League's downfall. Let it only be said that, in these moments of new creation, we want to clearly and decidedly state, in order to imprint the character of the new system being born: Light of light.

---

[4] On 20 July 1927.

The article then offers some insights into the new organization, and ends with an expression of faith in victory.

Here is an extract from an article by Corneliu Georgescu:

Light the Torch of Faith

Ancient chronicles tell us that, of old, the gods had sent down a difficult trial on ancient Hellas for her sins. From the wastelands of Asia, large armies, many hundredfold stronger than the Greeks, swooped down like a tempest on the country's plains, ravaging her fields, demolishing her cities, devastating her temples, and shattering her armies—which, though valiant, were too small in number to put up a successful opposition. Meeting no further resistance, the victorious Medes penetrated into the heart of Greece at Delphi, the location of Apollo's most famous temple. The temple priests were trembling with fright that soon the enemy would be able to desecrate the sacred temple. The grand priest alone was not afraid. Full of confidence in divine power, he turned to his fellow priests and said, "Do not fear. God has no need of armies. He will Himself defend us!"

And the grand priest and all the others set out to pray, and their prayer accomplished miracles. As soon as the confident armies of the Persians approached within a stone's throw of the temple, Mount Parnassus shook and rolled rocks down its slopes with a deafening thunder over the enemy, crushing him. The lightning coming down as if from nowhere, completed their ruin, so that from the grand army of but a moment earlier, hardly a few remained to tell of this heavenly miracle...[5]

Fighters! Light anew in your souls the torch of faith that victory and triumph shall be ours.

Then follows a letter of Radu Mironovici to one of his brothers in the village back home. Knowing him to be discouraged he tells him: "Certainly, we can be sad and grieved, but there is one right we do not have, that of

---

[5] As recorded by Herodotus, *The Histories*, Bk 8, secs. 35-39.

losing our courage and laying down our weapon." After this, he explains to him the disunity in the League and the founding of the Legion, thusly:

> Our house, that we all built with our own sweat, which was our shelter, has burned down... Only some smoke-blackened walls remain as a painful reminder of the little old house. What do you want us to do now? Rebel against God? This cannot be, for 'the Lord hath given, the Lord taketh away, blessed be the name of the Lord.'
>
> Shall we cross our arms and perish in misery, cold, rain, and wind? No! But, with faith in God, we shall begin to work, and little by little, should build for ourselves a new home twice as beautiful. Here it is, 'the Legion,' for which we have laid a first cornerstone.

Garneata's article is next:

Discord Among Brothers—The Enemy's Joy

> My heart full of chagrin, I take my pen in hand to share with others the torment of the disquieting thoughts that enveloped us in the face of our late troubles...
>
> The quarrel among brothers and the disagreements among leaders have become so evident that we can no longer hide them. Their consequences are likely going to discourage many, and the discouragement of those who placed their confidence in the League, is certainly a step backward, a step toward defeat.
>
> This is so obvious, because at no time in history was it ever evidenced that disunity led to anything else but misfortune, disaster...
>
> We shall know how to walk on the road we chose seven years ago, and just as determinedly. Our bones, accustomed to the harshness of prison days and misery, will feel good in battle trenches, on position against the adversary.
>
> Let the Jews, who today rejoice, believing the hour of their mastery had arrived, know that there is a corner in this country where, at any hour of the day or night, there is a troop watching, its face to the enemy.

Several items of information complete this first issue, together with the article "Dreams, Hopes, Reality" by engineer Gheorghe Clime, former vice-president of the League in Moldavia, from which I extract the final part:

> What do we need in order to reach this final goal?
>
> A fighting army led by a capable leader surrounded by devoted helpers. In this question, as far as I am concerned, though much older, I follow the action group of the young Corneliu Z. Codreanu, Ion I. Mota...
>
> Obviously, the contribution of many, of all those today dispersed in demoralized camps, is needed. Consequently, if someone in some corner of Romania has opened a list of subscribers, whether authorized or not, let him enter there my name also, with what I can give my life.

The Fundamental Principles of Legionary Ethics

The second issue of *The Ancestral Land* was published on August 15. In the lead article, entitled "The Legion of Michael the Archangel," I try to formulate briefly the first ethical norms of legionary life which we intend to strictly respect and affirm, and around which should gather all those who prize them. Anyone who would come and grow in our midst will have to grow up respecting them.

The following are the central ideas from that article, in the order in which I wrote them at that time. I will then elaborate on a few of them:

> First: "Moral purity."
> Second: "Disinterestedness in battle."
> Third: "Enthusiasm."
> Fourth: "Faith, work, order, hierarchy, discipline."
> Fifth: "The Legion shall stimulate the energy and moral force of our nation, without which there can never be any victory."
> Sixth: "Justice—the Legion shall be the school of justice and of the energy to enthrone it."
> Seventh: "Deeds, not words—You accomplish! Do not talk!"
> Eighth: "At the end of this school, a new Romania will emerge, along with the long-awaited resurrection of this Romanian people."

Disinterestedness in Battle

Defeating personal interest is another fundamental virtue of the legionary. This is in total opposition to the politician's position, whose single motive of acting and fighting is his personal interest alone, with all its degenerate byproducts—greed for enrichment, luxury, debauchery, or arrogance. That is why, dear comrades, from now on, for as long as a legionary life shall exist, you ought to know that wherever you feel arising, be it in the soul of some fighter or in your own soul, the snarl of this personal interest, there the Legion has ceased to exist. There, the legionary ends and the politician begins to show his fangs.

Look a newcomer right in the eye, and if you should detect a gleam of some small personal interest—either material, ambition, passion, or pride —know that he cannot become a legionary.

Nor shall donning the green shirt or adopting the legionary salute be enough for someone to become a legionary, not even if he "rationally" understands the legionary movement; but only if he leads a life in conformance with the norms of legionary life. For the Legion is not only a logical system, a chaining up of arguments; it is a "living faith." In the same way, someone is not a Christian if he simply "knows" and "understands" the Gospel but only if he conforms to the norms of life espoused in it, if he "lives the Gospel."

Discipline and Love

The entire social history of mankind is full of struggles, having at its base two great principles, each striving for prominence to the detriment of the other: *the principle of authority* and *the principle of liberty*. Authority has striven to expand to the detriment of freedom, and the latter has endeavored to limit as much as possible the power of authority. These two, face to face, cannot but mean conflict.

To orient a movement along one or the other of these two principles means to continue the historical trajectory of unrest and social warfare. It means to continue, on the one hand, the line of tyranny, oppression, and injustice, and, on the other hand, the line of bloody insurrection and of permanent conflict. Therefore I want to call the attention of all legionaries, and in particular that of newer ones, that they should not deviate from the movement's line because of a misunderstanding. In many cases, I noticed that as soon as a legionary received a rank, he stiffened into "authority," breaking away from everything that bound him to his comrades, and felt compelled to "impress" others by the use of his authority.

The legionary movement is based exclusively neither on the principle of authority nor on that of liberty. It has its foundations rooted in *the principle of love*. In it, both authority and freedom have their roots. Love is the peace between the two principles: authority and liberty. Love is in the middle, between them and above them, embracing the best of both and removing the conflicts between them. Love can bring neither tyranny, oppression, injustice, bloody insurrection, nor social warfare. It can never mean conflict.

There is also a hypocritical concept of the principle of love practiced by tyrants and Jews who, continuously and systematically appeal to the sentiment of love of their fellow men, behind which they continue to hate and oppress undisturbed.

Applied love means peace of soul in society and in the world. Peace no longer appears like the poor expression of a mechanical and cold equilibrium between the two principles, authority and liberty, condemned to eternal war and the impossibility of harmony.

Goodness and love are going to give us peace, not justice. For justice is very difficult to realize integrally. Even if an instrument of its perfect realization would be found, man, who is incapable of recognizing and appreciating it, would remain forever discontented.

Though one hundred men may love each other like brothers, it is possible that, faced with need for some action, they may each have a different opinion. One hundred opinions will never win. Love alone will never make them win. *Discipline is needed*. In order to win, all of them must adopt a single opinion, that of the one among them who is most experienced, their leader.

Discipline is the guarantee of success, for it insures the unity of effort. There are difficulties that can only be overcome by a united entire people, obeying a single command. Who is the imbecile who, in such an eventuality, would refuse to join the rest of his people, when they, as one, would heed the same command—under the pretense that discipline would 'wound his personality'? In such cases, when your country is threatened and when the nature of things urges you to endanger life and limb, to break up your family, to risk the future of your children, to renounce everything you own on this Earth, in order to save your Fatherland, it is ridiculous for one to talk of his 'personality being hurt.'

Discipline does not humiliate, for it leads to victory. And if victories cannot be attained except by sacrifice, then the submission to discipline is the smallest of all sacrifices a man can make for the victory of his nation. If discipline is a renunciation, a sacrifice, it does not humiliate anyone. For any sacrifice ennobles a man; it does not demean him. As our people have to overcome tremendous difficulties, every Romanian should joyously accept the education of discipline and be thus aware of his contribution to the victory of tomorrow.

There is no victory without unity; and there is no unity without discipline. Therefore our nation should consider it a hostile act, and condemn as dangerous to her victories and her very life, any deviation from the school of discipline.

Nationalist Movements and Dictatorship

Anytime there is talk about a nationalist movement, tendencies toward a dictatorship are systematically attributed to it. I do not wish to make a critique of dictatorships in this chapter, but I want to show that Europe's present-day national movements, such as the legionary movement, Fascism, National-Socialism, etc., are neither dictatorships nor democracies. Some fight us by shouting: "Down with Fascist dictatorship!" "Fight against dictatorship!" "Defend yourselves against dictatorship!" But these do not hit us. They are shooting off target. They can only hit the notorious "dictatorship of the proletariat."

Dictatorship presupposes the will of a single man forcibly imposed upon the will of the other subjects in a state. In other words, two opposing wills: that of the dictator or a group of men on one hand, and that of the people on the other. When this will imposes itself by constraint and cruelty, then the dictatorship is tyranny. But when a nation with a majority of 98 percent, in indescribable enthusiasm, a nation of 60 million or one of 40 million souls, approves and deliriously applauds the chief's measures, it means that there is a perfect accord between the chiefs will and that of the people. Moreover, they mesh so perfectly that there no longer exist two wills. There is only one: *the will of the nation*, the expression of which is the chief. Between the will of the nation and the leader's will, there exists only one relationship: a perfect rapport between them.

To claim that the unanimity obtained under the regimes of national movements is due to "terror" and "inquisitorial methods" is absolutely ludicrous, because the people among whom such movements arose have a highly developed civic awareness. They fought, bled, and left thousands who died for freedom; they never submitted, either to the enemy without or to the tyrant within. Why should they not fight and bleed also today, if faced by such terror? And then, one can draw votes or even majorities forcibly, by terror; one can draw tears or sighs; but it has never been heard nor will it ever be heard that one can produce enthusiasm and fervor by force. Not even within the most backward nation in the world.

Given that the national movement is not dictatorial in its essence, we ask ourselves then: What is it? Is it a democracy? Not at all, because the leader is not voted in by the electorate, and democracy is based on the eligibility principle. Or, in national regimes, no leader is selected by voting. He is acquiesced to. If these regimes be not dictatorships or democracies, what then are they? Without defining them, one must admit that they represent a new form of government, *sui genesis*, in the modern states. It has not been encountered before, and I don't know what name it will be given.

I believe that it has, at its basis, that state of spirit, that state of elevated national conscience which, sooner or later, spreads to the outskirts of the national organism. It is a state of inner revelation. That which of old was the people's instinctive repository is reflected in these moments in the people's conscience, creating a state of unanimous illumination that is encountered only in the great religious revivals. A people in its entirety reaches an awareness of self, of its purpose and destiny in the world. During past history, only flashes of such awareness have been noticed, but today we are faced with some such permanent phenomena.

In this case, the leader is no longer a "master," a "dictator," one who does as he "pleases," who leads "according to his whims." He is the incarnation of this unseen state of spirit, the symbol of this state of consciousness. He no longer does "as he pleases;" *he does what he must*. And he is guided not by individual or collective interests, but by the interests of the immortal nation which have penetrated the conscience of the peoples. It is only within the framework of these interests that personal and collective interests find their maximum of satisfaction.

The First Beginnings of Organization

The organization of units constitutes a new developmental stage in the legionary movement. Any movement, in order not to remain chaotic, must be cast into organizational molds. The entire legionary system of organization is based on the idea of "the nest"—namely, a group varying between three and 13 men under the command of a leader. We have no "members" in the sense of isolated individuals. There is only the nest, and the individual member is part of a nest. The legionary organization is not formed from a number of members, but a number of nests.

This system has not varied much in its essence, from the beginnings to the present day. It occasionally received needed improvements, for an organization must consider realities; it is like a child constantly growing, whose clothing must constantly be fitted as it develops.

I shall not dwell here too much on "the nest" because I treated that question extensively in *The Nest Leader's Manual*. However, what led me to choose this system? First of all, the needs of the movement. The leader of a movement must take reality into account in greatest earnestness. My basic reality was "the single man," a poor peasant in some village, crying; an unfortunate sick workingman; an uprooted intellectual. And then I gave each of these the opportunity to gather around him a group, according to his abilities, with himself as leader. That was the nest with its leader. It was not I naming him the nest's leader; it was his merits that put him there. He did not become a leader because I "wanted" him to be one, but only if he could gather a group, inspire it, and lead it in time—in contrast to all other parties where chiefs are often nominated on the basis of gifts. I succeeded in having a corps of small leaders "born" not "made," in whom leader's traits were obvious. That is why the leader of a legionary nest is reliable and dependable. The network of these nest leaders forms the whole skeleton of the legionary movement.

How did I acquire leaders over the larger units? I nominated no leader for village, district, or county. I told them: "Conquer and organize! And, as much as you can organize, you will be chief over." I just confirmed them as leaders in the positions to which their power, qualities, and aptitudes elevated them. We started with the nest's leader, and progressively he grew to village leader, district, town, and county leader.

The nest system also presents the following advantages:

a) It activates and puts to work the entire membership of a movement. In the other parties, where there are committees and members by village or county, it is only several committee members who work; the rest, 1,000, 2,000, 10,000, are inactive. In our system, thanks to the wide initiative the nest leaders have, within prescribed norms, and thanks to the obligation of each nest to write as glorious a page as possible in its record, as there are no separate members as such outside of the nest; everybody, absolutely every single legionary, works.

b) Solves all local problems. There are a host of items that a single man is unable to cope with and a whole organization is too large to examine, e.g. the digging of a small well in a village, the repairing of a little bridge, etc. A single man cannot do these by himself; an organization cannot busy itself with them; a nest, however, of 6, 8, or 10 men is the most suitable unit to execute them.

c) The nest is easily changeable: from a fighting unit into a working one, or vice-versa.

d) It creates a large number of units, consequently developing men specialized in the art of leading.

e) The effect of any defection or betrayal remains localized.

f) Finally, the nest is the best place for one to receive his legionary education. That is because men of the same age meet there, men of identical comprehensiveness and of like spiritual constitution. There, all are friends. A man who could not confess his troubles, bare his soul, before a youngster—either because of embarrassment or because he is reluctant to make him aware too early of the difficulties and worries of life—here in the nest, among friends, he can do it, just as he can take a reprimand or even a punishment.

The nest is a small legionary family, having love as its foundation. In *The Nest Leader's Manual*, I laid down the six laws by which this family should be guided. This family should not be governed according to the leader's whim—this would be dictatorship—but by laws:

1. *The law of discipline*. Legionary! Be disciplined! For only thus you can win. Follow your leader through thick and thin.

2. *The law of work*. Work! Work every day. Put your heart into it. Let your reward be, not gain, but the satisfaction that you have laid another brick to the building of the Legion and the flourishing of Romania.

3. *The law of silence*. Speak little. Say only what you must. Speak only when necessary. Your oratory should be deeds, not words. You accomplish; let others talk.

4. *The law of education*. You must become another person—a hero. In the nest, become fully educated. Get to know the Legion well.

5. *The law of reciprocal help*. Help your brother who fell into misfortune. Do not abandon him.

6. *The law of honor*. Go along only on the paths of honor. Fight, and never be a coward. Leave the path of infamy to others. Better to fall in an honorable fight than win by infamy.

But I want to emphasize once again, dear legionaries, and I call your attention to an essential thing: the meeting of a nest is incomplete if a cold atmosphere prevails; "What have we accomplished?" "What else is there to be accomplished?" "Let us do this or that." "Good-bye!"

Give free rein to your souls. Reserve a place for them in the meeting. Proceed with warmth. Give everyone the chance to open up his heart, unload his difficulties, anxieties, worries, with which life has burdened him. Let him share his joys. Let your nest be a place of consolation and of sharing joys. A nest meeting is successful when a man returns home after unloading there the burdens of his soul and is full of faith in his people.

Our Patron Saint is the Archangel Michael. We ought to have his icon in our homes, and in difficult times we should ask his help and he will never fail us.

A New Battle

In the 1 December 1927 issue of *The Ancestral Land,* we opened a new drive to seek funds for the purchase of a light panel truck to use in our travels. Again, we used the same system of general effort. Legionaries began organizing festive shows, conferences, and Christmas choirs, and to contribute. "The Vrancea Brotherhood of the Cross" of Focsani distinguished itself by collecting the sum of 50,000 lei as a result of a festive show sponsored by Gen. Macridescu. On 19 February 1928, that is, in ten weeks, this drive was successful. We bought a new panel truck in Bucharest for 240,000 lei, of which we put down 100,000 lei, the balance of 140,000 lei to be paid in twelve monthly installments. We left Bucharest for Iasi, with Stefan Nicolau driving "The Doe," as the boys baptized her, and Banea, Bordeianu, and Mironovici. The legionaries and our friends expected us at the edge of the city and we were welcomed upon our arrival amidst general joy.

In order to meet our monthly installments, we formed a Committee of 100 whose members were to contribute 100 lei per month for one year. This committee reached a membership of 50 within two months—mostly poor people, small employees, workingmen, or peasants who, parting with 100 lei per month, were making a real sacrifice. The girls of the Iasi

"Citadels" and in particular those of "The Iulia Hajdeu Citadel" of Galati, began to do embroidery work and sell it to collect money.

From the thriftiness these contributors imposed upon their spending for food and clothing, enough was being collected for the organization, which, by judicious use of the money, managed to stay alive and develop normally. But the Jewish press was yelling, "With what money do these gentlemen buy panel trucks? (The Jew, always in bad faith, made several *trucks* out of the *one* we owned.) Who finances this movement?"

Oh! Gentlemen, no one has "financed" it. No one, but the infinite faith of Romanians who, for the most part, are poor as Job. Not only were we not "financed" by capitalists, but I counsel anyone who leads a movement based on sane principles to refuse all offers of financing if he wishes his movement to survive. This is because a political movement must be constituted so as to be able to produce alone, out of the faith and sacrifice of its members, exactly as much as it needs to live and grow. For a normal and healthy development, a movement has the right to consume only as much as its members can provide; and its membership can only provide to the extent of their capacity for faith, that is, for sacrifice. Are you short of funds? Do not resort to outside financing, but go about increasing the faith of the membership. In fact, insufficient contributions on the membership's part is an indication of little faith. Out of funds? The organization is dead and it will soon collapse. Lacking faith, it will be vanquished by those that have it.

A leader who accepts the outside financing of his movement is like the man who accustoms his body to live on medication. To the extent an organism is administered medication, to the same extent it is condemned to being unable to react on its own. Moreover, when it is deprived of the medication, it dies; it is at the mercy of the pharmacist! Likewise, a political movement is at the mercy of those who finance it. These could cease their financing at any given moment and the movement, unaccustomed to living on its own, dies. A movement, just like an individual, in fact may sometimes need a larger amount of money. It then may borrow and repay the loan in time, but only if the certainty of being able to do so exists. Consequently, gentlemen leaders of movements—and saying this, I address myself to those who shall come after us—turn down those well-intentioned who offer to finance your movement. All those who can and do finance are the Jewish bankers, the very rich Jews, the big Jewish grain dealers, the great Jewish industrialists and merchants. They finance the political parties in order to exterminate the Romanians in their own country.

Quite soon, there will be no one to engage in financing—this world reeks of banker, of prey, of injustice and indecency! Neither Romanians nor, least of all, Jews. For this caste of bankers and tycoons, of business-men enriched as a result of business coups, these birds of prey who greedi-ly stalk human society, are going to be exterminated. Well-to-do people, rich people, to the limits of decency, there will be, but they will not be ca-pable of financing but only of helping a movement from their savings. This obligation to help, to help their nation in hard times, rests upon every Ro-manian and it will so rest forever; and such aid will always be welcome.

But my own material situation, as well as that of my comrades, was becoming worse and worse, more pressing. I became a burden on my poor father-in-law, who, not counting me, from his small salary could hardly feed and clothe his five children. With my wife, we occupied one room while the other seven members of the family shared the other two rooms. Understanding my predicament, and thanks to his great love formed and for the Romanian cause, he never said a word to me—though I saw as time passed that he was bending ever more under the weight of difficulties.

Then we decided that I would devote full time to the movement, and Mota, with the other three comrades of Vacaresti prison, would set up a law practice to make their living as well as to help me. They would com-mence shortly but they would meet with tremendous hardships. I looked back. Registered in the university ten years earlier, we had fought side by side with all student classes. And by and by, all of them found employ-ment, creating for themselves a small situation by which they managed to live; only we remained alone on the fringes of society, like some madmen lost in the middle of the world's ways. Although capable lawyers, my com-rades could only eke out a meager existence. They could not be hired by the railways, city hall, or the state; such places are reserved for those who desert the ranks of the national movement and cross over to the political parties—an encouragement to those lacking character. The honor of our lives dictated that we take no Jewish case to defend.

The road was tough for us, being ostracized in our own country and thus placed in the position where it was next to impossible to make a living.

The Summer of 1928

We spent the entire winter organizing nests. Spring saw the resumption of work in the Ungheni brickyard and the garden of Mrs. Ghica. We worked in these two places, making bricks and raising vegetables. We wanted to build ourselves another home, for we were not sure we could stay in the old one because a lawsuit was initiated to evict us. In this hard work, we became closer to one another, feeling ever closer to those who work with their hands and ever more distant from those who live by the labor of others.

This work was completing our education more than the lectures of some university professor. There we learned how to overcome hardships; we steeled our will; we strengthened our bodies and became accustomed to a tough and severe way of life in which no pleasure found its place, save that of spiritual satisfaction.

It was then that "The Brotherhood of the Cross" from Galati with Tocu, Savin, Costea, came to help, as well as other brotherhoods. Radu Mironovici learned to drive our panel truck very well and, helped by Eremeiu, carried paying passengers between Iasi, Varatec, Agapia, and Neamt monasteries. Yet, because of the summer, which is always poorer, I had to seek a loan from the Albina Bank of Husi, mortgaging my father's house for 10,000 lei, which I divided, part for the brickyard, part for the panel truck's monthly installments, and part for the legionary publications. Unable to repay this loan even to this day, my indebtedness reached the sum of 300,000 lei.

During that summer, we also entered the field of commerce in order to make some money for the Legion. The Jews have control over the vegetable marketing in nearly all markets in Moldavia. Three teams of legionary students were charged with marketing vegetables. These teams were buying merchandise on the Iasi market, loading 600 to 800 lbs. onto the panel truck, then descending like a plague upon the Jews, lowering prices to half.

August 1, 1928 was the first anniversary of our review's publication. Here is what I wrote:

> On August 1, *The Ancestral Land* celebrates one year of regular publication. This is not much. Several days ago, between 13 and 30 July, the town of Carcassonne (a fort in France) celebrated 2,000 years of existence. It may be that the Legion too, will have 2,000 years ahead of us! But the hardest of those is the first year, when one has to break virgin soil, to plow the first furrow. During these early days, a lot of difficulties came upon us, but our journal—sometimes richer, sometimes poorer, yet always great—stood firm, overcoming them.
>
> When a year ago, starting penniless, in the most critical moment of the national movement, we placed St. Michael

the Archangel's icon on the cover, we knew that our review would survive.

Fighting Misery

Towards fall, personal material difficulties became oppressive. My wife and I no longer had any decent shoes or clothing; my wife was wearing four-year-old shoes. We could no longer expect anything from my father because there were six other children besides myself, all in schools, and the fights he fought left him overwhelmed with debts. Only several thousand lei were left out of his salary to feed and clothe a large family.

I then gathered all my strength and decided that I, too, would commence law practice, intending at the same time to lead the movement. I opened my office in Ungheni, working together with my secretary, Ernest Comanescu. As a result, I was able to realize a small, very small, income with which I managed to take care of our needs and the few modest indulgences of our lives.

Six years had passed since we had limited our existence to only the strict necessities of life. For six years, I had not entered a theater, movie, beer hall, ballroom, or gone to a party. And now as I write, it has been 14 years since I have been to any of them.[6] I do not regret it. What I do regret is that after a life of such restrictions, some individuals have accused me of leading a leisurely existence. In this misery that lasted years, as in the tough trials in which my fate has put me, I had the steady support of my wife, who faithfully took care of me. She shared my numerous blows, experienced privations, and endured even hunger in order to help me fight on. I will forever be grateful to her.

The Liberal Party collapsed during the fall of 1928, as a result of the relentless assaults of the National-Peasants who threatened "violence" and "revolution." The National-Peasant Party succeeded them in power after eight years of political opposition. But they soon proved to be a great disappointment to the whole country. They would begin to steal, just as the Liberals did; they would engage in "scandalous business deals" just like Liberals; they would use the gendarmerie to "terrorize" and even shoot down their adversaries or those who would express dissatisfaction, just like Liberals; and they would set up their own bankers, just like Liberals.

---

[6] In early 1936, at 36 years of age.

But particularly, they would fall under the continual influence of international finance, to which they began yielding up—little by little, for years, for decades—the riches of Romania, in exchange for ruinous loans.

The First Assembly of Nest Leaders; Forming the Legionary Senate

On 3-4 January 1929, I convoked the first national meeting of nest leaders in Iasi. Forty to fifty participated. The meetings were held in the house of Gen. Ion Tarnoschi who, on this occasion, during a touching ceremony, with tears in his eyes, was now receiving a little sack of earth that included the blood of his own soldiers and officers. "How I wish God gave me enough days to live to see the hour of Romanian deliverance. But I do not think that I shall live that long," he told us.

From the discussions we had and from reports by each representative, we became convinced that the system of "nests," unused in our country up to then, could catch on and yield good results. Certainly, there are problems and awkwardnesses that are inherent in any endeavor. However, it was enough for me to find out that, in one year's time, without any other education, but only on the basis of appeals and directives given in our review, isolated nests had been formed—active nests, in all regions and social strata. I told myself. "The system passed the exam. It works." This meeting of January 3-4 proved the correctness of my principles of organization. Consequently, what we had to do now was to continue steadily along the same lines.

I realized, at the same time, that the movement was catching on particularly among youthful ranks; that the system of dynamic education—education in parallel with action—is much superior to the static one. Therefore we should continue this system for another year, not yet trying to reach out to the masses, and dismissing the idea of an electoral campaign.

It was also then that the Legion's Senate was set up: a forum made up of men over 50 years of age—intellectuals, peasants, or workingmen, who had led a life of great correctitude, had showed great faith in the legionary future, and great wisdom. They would be convened at difficult times, any time it was felt their advice was needed. They were not to be elected but designated by the head of the Legion, and later passed on by the rest of the Senate. The title of Senator was the highest honor to which a legionary could aspire. The Senate then was formed by Hristache Solomon, Gen. Dr. Macridescu, Gen. Ion Tamoschi, Spiru Peceli, Col. Cambureanu, and Ion Butnaru. Several months after its constitution, the illustrious university Professor Traian Braileanu took his place in the Senate.

CHAPTER 6

TOWARDS THE POPULAR MASSES

Among the Moti

The Moti still live in the mountains of central Transylvania. Old as those mountains, they have lived for centuries in the same way, always dominated by two characteristics: poverty and liberty. They are the only Romanians, perhaps the only people on Earth who have never known throughout their history a single day of happiness and plenty, and the struggle for liberty. Their whole life has been a struggle for liberty. They gave us Horia, Closca, and Crisan, and they supported the revolution of 1784; they gave us Avram Iancu, and fought in 1848. History has recorded over 40 uprisings in their mountains against Hungarian domination; all of them drowned ultimately in their own blood. Yet, their steadfastness could never be broken. Lately the tribune voices of Amos Francu and Capt. Emil Siancu, Moti themselves, ring out in vain like a cry of alarm. There are gold mines in their mountains. One by one, their exploiters were getting rich, while they remained unclad and without bread: "Gold lies in our mountains' core, While we beg from door to door."

The gray rock is bare. Nothing grows on it; neither wheat nor corn. The only wealth there is, is the gold in the exploiter's hands, and the only possibility of making a living is in the timber of the forests. The calvary of foreign domination lasted 1,000 years. One thousand years of endurance, hoping that someday Greater Romania would be born to save them, to finally look after them and their children, to redress the long and killing injustice, to come and reward them for their millenary patience, suffering, and struggles. Only those who are motherless know not consolation. Only those who do not have a Fatherland know neither consolation nor recompense. The Fatherland always rewards its children—those who have been awaiting its justice and believed in it, and those who have fought and suffered for it. It was inconceivable that the Moti would not be recompensed for their immense patience, suffering, and bravery!

But after the war, every man, especially every politician, busied himself with his own "self," his own material, electoral, political situation. Thus the Moti were forgotten. Whoever busies himself with his own "self" cannot busy himself with "others." And whoever is surrounded by present worries cannot place himself, his thoughts and feelings, in history, so that working in the name of his Fatherland, he would see to it that the great redress and historical rewards that are owed to its brave men are given.

Not only were they forgotten, but they were delivered as prey to the Jewish usurers who, in their race for profit, infiltrated their mountains. They stole their only livelihood by building mills high up in the mountains and felling their forests, leaving them with bare rock.

"O Iancu, why don't you come back from the dead to see our mountains bared?" In their song of despair, they call out to Iancu, their hero, to see his mountains despoiled, his forests "shaved" by the bands of "little Jews;" this, during an administration of Greater Romania, in the days of the people's long-awaited victory. Verily, what frightening tragedy: to resist for ten centuries against all iniquities, and now to die of misery and hunger in the Greater Romania you awaited for a millennium!

It is she you have expected. She was the only moral support that sustained you. Now this hope too, falls to the ground. You did not have any bread, but yet you hoped. For this population, Greater Romania did not turn out to be an invigoration, a triumph, a coronation following a thousand years of suffering, with joyous reward from all their people. For this, someone with a soul like Stefan the Great was needed, not the pygmy soul of the Romanian politician. Greater Romania meant a collapse into mortal despair for the Moti people. These politicians stain the face of our nation. A nation, over and above any other interest, has the duty to fulfill certain moral obligations. If that nation does not meet them, its face remains stained.

Touched by the letter of a teacher from Bistra, near Campeni, I boarded a train in order to go there and examine the state of affairs for myself. Riding a small mountain train, I was coursing with shrinking heart through the valleys of the Apuseni Mountains, where death had frolicked in scores of battles and where the ghosts of Horia and Iancu wander.

I approached a Moti peasant in a railway station. He had at least 20 patches on his coat, a sign of unparalleled poverty. He was selling wooden barrel hoops he had made for a pittance. His eyes were sunken, his cheeks drawn in. A gentle physiognomy. His look was shy; one could read no particular thoughts on his face, but in his eyes was pain, and I saw not only a hungry man but one tortured by hunger. There was no sense of life in these gentle eyes that inspired pity, no preoccupation; they were just blank.

"How do you manage in these parts?" I asked him.

"Well! Well, thank you."

"Can you raise corn and potatoes here?"

"Yes, we can."

"Do you have everything you need, food…?"

"Yes, we have…we have…"

"Then, you don't have it too bad…?"

"No!… No!…"

He sized me up several times, showed himself very little disposed to conversation, for who knows on what shores of despair his mind was wandering—and in his inherited racial nobility, he did not wish to explain to a stranger.

Finally I arrived at Bistra. I called on the teacher in the village who had written me. I only stayed a day. In the poor homes of the Moti that I visited, I saw their many little cold children huddled together—waiting for two, three weeks, or sometimes a month or more, for the return of their parents. The adults had gone on the road with horse and wagon to bring back to them a sack of corn meal in exchange for the wooden hoops and barrels they make, and then sell hundreds of miles away in other parts of the country to which God had been more generous. It is only for a few months of the year that the Moti stay at home; the rest of the time they are on the road. The teacher told me this:

> Not even during the Hungarian domination could the foreigner settle here. But nowadays, a lumber mill has been set up, owned by a Jewish company in Oradea, which grabbed our forests and cut them down. Throughout their poor lives, the Moti have eked out a livelihood by making barrels and barrel hoops. But from now on, they will be deprived of this. They are condemned to die.
>
> Hunger and other necessities force them to work for the Jews, felling their own trees for 20 lei per day, a trifle. That is all that is left to them out of all that richness that is extracted from their mountains and taken down their valleys in long trainloads. And when the timber is all cut down, that will be the end of us too. But there is something that is even sadder. We have lived a life of virtue for hundreds of years. The Jews brought with them the sins of debauchery. There are over 30 Jews employed at this lumber mill.
>
> And Saturday evening when they get their wages, they take the girls and women of the Moti and dishonor them in nightlong orgies. Moral and physical illnesses consume our villages, in addition to poverty.

And one cannot say anything. No protest can be attempted because these Jews are on such good terms with all the politicians that they are virtually all-powerful masters. Local authorities are at their bidding, from gendarmes all the way to the top.

If you try to say something, you are immediately accused of urging one part of the citizenry to "hatred" against the other citizens; that you "disturb social harmony" and "the brotherhood" in which the Romanians have always lived with the "peaceful Jewish population;" that we are not good "Christians," for Jesus Christ said: "Love your neighbor, even him who wrongs you…" etc.

If you utter one single word, you are arrested as an "enemy of the State's security" and as an inciter to "civil war." You are insulted and even beaten. They control the authorities and you must keep quiet and watch the whole tragedy of your people. It would be better for God to blind us so we would no longer see with our own eyes; so we would know nothing.

My blood was boiling in my veins. The idea occurred to me anew of grabbing a weapon, going into the mountains, and mercilessly starting to shoot into the bands of enemies and traitors. The Romanian authorities and laws of Greater Romania condone such crimes against the Romanian nation, her honor, and her future, and these laws and sold-out authorities have stripped her of any hopes for justice and for salvation. I returned to Iasi with an aching heart, borne down by the burden carried by this people.

How terrible is the alienation of the leading class of a people, of its political and cultural class! Literati and writers consecrate their efforts to all kinds of irrelevant topics. Countless books are published that fill the bookstores shop windows. What shall the future's verdict be regarding these men, if for such a historical tragedy as that of the Moti, unfolding under their very eyes, they found not a single word of protest that could also serve as an alarm signal to people dazed by all the scandalous literature that puts them to sleep and clouds their future and life?

In what light shall the nation look at these writers and literati, whose mission, the most sacred one, is precisely that of denouncing the dangers that threaten its moral and physical being, and of lighting the way for its future? And how will this leading political class of "orators" in Parliament or anywhere else be looked upon, which has deserted its most elementary obligation to watch over the nation's life and honor?

As I was going down on the little train from Bistra toward Turda, the director of the sawmill in Bistra also entered the same compartment; a fat Jew hardly contained by his clothing, who gave the impression of a life abundantly lived. I do not believe that one like him ever knew hunger in his life, even once. A young man approximately of my age also entered the compartment at the next stop. From the very first, I realized they were friends on very good terms and that the young man was Romanian. The Jew poured himself some coffee out of a thermos bottle and took out some slices of cake from a packet. He began to eat; I observed a wolf's appetite. He began gulping before realizing he had not invited his friend to partake, and immediately did so. The young man took a slice of cake and a cup of coffee and began eating somewhat timidly, showing himself grateful and respectful to the rich Jew for the "attention" accorded him.

It was about five o'clock in the morning, not quite light yet, on the Friday before Easter: Passion Friday. Saddened, I asked myself: "Who, I wonder, is this scoundrel of a young Romanian who, on this day when the whole Christian world fasts, eats cake side by side with the Jew, the torturer of Romanians?"

From their talk, I learned he was a forestry engineer. The Jew showed a compulsive inclination to talk. He talked and joked continuously. Then he produced a record player and began playing records, everything on them most indecent. I sat in a corner of the compartment and listened without a word, looking out the window. The day was beginning to break and I could see, on the road paralleling the railroad, a long line of horse-drawn wagons, and at the head of each, a Moti man, trudging quiet and sad. Loaded with charcoal, they were headed for the market of Turda, a 40-mile ride, to sell it and buy, not new clothes or toys, but a few pounds of cornmeal to take home to their children, for it was Easter time. This is the only joy they could bring their children.

My heart groans with pain and anxiety. It is not enough that these robbers take the Moti's bread; they also desecrate and insult, on this Passion Friday, their poverty and faith. They pass by singing and insulting, on these roads of millenary suffering on which—out of respect for human suffering and pain—no man should tread, except in the deepest quiet and decency, heads uncovered before the hungry and ragged people who walk heavily under the sentence of their merciless fate. When it was daylight, our eyes met, the young man's and mine. I could see that he recognized me. Uneasy, he lost his composure. I too, recognized him. Back in 1923 I had seen him as a Christian nationalist student. He was in the front lines of a demonstrating student group, singing... "And we shall crush the Jews under our heels, or else shall gloriously die," etc.

I reflected, full of bitterness. If all the youth who fight today become like this tomorrow, then this people of ours must perish; through Jewish conquest, floods, earthquake, or dynamite—it does not matter which—but perish it must.

The Summer of 1929

Two marches were organized this summer: one with the young men in the Galati and Focsani "Brotherhoods of the Cross," and one with legionnaires. I wanted to take them on the roads I had so often trod, to spend with them as much time as possible, in order to observe and study them, as well as to show them the beauties of our country. This time, as in all future marches that I shall take, I shall seek to initially develop in the young legionnaires their *will*. I will do this by long marches in which everyone will carry heavy loads through rain, wind, heat, or mud; in formation and in step, with talking forbidden for hours; through a Spartan life, sleeping in forests, eating simple fare; through the obligation of being severe with themselves in all respects, beginning with their bearing and gestures; through creating for them obstacles they would have to overcome, such as climbing over huge rocks or getting across streams. I was trying to turn them into men of strong will, who were to behave in a manly fashion under any difficulty. Therefore, I never permitted the avoidance of an obstacle; it had to be overcome.

In place of the weak and defeated man who bends with any passing wind, a type now predominating in both political life and the professions, we must create for this people a conqueror, unbending and undaunted.

By instructing them in common, I shall seek, on the other hand, to develop an *esprit de corps*, a sense of unity. I have noticed that the instruction in common has a great influence upon a man's intellect and psyche, rendering order and cadence to his disorderly mind. By imposing punitive measures, I shall seek to develop, in fine, a sense of responsibility and the courage to assume that responsibility for his acts. There is nothing more disgusting than the man who lies and shuns his responsibility.

I punished regularly, without exception, any infraction. I punished a youth in Vatra-Dorhei for having caused a disturbance in a public park. Something of a more serious nature happened at Dorni Cozanesti, not so much in itself but rather as an indication of the state of spirit the case revealed. Four youths went to a Jewish tavern, ordering sardines, bread, and wine; and after they ate well, they stood up. Instead of paying their bill, one of them heroically brandished a revolver, threatening the life of the Jew if he should squeal, for—he added—they were from Corneliu Codreanu's group.

I punished him. Had I not done so, it would have been this youth—not the Jew from whom a can of sardines had been stolen—who would have morally destroyed himself. As a matter of fact, among legionnaires, punishment cannot cause resentment, for all of us are fallible. In our concept, punishment means a man of honor has to make good on his error. Once the punishment is fulfilled, man is free of its burden, as if nothing had happened. In most of the cases, this punishment takes the form of some work—not because labor would be in the nature of a condemnation, but because it offers the chance of amending through a good deed the wrong that has been committed. That is why the legionary receives and carries out punishment with serenity.

More than two years had passed since the Legion came into being. Our nests multiplied all over the country. The need was now felt to strengthen the movement by using and stimulating these small nuclei to work. The only legal way to bring about nationwide measures for solving the Jewish problem was through political avenues. This presupposed a contact with the masses at large. Whether good or bad, this was the method that the law placed at our disposal, and which sooner or later we had to follow. We fixed the first legionary public meeting in Tg. Beresti in the northern Covurlui county on December 15. The decision was taken on November 8, when a new series of legionnaires from various parts of the country, took their vow on the anniversary of the Legion's patron saint.

At the same time, I sent Totu into Turda county where, together with Amos Horatiu Pop, he was to intensify the legionary propaganda and also organize a meeting.

December 15, 1929

On the evening of December 14, I was in Beresti. Lefter, Potolea, Tanase Antohi, and others were expecting me at the depot. The market town of Beresti is a real wasp's nest of Jews; houses and shops crowded together. The only street runs through the middle of town, with the mud ankle deep, and some boardwalks along the sides. I was to stay at Potolea's.

The next morning, the Galati prosecutor and a gendarme major came to tell me that I was not permitted to hold the meeting. I told them: "The interdiction you confront me with is neither right nor legal. Anyone has the right to hold meetings in this country: Germans, Hungarians, Turks, Tartars, Bulgarians, Jews. Is it only I who do not have this right? Your measure is an arbitrary one; being illegal, I shall not obey it; I shall hold the meeting at any cost."

Finally, after some discussion, they approved my holding the meeting on the condition that we not cause any disturbance. What was I to do? What kind of disturbance? Break into people's homes? This was my first public meeting. Was I not fully determined to keep it in perfect order and thus retain the privilege of holding others?

At the determined hour, a very small number of people gathered, hardly one hundred. I learned from them that a lot more people had wanted to come but they were prevented from leaving their villages. The whole meeting lasted only five minutes. Lefter spoke one minute, Potolea another, and I the rest. I said: "We came to hold a rally, but authorities forcibly prevent our men from coming. Against all orders, I shall hold ten rallies! Let someone bring me a horse and I will ride from village to village throughout the whole district of Horincea."

In fact, through all that mud, the only means of locomotion was the horse. Two hours later, a horse was brought and I started off. After me on foot came Lefter with four other legionnaires. We reached the first village, Meria. There, in the church yard, in a matter of minutes, everyone was gathered—men, women, and children. I said but a few words and I outlined no political program:

> Let us all unite, men and women, to carve for ourselves and for our people another destiny. The hour of Romanian resurrection and deliverance is approaching. He who believes, he who will fight and suffer, will be rewarded and blessed by this people. New times knock at our gates! A world with an infertile and dry soul is dying, and another one is being born, belonging to those who are full of faith. In this new world, everyone will have his place, not based on his schooling, intelligence, or knowledge, but above all in accordance with his faith and character.

Then we went on. Less than three miles away, we came to Slivna. It was getting dark. Yet people were expecting me with lighted candles. A nest of legionnaires headed by Teodosiu came out to meet me at the edge of the village. I spoke there too. Then I headed for Comanesti, with the Slivna nest of legionnaires leading the way. These were roads I had never traveled before. Here too, people were expecting me with lanterns and candles, while the young men sang. People were receiving me joyously no matter to what party they belonged. We were strangers, yet it seemed we had been friends for ages. Enmities melted. We were all one soul, one people.

The next morning, I resumed my ride. But this time I was not alone. Three other riders asked me if they could come along. On the edge of the neighboring village, Ganesti, we stopped at Dumitru Cristian's. He was a man about 40 years old with a pair of eyes hidden under dense brows. He had been a fierce nationalist fighter since early student battles. Now, in an instant, he unhitched his horses from the wagon, put the saddle on one of them and came with us. Soon our number grew larger with Dumitru and Vasile Popa, Hasan, and Chiculita. As we rode from village to village, the number of riders increased to twenty. Most were between 25 and 30 years of age, a few being 35 or 40, the oldest, Chiculita from Cavadinesti, was about 45.

When our numbers had so increased, we felt the need for a distinctive insignia, a uniform. For lack of something better, all of us placed turkey feathers in our hats. And so we entered villages singing. It seemed—as we went singing, our horses trotting along the hills' crests near the river Pruth where so often, long ago, our ancestors passed and fought—that we were the shadows of those who of old had defended Moldavia's territory. The live ones in the present identified with the dead of the past; we were the same soul, the same great unity of Romanianism carried by the wind over the crests of the hills. The news of my arrival, carried by word of mouth, had spread through all the villages. Villagers were expecting us everywhere. Everyone we met on the road was inquiring: "When are you going to come to us too? People waited for you yesterday, well into the night."

In those villages, as I sang and spoke to the people, I felt how I was penetrating into those undefined depths of soul where the politicians with their borrowed platforms could never descend. There, into those depths, I plunged the roots of the legionary movement. No one will ever be able to pull them out.

Thursday was Market Day in Beresti. At 10 o'clock in the morning, about 50 of us riders appeared on the top of the hill above the market town. From there we descended into the town in formation, singing. Townsfolk received us with great enthusiasm. Romanians came out of Christian homes, pouring pails of water across our path—an old custom wishing us in our travel the fulfillment of all our hopes. Again we went into the yard of Nicu Balan, where the first rally was supposed to take place. There were over 3,000 people this time.

This Horincea Valley, with its places and people, remained dear to me. After Focsani, it was to remain the second strongest pillar of the legionary movement.

In Transylvania, at Ludosul-de-Mures

We left for Ludos on the Friday before Christmas, at 5 o'clock in the evening. There were four of us in the panel truck: Radu Mironovici driving, Emil Eremeiu, an acquaintance, and I. Extremely cold weather had forced train cancellations. That night we almost froze to death, although we filled our panel truck with straw and covered ourselves with it. We traveled the route: Iasi, Piatra-Neamt, Valea Bistritei; and at 4 o'clock in the morning we reached the crest of the Carpathian Mountains. We arrived in Ludosul-de Mures at 11 o'clock that Christmas Eve, after more than 24 hours of driving. Here we had a good rest at Amos's house.

We went to church Christmas morning, then visited the little town. It was larger than Tg. Beresti; situated about 18 miles east of Turda, the county's capital. This town too, is full of Jews, though not reaching the Beresti percentage. Here too, Judas, settled in the market place, spread his web like a spider over the whole Romanian region. The poor peasants will be caught in this web, twirled around and dazed, then sucked dry of all their possessions.

On the morning after Christmas, we got started, the panel truck carrying ten legionnaires up ahead, then I with some 20 riders on horseback—Amos, Nichita, Colceriu, Professor Mattei, and others, all of us wearing turkey feathers in our hats. On the road, we were looked upon curiously, as the people we met were not aware of our purpose. But we were riding as if we were invested with the greatest authority, for we felt we were coming in the name of the Romanian people who ordered us to do so. In Gheta, Gligoresti, and Gura-Ariesului, people were gathered in as large numbers as in the Horincea Valley. Here too, we outlined no political program. We just told them we came from Moldavia to stir to life again the suffering soul of Romanians, for one thousand years of slavery, injustice, and entombment had been long enough.

Greater Romania was realized with much sacrifice, but it seems that foreign domination and the old injustices extended into this new nation. Ten years of Romanian administrations had not succeeded in healing our painful wounds nor had they corrected the injustices of centuries. They gave us a semblance of unity, but the Romanian soul still was split into as many pieces as there were political parties. The resurrection of this people is seething underground, and it will soon erupt, lighting with its light our whole future and the dark past. He who believes shall conquer!

Again I had the feeling that I was descending into their hearts. Although I was hundreds of miles away from Moldavia, in regions that had been, for centuries, separated from us by borders, there too I had found the same soul, exactly the same as in the Horincea Valley near Pruth. The same soul of the nation, over which I understood that no manmade frontier whatever had ever been drawn. The same breath flowed from one end of the nation to another, from Dniester to the Tisa, in total disregard of manmade frontiers, just as the underground water flows without regard to any obstacles man has raised on the surface. There, in the depth, I found no political parties, no enmity or clashes of interest, no "blind disunity" of fratricidal fights, but only unity and harmony.

On the second day after Christmas, we again took to the road. We stopped at a church on our way to say a prayer in remembrance of Michael the Brave, Horia and his men, and Iancu, so they would know too that we were treading today on the paths on which their bodies were tortured and ripped apart. It was the feast of St. Stefan; therefore I lit a candle for the repose of Stefan the Great's soul; through him, our people reached the greatest glory. I consider him equal in rank with Napoleon, Julius Caesar, and Alexander the Great.[1]

No matter where my steps are going to carry me or into what battles I shall engage, if above me, I feel the shadow of St. Michael the Archangel and below me, those of our 20 beloved martyrs of the family of the legionary movement, on my right I shall also feel the soul of Stefan the Great and his sword.

In Bessarabia

On 20 January 1930, I sent Totu, Crang, and Eremeiu, with a team in the panel truck, into the county of Tecuci, while on January 25, I myself was again in the Horincea Valley in the midst of my riders. On the evening of the 26th, after passing through Rogojeni, we entered Oancea. In both villages we were received warmly and with high expectations. We were lodged in Oancea by the Antachi family. The next day, a Monday, it was

---

[1] Stefan the Great (ca. 1435-1504) was Prince of Moldavia, ruling that region for nearly 50 years. He was venerated by nearly all Romanians afterward, and is still today considered one of the greatest Romanians in history.

market day in Cahul, on the left bank of the Pruth. Therefore we decided to go into Bessarabia, where the Jews were more numerous and provocative.

In Cahul, as in the other Bessarabian market towns, Jewry is communistic—not because of "love for the people" but because of hatred for the Romanian state, which, only through the triumph of Communism, could be toppled and placed under the heel of total Jewish domination. Communism's triumph coincides with Judaism's dream of ruling and exploiting the Christian nations by virtue of their theory of the "chosen people" that is at the base of the Jewish religion.[2]

We made some white cloth crosses that evening, about eight inches high, that were sewed on the riders' coats. I was given a wooden cross to carry.

At ten o'clock the next morning, I crossed the Pruth at the head of 30 riders, carrying the cross against the heathen power that was strangling Christian Bessarabia. After covering close to three miles, we entered the town. The Christians came out of their houses and followed us. They did not know us, but saw the white crosses on our coats and the feathers in our hats. We rode along the streets singing: "Awake, awake, ye Romanian!"

We stopped in the public square. Over 7,000 peasants gathered around us in no time at all. None among them knew who we were and what we wanted, but all of them had the premonition we had come to save them. I began to talk to them in the same vein I used in the Horincea Valley and Turda. But two minutes later, Popov, a policeman, accompanied by local authorities, made his way through the crowd and stopped me: "You are not allowed to hold a public meeting in this square…" "The Romanian people are allowed to do that anywhere."

The authorities wanted to prevent us from talking; the people wanted to hear us.

"My good people," I said to them. "This is the way it is; the law forbids us from holding meetings in public squares. Let us go to the edge of town or into someone's courtyard."

I signaled the riders, and we started for the edge of town. An army cordon stopped the crowd. Several minutes later, I was confronted by a soldiers' detachment with bayonets, headed by a colonel, Col. Cornea. He drew his revolver and pointed it at me: "Halt, or I fire!" he said.

I stopped.

---

[2] Recall Deuteronomy (7:6): "For you [Jews] are a people holy to the Lord your God; the Lord your God has chosen you out of all the peoples on earth to be his people."

"Colonel, why should you shoot me? I have done no wrong. I too, carry a revolver, but I did not come here to fight anybody, least of all the Romanian army."

I argued with him for almost an hour, but all that proved futile. I stayed there an hour, taking all possible insult and ridicule. I could have replied to him in the same tone of voice, or fought him, but I had to muster an iron will, for otherwise I would have fallen into a sadder predicament—that is, with myself, a Romanian nationalist, fighting the army of my own country and being watched by communist Jews.

The colonel began hitting us and our horses with his saber, and the soldiers jabbed us with their bayonets; then the prefect arrived. I dismounted and accompanied him to the Prefecture. He was a civilized man. The colonel came as well. I told him: "I respect your rank; that is why I did not answer you. But it does not matter. We will see you again next Monday at the same place."

Then I left. A sergeant brought my horse. Cristian and Chiculita were expecting me at the gate, on foot. They then brought their horses and we returned the same way we came, chased from behind by police and accompanied by the insulting glares of the Jews. At the edge of town, we met the rest of the saddened riders, dejected by the defeat we suffered. A bit further out, a few peasants who sneaked out of town asked us who we were. "Go back and tell the people that we will be back again next Monday. All the Christians in the county should come to Cahul."

We took a beating. We were in no mood for singing. We were going back and no one said a word.

When we got back to Oancea, we made ten posters announcing that Monday, February 10, we would again come to Cahul. These were sent by horse riders into several points of the county. Then we returned to Ganesti, to Cristian's home, where we arrived around midnight after a hard trip, a night so dark we could not see two paces ahead, whipped in front by a cold rain lashing our faces and from behind by the recollection of our stinging defeat.

I spent the night at Cristian's, and in the morning I left for Beresti. There I issued a directive to the legionnaires in the Ilorincea Valley, Galati, Iasi, Bucharest, Focsani, and Turda, informing them of our defeat at Cahul and saying that, since this is now a matter of honor, all of us must go back there and win; they must report there in the greatest possible numbers. The meeting place—Oancea—where they should arrive no later than Sunday evening, February 9. At the same time, I so informed the team of Totu, Cranganu, and Eremeiu, who at the time were in the county of Tecuci. I also wrote a letter to my father in which I asked him to give us a hand.

The legionnaires put some money together for me and I left for Bucharest to see Mr. Ioanitescu, Under-secretary of the Ministry of Internal Affairs. I told him what had happened at Cahul and requested permission to hold another rally there—a legal request—assuming the responsibility for conducting this rally in perfect order, provided the authorities did not provoke us. After demanding some additional clarifications, our rally was approved. We needed no approval for such a rally, as it was not required by law, but I wanted to be covered by official permission, thus to parry any possible tendentious interpretation of my action.

On Sunday morning, I was in Oancea once more. Lefter went to Cahul in order to determine the meeting place with the authorities. There was much excitement in Cahul, as news had come to the authorities that thousands of peasants from all parts of the county were headed for Cahul for the rally. Two truckloads arrived during the day from Focsani, the groups led by Hristache Solomon and Blanaru; from Turda, Moga, and Nichita; from Iasi, the legionnaires with Banea, Ifrim, and Father Isihie; from Galati, Stelescu with the Brotherhood; a student delegate from Bucharest; and Pralea with the nests from Foltesti.

Then came on foot, or with wagons and riding horses, those from Beresti, and the legionnaires from the Horincea Valley. My father too, came. By evening, over 300 legionnaires had arrived; they were lodged in Oancea. And more kept coming. Being concerned lest the pontoon bridge over the Pruth might be unhooked by authorities in order to prevent our crossing, I dispatched 30 legionnaires to occupy both ends of the bridge.

On Monday at 8 o'clock in the morning, I sent into Cahul a team of 50 legionnaires under the command of Potolea, to police the rally. In the meantime, new interventions were attempted in order to prevent us from going ahead with the rally. This was an impossibility. At 10 o'clock we formed a column and started out.

In the first group, 100 riders carrying a flag, all with feathers in their hats, many wearing green shirts. Each had a white cloth cross sewn on his coat. We looked like some crusaders who marched in the name of the Cross, against a heathen enemy, to free the Romanians. In the second group came over 100 pedestrians in a marching column with their flag. In the third group there followed about 80 wagons, 4 to 5 men in each, most from Oancea, also carrying a flag.

We seemed like an army ready for battle. When we approached the edge of Cahul, a sea of uncovered heads welcomed us, with no hurrahs or music, in an impressive church-like silence, we rode through this crowd of peasants. Some of them were crying.

The Bessarabian peasant population, too, since the unification of Romania at the end of the First World War, had felt no improvement in its lot. For, though delivered from Russian occupation, it fell under the domination of the Jews. It was purely and simply prey to the Jews. For 12 years, they had been exploited and bled by the communist Jews in a worse manner than the most tyrannical regime known in history had ever exploited any human society.

The Bessarabian cities and market towns are real colonies of leeches, clinging onto the exhausted body of the peasantry. And, the epitome of shamelessness, these leeches dared disguise themselves as fighters against people's exploitation, against the terror oppressing the people. These then are Bessarabia's and Romania's communists.

Moreover, these leeches, bloated by the sucked blood of Romanians, keep up in their press, of which *The Truth* and *The Morning* are the main papers. They write in the following style: "We have lived [the leeches!] in the best brotherhood and harmony with the Romanian people. Only some enemies of the people, of the country, some right-wing extremists, want to spoil this harmony."

There were over 20,000 peasants at the rally. Certainly this was the greatest assemblage of people this town had ever seen since the beginning, and all without any manifestos or newspapers to publicize it. The rally was conducted very solemnly. On one side, the riders were placed in a row; on the other, the column of pedestrian legionnaires.

The peasantry listened with heads uncovered. There was not one word, not one gesture to disturb this solemnity. This time Col. Cornea did not keep the rendezvous we promised him. This Bessarabian peasantry was expecting a word of consolation, and they came to this rally in such overwhelming numbers, not urged by me but by their great suffering. I told them:

> That we will not abandon you to the Jewish slavery now oppressing you; that you will be free, master of the fruit of your labor, master over your land and country; that the dawn of a new day for the people was approaching; that in this fight we have begun, all we expect you to give is *faith*—faith to the death—and in exchange, you will receive justice and glory.

Then spoke Lefter, Potolea, Banea, Ifrim, Father Isihie, Victor Moga, Tarziu, and Hristache Solomon. My father spoke for two hours at the end, unsurpassed in style and depth, and in the people's language. When speeches were over, I advised the peasantry to return to their villages in perfect order and quiet, calling it to their attention that if we were to end this imposing assembly with the slightest disorder, we would render a great service to the Jews. People wanted us to go with them. From all sides they wished us: "May God help you!"

Accompanied by the affection of these peasants, we left for Oancea where we parted ways. From that moment of the rally in Cahul, my father entered into the legionary movement.

Everyone went home in perfect order. Our victory was great, particularly by virtue of the peaceful and orderly manner in which the rally progressed and ended.

But the Jews of Cahul needed a scandal, a disturbance, a disorder at any cost, in order to compromise our movement and initiate governmental steps against us. Seeing that people left for their homes in a peaceful manner, two Jews, surely set up by their rabbi, broke the windows of a store— *their own*. Had the local authorities and some people not caught them in the act and taken them to police headquarters, the Jewish press, *The Morning* and *The Truth*, would have printed such headlines as: "Great devastation at Cahul," "How much the country loses in the eyes of the people abroad!" etc.

I have given this case, seemingly of minor significance in itself, because of its immense importance for those who wish to understand and know the Jews' devilish system of fighting. They are capable of setting a whole city on fire and then throwing the blame on their adversaries, in order to undermine an action that otherwise would lead to the ultimate solving of the Jewish problem. Therefore, I warn the legionnaires not to permit themselves to be provoked, for we will win only by maintaining the most perfect order. Disorder, for us, does not mean a conflict with the Jews but with the state. But it is exactly this that the Jews want to push us: into a permanent conflict with the state. That is why, as the state is stronger than we, if we were to be lulled or pushed into conflict with the state, we would be crushed; and they would continue to remain impartial onlookers.

My dog Fragu welcomed me at the gate upon my return to Iasi; I had him since 1924, a witness to all my trials and fights ever since. In Iasi, I took care of all current questions of organization, including correspondence with nests, which Banea—the head of the legionary correspondence—presented to me in perfect order. He began to grasp my way of seeing things very well in the past two years, and so he could himself handle many questions during this period when I rarely came to Iasi.

Return to Bessarabia: Advent of the Iron Guard

I stayed at home only for a week because the Bessarabian peasants sent delegates, letters, and telegrams, asking that I return to them. One cannot imagine the hopes they put in this movement of ours, and their faith. During the two weeks following the rally in Cahul, the news about the legionnaires spread like lightning among all Christian people of southern Bessarabia, from village to village, all the way to the banks of the Dniester; news of a beginning of deliverance from the Jewish slavery had inflamed the hearts of the poor peasants. Up to then, they placed their hopes in the Peasant Party, believing that when this party came to power, they, the peasants, would receive justice. But after eight years of hardships, battles, and hopes in this party, they discovered something frightening for their souls: that they had been betrayed and cheated; that Jewish interests lurked behind the name of the Peasant Party—the party of "The Romanian Peasant with Jewish sidelocks," as Professor Cuza baptized it.

I was seized by anguish upon seeing the faith in their hearts crushed that way, when, after eight years, they could see that their good faith had been betrayed. I went back to Beresti again, and from there by car to Rogojeni on the banks of the Pruth, where I was expected by over 200 riders headed by Stefan Moraru and Mos Cosa. They came from all the surrounding villages. "Let us march all the way to the Dniester," said one of them. "Yes! We will march," I replied.

It was then that the notion struck me to stage a grand expedition over the whole of southern Bessarabia from Tighina to Cetatea-Alba. Back in Iasi, the thought troubled me constantly as to how we could cross Bessarabia all the way to the Dniester? There existed one great difficulty: how best to proceed so that the authorities would not oppose us, to avoid fighting the state, the army?

It occurred to me that if I launched a new national organization for combating Jewish Communism, an organization inclusive of "The Legion of Michael the Archangel" and any other youth groups not affiliated with any political party, we might succeed in getting into Bessarabia. What name should we give this new organization? I debated this question with legionnaires, in the lobby of our home. Some said: "The Anti-Communist Falange",[3] others proposed other names. Cranganu said: "THE IRON GUARD!" "Let this be it!"

---

[3] A reference to 'Falangism,' a Spanish quasi-fascist movement.

Now we began preparing this anti-communist action backed also by workers. Actually, by "anti-communist action" I do not mean an "anti-worker" action; when I say "communists," I mean Jews.[4] In order to obtain authorization for entering Bessarabia and thus avoid any possible trouble with local authorities, I had an audience several days later with Mr. Vaida-Voevod, at that time Minister of Internal Affairs. He was the second politician of high rank whom I consulted; Ionel Bratianu was the first. He kept me there for three hours. I realized he was erroneously informed, both with regard to our movement and to the Jewish problem, which he did not know in its true light. He took us for some rambunctious youth inclined to solve the problem by breaking windows. I explained to him then how we saw the Jewish problem; how we consider it a life-and-death problem for all Romanians; how their number is overwhelming and inadmissible; how they destroyed the middle class and Romanian towns. I told him what the proportion between Christians and Jews was in Balti, Chisinau, Cernauti, and Iasi; and the danger they represent in our schools, threatening the alienation of the Romanian leading class and the falsification of our culture.

I also explained to him the manner in which we envisioned solving this problem. He understood from the very beginning what I was talking about. But, though a man of his stature readily understood the gist of the matter, yet, I believe he will never be able to completely understand us, for such is the nature of things; the eyes of 1890 no longer see as do those of 1930. There are calls, urgings, mute commands that only the youth hear and grasp because they address themselves only to it. Each generation has its own mission in life. That is why, perhaps, he will not trust us completely.

I obtained approval for our march into Bessarabia—after, naturally, assuming full responsibility for maintaining complete order. Several days later, I put out a manifesto addressed to all the youth of the country.

Troubles in Maramures

Meanwhile, great turmoil erupted in Maramures. This is another corner of Romanian soil over which death had spread its wings. There, Jewry had invaded villages, imposed its control over fields, mountains, and sheep corrals. Romanians, in a state of virtual slavery, retreated step by step before this Jewish invasion and gradually perished, leaving the estates they

---

[4] Communism was indeed a predominantly Jewish movement from the very beginning, in the founding works of the German Jew, Karl Marx. And as noted already, Bolshevik communists were heavily Jewish among the leadership.

had inherited in the hands of the invaders. No government shows an interest in them any longer, no law protects them.

It was early in June 1930 that a wagon drawn by two horses stopped at the gate of my house in Iasi. From it descended two priests, a peasant, and a young man. I asked them to come in. They introduced themselves: Orthodox priest Ion Dumitrescu, Greek-Catholic priest Andrei Berinde, and the peasant Nicoara.

"We come by wagon from Maramures. We have been on the road for two weeks; we are both priests in Borsa, one Greek-Catholic, the other Orthodox. We can no longer bear to see the misfortune of the Romanians of Maramures. We wrote memorandum after memorandum which we sent all over, to Parliament, the government, cabinet ministers, the Regency, with no reply from any of them. We do not know what else to do. We came by wagon here to Iasi to ask Romanian studentry not to abandon us to our fate. We speak in the name of thousands of peasants from Maramures who have grown desperate. We are their priests. We cannot close our eyes to what we see. Our people are dying and our hearts are breaking with pity."

I hosted them for a few days and told them: "The only solution I see is to organize them and try to boost their morale. They should know that they are not waging this battle by themselves; that we are behind them, fight for them, and that their fate depends on our victory." Eventually, I sent Totu and Eremeiu to organize them; and later Savin and Dumitrescu-Zapada. Thousands of peasants from Borsa and all mountain valleys were enrolling in our organization.

The Jews, realizing the danger of a Romanian rebirth, started provoking people. Seeing that their tactics failed, they resorted to an infernal means. They set fire to Borsa, blaming Romanians for it. Jewish newspapers immediately began yelling, demanding energetic measures be taken against the Romanians who, they were saying, were preparing pogroms. Both priests were attacked by Jews, insulted, struck, then chased several miles and stoned. To cap it off, they were both arrested as "agitators" and thrown into jail in Sigherul Marmatiei. Also arrested were Savin and Dumitrescu-Zapada and several score of leading peasants. Totu and Eremeiu too, were arrested in Dorna and locked up in the Campul-Lung prison. *The Truth* and *The Morning* set off a real cannonade of lies and calumnies heaped upon the priests and the others arrested. All protests, telegrams, memoranda, etc. remained fruitless, as they were drowned out by the Jewish howls, noise, and pressures.

The March into Bessarabia is Forbidden

In view of the march we were to make, I issued an "order of the march" that I printed in *The Ancestral Land.* I extract from it:

Comrades,
1. We shall cross the Pruth to the tune of the old Romanian hymn of unity: 'Come, let us join hands together, those of Romanian heart.'
2. The march will last one month.
3. We will form seven powerful columns, 14 miles apart.
4. The crossing of the Pruth will be done at seven points, the right flank column aiming to reach Cetatea-Alba; the left flank column, Tighina.
5. The mode of advancement will be marching on foot from the Pruth to the Dniester.
6. The date of departure, July 20 in the morning. The crossing of the Pruth at an hour to be announced.

When Jewry learned about our plan to enter Bessarabia in order to awaken the conscience of Romanians, the Jewish press launched a hurricane of attack against us. Calumnies, lies, and incitations came upon our heads unremittingly for a whole month.

These attacks were directed in the same measure against Mr. Vaida. The Jews were demanding that Mr. Vaida be forthwith demoted in the Ministry of Internal Affairs, in fact "thrown overboard" because he dared consent that we, Romanian youth, enter Bessarabia in order to bring a Romanian word of consolation and hope to our brothers across the Pruth. Bessarabia has been economically and politically delivered into absolute domination by the Jews. Any effort for Romanian emancipation, any mention of this black rule, was considered a crime.

Under the pressure of attacks and intrigues in the Jewish press, the march into Bessarabia was forbidden on the very day that legionnaires from all parts set out toward the Pruth. On that occasion, I wrote the following statement of protest, which I had distributed throughout the capital:

THE LEGION OF MICHAEL THE ARCHANGEL
"THE IRON GUARD"
AN APPEAL AND A WARNING

ROMANIANS OF THE CAPITAL,

The march of 'The Iron Guard' that was to take place in Bessarabia was stopped. The enemies of a healthy and powerful Romania have triumphed. For a full month little Jews from *The Fight*, *The Truth*, and *The Morning*, these poisoners of the Romanian soul, have threatened, insulted, and slapped our souls, here in our own land. From ticks latching into the bosom of this nation, they became the only ones who could understand the superior interests of our Fatherland, and turned themselves into uninvited censors of all its administrative acts.

At Turda, they demanded the government stop our demonstration, claiming that Transylvania was being set afire; at Cabul, that revolution was being started in Bessarabia; at Galati, that slaughters and pogroms were going to begin. They turned out to be contemptible provocateurs in each case, for the Legion kept perfect order and discipline everywhere. We were headed today towards the Dniester in order to turn Bessarabia's face toward Bucharest, but this did not please these mercenaries of Communism. Bessarabia must continue to remain prey to Bolshevism and look to Moscow so that they can continue to terrorize Romania's entire political life.

ROMANIANS,

The venal and perverse political system, this pus infecting our lives, aids and abets them—out of selfish petty electoral interest and out of a demeaning spirit of servility—in their work of dismembering our country and alienating our ancestral land. It was this selfish interest and this spirit that have been placing Romania into the hands of foreigners for the past 60 years.

Look, today, the martyrs of Maramures and Bucovina are beginning to stir! They cry out along their roads about the bitterness of slavery into which they were pitched by the treachery of all the country's leaders—not that they had been forgotten by them, but that they had been sold out.

Does it not seem to you at least strange that no voice has been found in this country to come to them with a word of consolation? And does it not seem to you to be at least a shamelessness to reduce the entire affair in Maramures to the 'instigators' Nicolae Totu and Eremeiu? Are they the ones who are guilty? What about the politicians who, for 12 years, have been cheating these Maramures peasants daily—are they not guilty? What about the hundreds of thousands of roving Jews who descended upon them like locusts to take away the land they inherited from their ancestors, and to enslave them? Are these not instigators and provocateurs? What about the [Jewish] gentlemen from Sarindar St. who ridicule our pride in being masters in our own country; are they not provocateurs?

ROMANIANS,

Here is a typical example that shows the real cause of the 'disorders' in Bucovina and Maramures. *The Universe* of 17 July 1930 published the following statistic: "At Cernauti… children of school age in the elementary schools: 12,277, of which only 3,378 are Romanians (boys and girls) while the rest are foreigners." What other proof of the domination of the Romanian element in the northern part of Romania do you need? Where do you want the soul of the Romanian people to run from this huge and murderous invasion?

Why is it that no politician has come out to tell His Majesty the truth?

YOUR HIGHNESS,

These unfortunate people do not ask for bread. They demand justice! They demand deliverance for the Romanian soul on the verge of dying because it is being suffocated both in Maramures and Bucovina. They demand that measures be taken against the hundreds of thousands of Jews, gorged, rotund, and white as worms, who defy them daily in their poverty, being protected by all Romanian local authorities.

GENTLEMEN [JEWISH] JOURNALISTS FROM
SARINDAR STREET,

Certainly, the Romanians know all too well that such a problem will not be solved by violent demonstrations; but, having reached the limit of their endurance, they wish to impose a Romanian leadership for Romania; to force Romanian legislation, laws for the protection of the Romanian element in Romania.

Would you like, through your continuous insults that wound our Romanian souls, to see me some day at the head of the holy rebels from Maramures? You had better know that, at that instant, your last hour has struck!

In any case, if you consider the existing laws inadequate to simmer you down, I declare to you that I have enough power to put you in your place and make you understand in which country you live. If you do not quiet down, I shall call up against you all that is alive in this country, determined to fight with all the weapons that my mind can call up.

ROMANIANS,

A New Romania cannot be born from the back rooms of political parties, just as Greater Romania was not born from the calculations of politicians, but on the battlefields of Marasesti and the deep valleys, upon which cannon rained steel. A New Romania cannot be born except by battle; from the sacrifice of its sons.

That is why I do not address myself to politicians but to you, Soldier! Rise up! History calls you again! As you are. With your broken arm, with your fractured leg, with your bullet-riddled chest. Let the powerless and the imbecile tremble. You, engage courageously in the battle.

Soon 'The Iron Guard' will be calling you to a great rally in Bucharest for the defense of Maramuresans, the children of Dragos-Voda and of the Bucovinans, the sons of Stefan the Great and the Saint. Write on your banners: 'The foreigners have invaded us,' 'The alienated press poisons us,' 'The political system kills us.'

Blow your trumpets in alarm. Blow them with all your power. At this moment, when the enemy invades us and the politicians betray us, Romanians, shout with trepidation as of old on mountain paths in hours of storm.

Fatherland! Fatherland! Fatherland!

— Corneliu Zelea-Codreanu,
Head of the Legion

The Attempt on the Life of Minister Anghelescu

On the evening of the day that my manifesto was posted, I was at the student center talking with several students. The young Beza appeared. All of a sudden, he ripped off his insignia of the "Vlad Tepes" organization to which he belonged, pitched it away and said: "Henceforth I shall have nothing to do with 'Vlad Tepes' anymore; I resign." This gesture on his part did not impress me. First, because the "Vlad Tepes" League seemed to lack earnestness, more especially the youth in that league, whose existence I doubted from the start. A resignation from such a youth group left me completely cold.

Several minutes later, this youth again joined our discussion saying he would like to become a legionary, if I had no objection. My vague reply avoided a direct refusal. Legionary dogma imposes reserve toward anyone new seeking to join the Legion, and this applied particularly in the present case. Several weeks earlier, I had seen Beza in a small restaurant where he asked me whether it would not be advisable to shoot Stere. Then too, I did not take him seriously.

Upon leaving, he asked me to spend the night at his place. I refused. Instead, I spent the night with the medical students. Th next day around noon, I heard the newspaper street vendors: "An attempt on the life of Minister Anghelescu!" Who? *Beza*. How? He fired several shots, superficially hitting his victim. Why? I did not know. Inquiring, I learned that a conflict arose between Macedonians and Anghelescu around the Law of New Dobrogea that infringed upon Romanian interests in that province. I had never met Anghelescu.

Two days later, I was summoned before the judge preparing the case. "Iron Guard" manifestos were found on Beza. I declared that I had no knowledge whatever of and no connection with this attempt, nor did I know his motive. I was released. As I left, I pondered how easily misfortune can befall a man. Had I accepted Beza's invitation to sleep at his place, I would have become the moral author of his crime. Any argument presented to defend myself would have been dismissed—particularly in view of the fact that this attempt coincided with the denial of our march into Bessarabia.

To my great astonishment, the next day I read the half-page headline in *The Morning*: "Corneliu Codreanu condemns Beza's act." I was dumbfounded. Consequently I went to see the judge who had interrogated me the day before. "Your honor, I am very astonished that such incorrect information could originate with your office from a secret interrogation. I did not condemn Beza's act. It is not for me to do so!" "I have released no such information. This is an invention of the press."

Then I said to myself: Should I let myself be insulted by the Jewish press? Even if I knew Beza for such a short time, though I had no connection of any kind with him, no one can compel me to be such a scoundrel as to jump on him, in such a case as this, to condemn him. I do not want to do it. Let anyone else but me do it, because I do not know what the matter is and because of my past, in which I had worn the same shoes, precludes me from condemning others. I shall write another warning. The same day, I printed a manifesto that I distributed throughout the capital:

THE SECOND WARNING

Because the press dared again becloud the truth, claiming I 'condemned' Beza's gesture, I insist on giving the following clarification:

If Minister Anghelescu might have reason to be defended, I believe that the youth Beza has as many reasons at least, both in the courts and before the conscience of his countrymen.

I declare that I am not going to defend the former by condemning the latter, but that I will defend the young Beza and his cause with all my heart and all my power.

As for you, gentlemen from Sarindar St., write on the list of settlements to come, this second warning.

— Corneliu Zelea-Codreanu

As a result of these two warnings, my relationship with Mr. Vaida was ended. Vaida became angry with me, but I could not proceed otherwise than as my conscience dictated. Summoned again before the same judge, I was arrested. So there I was again in the Black Maria, headed for the Vacaresti prison. There were seven other youths in the same van, to whom I introduced myself: Papanace, Caranica, Pihu, Mamali, Anton Ciumeti, Ficata, and Ghetea. They issued a declaration of solidarity with Beza. I walked again under the same gates as seven years earlier with my old comrades, and by coincidence I was placed in the same cell I occupied then. I entered the church the next day to view St. Michael's icon from which we started but children, seven years before.

There in prison, I got to know well certain Aromanians who came from the mountains of Pind. They exhibited a high culture, sound moral health, were good patriots, built to be fighters and heroes, and willing to sacrifice. There I came to know better the great tragedy of the Macedo-Romanians, this Romanian branch that, for thousands of years, alone and isolated in its mountains, has defended—weapons in hand—its language, nationality, and freedom.

It was then that I met Sterie Ciumeti, whom God chose for his good soul, pure as dew, to become, through his tragic torture and death, the greatest martyr of the legionary movement, of legionary Romania. There, our thought and hearts united forever. Henceforth we would fight together for our whole people, from Pind to beyond the Dniester.

No amount of complaining, petitioning, or intervening before an administration that has been deaf to all Romanian problems, will ever solve Romanian problems anywhere without a strong Romanian nation being in control of her own house. When that happens, these Romanians, scattered outside our borders, will be brought back into Romania. For the blood of all is needed here where Romanians are faced by death. And it is well to note that, in this struggle, the governments that opened the country's gates to thousands of Jews, at the same time did not permit Romanians from abroad to come in.

All hidden forces were at work, bearing down on justice, in order to secure my conviction. My recent arrest and incarceration in Vacaresti caused great rejoicing among the Jewish ranks. Every impertinent little Jew was attacking and insulting me in every paper. To please the Jews, even Romanian newspapers run by the political parties attacked me.

The date of my appearance in court had been set. I began the necessary preparations. I was waiting for Nelu Ionescu, who defended me in every trial since 1920, to arrive from Iasi. My defense was joined also by Mr. Mihail Mora, upon the insistence of students.

My trial, as always, was a Judaic attack trying to secure my conviction, no matter how small—demanded the Jews from *The Truth*—so they could say that the movement I lead is anarchical because it uses illegal means of action. The halls of the Ministry of Justice were full of Jews running to and fro with intercessions of all kinds.

However, Romanian justice, inflexible and undaunted, acquitted me. But the prosecutor appealed; therefore, I remained in prison.

This time the pressures and the interventions of the Judaic power were increased. Again I was taken to the Court of Appeals. To please the Jews, Prosecutor Praporgeseu placed me in the same box with embezzlers, horse thieves, and pickpockets. For three hours, while their cases were judged, I was the object of ironical and defiant glares from scores of Jews.

My case was the last to be considered and, as earlier, it was Mr. Mihail Mora and Nelu Ionescu who pleaded it. The verdict on the appeal was a new acquittal. After close to one month and a half of imprisonment, I was released. I left for home.

Following all this, together with Nelu Ionescu, Garneata, Mota, and Ibraileanu, I left in our panel truck for Sighetul Marmatiei to look into the fate of the two priests who were jailed in frightening misery. No one was coming to see them, even to bring them food. Father Dumitrescu's wife was sick; he had two small children. Their home was a breadless, money-less, impoverished home; they lived on charity—such is the fate of Chris-tian priests, sworn to defend the cross, the church, and their people! The lot of the other ten imprisoned peasant leaders was just as bad.

On the outside, Jewry was jubilant. Money was being collected both at home and abroad; the government gave money to the "unfortunate Jews" of Borsa so that they could build new two-story stone homes, while the poor Romanian peasants were eating bread made from sawdust meal mixed with oatmeal.

I, who then saw this Romanian Maramures groaning and writhing in the throes of death, cannot but urge every politician, every member of the teaching corps, every priest, all university students and secondary school students, and every preacher of humanitarianism—all who come here to censure our political life—"Go, all of you, and observe Maramures. Name anyone in the world as an arbiter to tell us if it is tolerable that in Romania something like that happening in Maramures, can happen to Romanians."

At the end of four months, the priests were transferred to the prison in Satu Mare. There, a trial was held in which some 50 peasants and peasant women with children in their arms were involved, as well as 20 Jews. Pro-fessor Catuneanu, Ion Mota, a local attorney, and myself, formed the de-fense of the accused Romanians. The 20 Jews were represented by four Jewish attorneys. After eight days of proceedings, all were acquitted, since all charges leveled at them were proven false.

Dissolution of the Legion and the Iron Guard (11 January 1931)

Meanwhile, Mr. Vaida, under pressure by Jewish attacks, was dismissed from the Ministry of Internal Affairs, being replaced by Mr. Mihalache—who, as his late attitude indicated, let it be known that he would not hesi-tate to use "strong arm" methods against us. This moment had arrived.

The youth Dumitrescu-Zapada, who was arrested in Sighet, was ex-asperated by the lies, attacks, insults of the Jewish press. Without asking or telling anyone one word, he grabbed a revolver he happened to find, went to Bucharest, entered Socor's office, and fired one shot. But the revolver was defective; it could not be fired the second time. This happened around Christmas time [1930]. It was a year in which I had not spent even a month at home. I wanted to spend the holidays with my family. I was at Focsani preparing to leave for home when I read in the papers what happened in Bucharest. Immediately I was summoned to come before Judge Papadopol at the Tribunal. It was proven I had no connection at all with the shooting. I could go my way.

I returned to Focsani where, by orders from Mr. Mihalache, for no reason, I was surrounded by police in Hristache Solomon's house and kept incommunicado for eight days. Mr. Mihalache then dissolved the Iron Guard and the Legion through a decree of the Council of Ministers. Searches were made of all our headquarters; all our records were seized; all our offices sealed. At home in Iasi, as well as in Husi, even my pillows and mattresses were ransacked. For the fifth time, my house was rifled, everything connected with the movement being taken away, down to the smallest notes I had. Sackfuls of documents, letters, and papers were confiscated from our homes and taken to Bucharest. But what could they find in our homes that could be illegal or compromising? We had been working in broad daylight and anything we had to say was said out loud. We confessed our faith strongly before the whole world.

On January 9, I was taken by agents from Focsani to Bucharest, and there, following a 12-hour interrogatory, I was placed under arrest and sent again to Vacaresti. The second day, the following legionnaires were brought in from the counties in which we were most active: Lefter, from Cahul; Banea, from Iasi; Stelescu, from Galati; Amos Pop, from Turda; Totu and Danila.

This was another hard blow to the leadership of a Romanian organization that had done nothing illegal, but only was trying to lift its brow against the Judaic hydra. Yet another attempt on the part of this people to rise up through its youth, from its slavery, was going down under the blows of a Romanian Minister of Internal Affairs, with the unanimous applause of Jewry, both at home and abroad.

This time too, the fury to destroy us was mercilessly unleashed. No means were spared to annihilate us; no infamy. And we were guilty of nothing. The Jewish papers in which we were violently attacked, ridiculing us and the truth, reached us in prison, and we could do nothing, we could answer in no way. With arms crossed, within the four prison walls, we watched how insults and all kinds of accusations were hurled at us.

It is sufficient to give one example showing the extent of the infamy of the Jewish press at that time, from the many attempts made, with the intention of setting public opinion against us to force our condemnation. I call the attention of the reader to the fact that I never planned, wrote, or signed such an order. No word in it belongs to me. It is wholly invented by Jewry. Here I reproduce in full the contemptible lie as printed in *The Morning*, which was then copied and commented on by the other papers:

AN EDIFYING DOCUMENT

With regard to the aims and means used by the 'Archangel Michael' organization, we are in position to publish a sensational document issued by the Legion in Iasi. The matter pertains to a circular sent to Campul-Lung and Ludosul Mare by the Legion 'Archangel Michael' in the capital of Moldavia:

The Legion 'Archangel Michael' Headquarters Iasi
The Cultural Christian Home
245/930 ad circulandum
Address your reply to Corneliu Zelea Codreanu
20 Florilor St., Iasi

To Second Battalion, Campul-Lung
Third Battalion, Ludosul de Mures
We have the honor to bring to your attention the following: Considering that both civil and military authorities have relaxed their vigilance because we had intervened with some highly placed officials—both in the Ministry of Internal Affairs and in … (another highly placed individual, N.R. is mentioned here)—we must take advantage of this opportunity to double our propaganda and instigation efforts, for this favorable situation may one day be reversed.
Consequently, with no further hesitation or loss of time, you shall do the following:
1. Make lists of all legionnaires who have taken their vow, by companies and platoons. These lists should be of defense before national and world opinion forwarded to the Legion by November 1 of this year to be totaled by regions.

2. The Second Battalion shall convoke in Campul-Lung the important leaders: Robota, Popescu, Serban, Despa, and in total secrecy, Commissar Nubert of Vatra-Domei and the chief of the gendarmes post of Poiana Stampii, Paduraru Gheorghe. You shall inform them that the Legion took the decision to change the plan of action.

Henceforth we shall work conspiratorially in absolute secrecy; you shall no longer hold public meetings or engage in propaganda—you shall get in touch with all legionnaires who are nest leaders—instructing them to sustain the present state of revolt among the peasantry. The decisive coup will be delivered this fall during the Mironeseu government change.

3. Third Battalion shall convoke Professor Matei, Moga Victor, Moga Tanase and the platoon chief of Grindeni—and from Urea you shall call only the merchant Moldovan. Secretly you shall call the gendarme instructor Sgt. Constantin of the Ludos post-inform them…(as in the Second Battalion).

4. You shall take out for exercises the legionary youth twice each week—on the village grazing grounds or elsewhere—preparing it and explaining our noble aim, encouraging it.

5. The chief of the Third Battalion's Staff shall terminate the mission he was charged with both verbally and by secret order No. 7/1930 to carry out as soon as possible; if the quantity of dynamite sent is insufficient, he is to demand more from the individual in question.

6. You shall also tell the above, by letter, to Dr. Iosif Ghizdaru of Sighisoara and also send him a detailed report on the activity in Ludos. A Fourth Battalion shall come into being in Sighisoara under the command of Dr. Ghizdaru. This order is to be burnt immediately after being read. Be careful, an army of Jewish spies is on our tracks; do not talk to anyone or see anyone who does not display my signature.

Courage; long live the Legion and with God, forward!

Iasi, 7 October 1930
Commander of the Legion
(SS) Corneliu Zelea-Codregnu
Chief of General Staff,
and Secretary (ss) Garneata

It is obvious from this circular that the Legion 'Archangel Michael' has prepared criminal actions, supported by a certain number of public officials. Though late, the authorities have the duty to identify absolutely all these public officials who place themselves in the service of this criminal action of the Legion 'Archangel Michael' and apply the most severe penalties.

Arrest Warrant

I realized that the situation was difficult; our organization dissolved, headquarters padlocked, searches everywhere. The public, completely dazed as a result of Jewish outcries and stupefied by their accusations heaped upon us, was inclined to take as real all these odious frame-ups. Moreover, in prison we were living in misery, cold, dampness, lack of air and light, and lack of blankets. It was due only to insistent interventions on our behalf that some straw was issued to us to stuff our mattresses and some mats to cover the dampness of the walls.

Thus we began 1931 in prison under a rain of Jewish lies, insults, and blows. This time too, I took my new prison comrades, who were sharing this trial with me, to see the icon and all the places that were full of memories. Certainly the situation was difficult for them too. But they had to answer only for themselves, and this responsibility was much smaller. The 'enemy' who had to be shattered and destroyed, was I. I felt that black clouds were gathering anew over our heads, that an enemy world was coming down on us anew with even more determination to annihilate us.

The only support in the midst of all these infernal machinations and gigantic assaults, was to be found in God. We began to fast each Friday, total fast; and to read each midnight the Akathist of Virgin Mary. Outside, legionnaires in the capital were doing their utmost to enlighten public opinion, which was misled by the Sarindar St. press.

At the same time, the devoted and undaunted Fanica Anastasescu— always present at my side in all my trials—tried to improve our material prison lot. Here is the accusation leveled at me:

ARREST WARRANT NO. 194:

Whereas the acts of criminal procedure drawn up against
Corneliu Zelea Codreanu, attorney in Iasi, aged 31, warned
that he committed the act of trying to engage in an action directed against the form of government established by the
Constitution and tried an instigation from which a danger for
public safety could have resulted by organizing an association, 'The Legion of Michael the Archangel,' 'The Iron
Guard,' having the aim of setting up a dictatorial regime
which was to have been imposed at a given moment wished
by him, by violent means, toward which his partisans were
prepared and urged through quasi-military drills, orders, directives, and speeches, as well as through publications, posters,
emblems, discourses during organized or public meetings.

Whereas, this act is specified by Art. 11, Paragraph 2 of
the Law for the suppression of some new infractions against
public order, as punishable by imprisonment of from six
months to five years and a fine of from 10,000 to 100,000 lei
and with loss of civil rights.

Considering that from the investigation conducted, serious charges and grave indications of guilt result against Corneliu Zelea Codreanu; and that in order to prevent the above
named to communicate with the informers and witnesses
which are to be questioned; as well as in the interest of public safety; it is important for the preparation of this case that
the accused, until further disposition, be placed in detention.

For these reasons: We mandate all agents of the public
force, that in conformance to the law, they arrest and take to
the arrest house of the Vacaresti prison, said Corneliu Zelea
Codreanu... Given in our office today January 30, 1931.

Investigating Judge Stefan Mibaescu
(Dossier No. 10-193 1)

The Trial (27 February 1931)

This rain of accusations continued uninterruptedly for 57 days, disseminated daily in millions of newspapers through villages and towns. We had no
chance whatever of responding. No ray of hope from anywhere. No one
had the capability of coming to our defense and to denounce the Jewish
conspiracy that sought our condemnation and burial and that of our

movement. We watched how the authorities, prosecutors, the Siguranta, and this gentleman named Mihalache, Minister of Internal Affairs, who—though all knew from the investigations they made that we were guilty of nothing; that no munitions, weapons, dynamite deposits were found, etc.—still persisted in their dishonorable attitude, leaving a few apprehended men prey to Jewish insults and ridicule—men unable to defend themselves. Because state security was involved, they should have heeded their elementary duty to quiet public opinion by issuing a communique denying the discovery of caches of munitions, denying the country was on the brink of civil war, etc.

It was under these inauspicious circumstances that our trial date was set for Friday, February 27. Some of the defense attorneys felt that introducing a motion for the postponement of the trial was advisable in view of the agitated atmosphere; that in the meantime, we call to the witness stand officials of security units to compel them to tell the truth under oath.

We declined this proposition; we would go to trial without witnesses.

Counselor Buicliu presided, assisted by Judges G. Solomonescti and I. Costin; the prosecutor was Procop Dumitrescu. We were defended by Professor Nolica Antonescu; attorneys Mihail Mora, Nelu Ionescu, Vasiliu-Cluj, Mota, Carneata, Corneliu Georgescu, Ibraileanu. Both the audience and the magistrates expected to see some proofs against us: bombs, munition deposits, dynamite, weapons. But nothing, absolutely nothing was produced in evidence.

Half an hour after our testimony was completed, the entire farce collapsed. Finally, we could speak, full of the indignation which for two months had been building up within us, hour upon hour. All that barrage of lies was broken in the face of truth. All the chains with which they shackled us came apart: our lawyers defended us brilliantly. Though the trial continued into the second day, sentencing was delayed for several days. At the appointed time for the verdict to be handed down, we were again taken to the Tribunal. The verdict of unanimous acquittal was read to us.

Here are the terms of this verdict of acquittal, detailing the actions, on the basis of which the dissolved "Legion of Michael the Archangel" had been brought before the law:

> Considering that the chief prosecutor's investigation results in the fact in the dossier that the adherents of the Legion had indeed been recruited only from among determined people: peasants, students, and high school youth; that, for instance, the dossier speaks of nests of legionnaires or 'white vultures;'

it speaks of a probationary status, vow or oath, five fundamental laws, one of which is a law of secrecy; that the Legion is militarily organized with a uniform, baldrick, scarves,
programs of physical education, and military drills, signaling
exercises and Morse code, etc., still, it has not been established that recruiters and recruited have engaged in any action against the present form of government established by
the Constitution, or in an action which might result in some
danger to state security.

That the fact alone of being constituted into such an organization cannot be construed as an infraction, even if it
might in someone's conception be considered such a danger.
For, as long as the organization was not an occult one, administrative authorities could have stepped in either to stop it
or to dissolve it.

That even in the supposition that it would have been established that the organization had copied the Fascist system
as a form of make-up, even then its members could not be
considered liable to the penalty stipulated by the text of the
law on the basis of which the accused have been brought to
trial; because no matter what its form, an organization in its
static stage does not present any danger to state security; it
could at most be the object of preoccupations of preventive
measures on the part of administrative authorities, but not of
any repressive measures which are in order only when such
organization initiates some action.

Furthermore, it cannot be said that just because several
legionnaires had gone through villages in order to seek ad-
herents, advising the people to organize, to trust the Legion's
movement, etc., one can produce proof that they intended to
endanger state security—propaganda being a means for
forming and replenishing the cadres of a political organization such as this; or that the inception of so-called nests of
high school students—formations outside the organization
proper—meant any threat to state security, if one considers
that in the organization's program one recognized the awakening of national conscience together with precepts of physical and moral education befitting a school program, as long
as there was no undue agitation.

Considering that the accused cannot be blamed for having sought to change by their action the present form of government—for, from the dossier, this fact not denied even by the representative of the Public Ministry—it is obvious that both the accused Corneliu Z. Codreanu and the others, as well as all the members of the organization, preached the need for a strong government to replace the parasitic political parties, and recognized the kind authority who was spoken of with all due respect and whose collaborators—as attested by their manifestos—they wished to become.

Also, as long as one speaks of collaboration with the head of the state, one cannot talk of toppling a form of government that the sovereign had not sanctioned ...

Whereas, for these considerations the subversive action (which as a matter of fact has not been proven from any angle as being subversive) of which the defendants are accused does not fall within the dispositions of Art. 11 ...

Whereas the march the organization had planned to make into Bessarabia had not taken place; that it would not have taken place if the authorities had not consented—consent that the accused as a matter of fact claim was obtained but later rescinded; that in such circumstances, it is superfluous to retain the claims of the accused that they intended first to test the resistance of legionnaires and second to awaken the national conscience of the populace penetrated by foreign elements.

Whereas it was also claimed that all the acts of the accused have to be looked at in the light of their antecedents...

Whereas as long as the fact for which the accused were brought to trial cannot be established, one cannot speak of the acts of Corneliu Zelea Codreanu, Danila, etc. as determining the degree of guilt, because the antecedents are of interest in establishing the degree of punishment and not in forcing a condemnation ...

That such being the case, the accused are innocent of the allegations brought against them and in consequence they are to be acquitted.

We returned joyously to prison, there to pack our bags and await the order to be released. We waited; 8 o'clock in the evening came, 9, 10, 11, o'clock; we jumped at each step we heard outside in the yard. Finally, we went to sleep with our bags packed.

The next day, again we waited. Only on the third day did we learn that the prosecutor appealed and therefore we would have to stay in prison until the appeal was considered. Once more, days began to drag slowly.

The new date was set for 27 March 1931 at the Court of Appeals. The days passed slower and slower. Finally they took us by van to the Palace of Justice, Section 11 of the Court of Appeals, presided over by Mr. Ernest Ceaur Aslan. The same defenders did their duty, combating successfully the thesis of Prosecutor Gica Ionescu, who laced the indictment with insulting outbursts full of hatred. Sentencing was postponed for several days. Back to Vacaresti, where we waited.

Recalled, we were told of a new acquittal, unanimous. After 87 days of imprisonment, we were finally released because we were found to be innocent. Who, I wondered, was going to punish our detractors? Who, I wondered, will avenge all the injustices, blows and suffering we had undergone?

But the prosecutor took the case even higher, to the Supreme Court of Appeals. Later, when the case came up for consideration, this court too, unanimously upheld the acquittal of the lower courts. Here we were, with two decisions: one, that of Mr. Mihalache, by which "The Legion of Michael the Archangel" and "The Iron Guard" were dissolved as subversive organizations, dangerous to the existence of the Romanian State; the other, that of the whole of the Romanian juridical system, Tribunal, Court of Appeals, and Supreme Court of Appeals, which unanimously declared these youth to be innocent, and that the Legion and the Guard did not represent any threat to public order or state security. Despite all this, our headquarters continued to remain padlocked.

Jewry, which was again beaten, lay low, in the shadows, preparing other lies, other attacks, other infamies. Oh Lord! Oh Lord! How come this people does not see that we, its children, are left prey to the enemy blows that fall upon us, one after the other? Oh Lord! Oh Lord! When will the people wake up and understand the great storm and the cabal directed against them with so much hatred, determined to stun them and slay them?

The Legionary Movement in the First Elections (June 1931)

The National-Peasant administration fell in April. The Iorga-Argetoianu government came to power. Since the Legion was dissolved, I registered my movement with the central electoral commission under the name of

"The Corneliu Z. Codreanu Group," choosing as its electoral symbol the iron grid.[5]

But the new designation, as expected, did not catch on. People, press, enemy, government, continued to call it "The Iron Guard." We had to take part in the elections so as to avoid the imputation of being different from the rest of the people, or that we did not take advantage of legal channels. June 1 was election day. With great material efforts, and borrowing many funds, we succeeded in registering lists of county candidates.

The campaign had begun—on our part, the most legal and most delicate campaign. In the two counties in which the candidacy of the Minister of War and that of the country's Prime Minister were announced, we did not come up with any lists; thus, of the few counties that we could have counted on carrying, we had to abandon two, Focsani and Radauti.

On top of this, government, local authorities, and their hit men continued to set upon us. Our communications were blocked; in the end, even some of our votes were stolen from the ballot box. Yet we obtained, after a tough fight, 34,000 votes. Cahul came in first with nearly 5,000 votes; then Turda with 4,000; Covurlui with its three sections, Beresti, Ganesti, Oancea, with nearly 4,000; Ismail with 6,000; etc. Since 15 December 1929, when I went to the first rally in Beresti, until June 1931, I was in continuous battle and imprisonment; I do not believe I spent two months at home, were I to add up the brief stops there.

The Campaign of Neamt (31 August 1931)

Twenty days after the elections, I learned that a seat in Parliament had been declared vacant in the county of Neamt. After I looked over the situation, I decided to enter the battle. We had only 1,200 votes in this county in the previous elections. This time, the Liberals, the National-Peasants in common front with the Averescans, and the Georgists were entering candidates for this vacancy.

The press intended to confer particular significance on this election because the battle promised to be a fierce one and its outcome would indicate the succession to power. There were concentration of forces; people even ventured prognostications. Some gave victory to Liberals, others to National-Peasants. In the midst of battle, some would place bets.

Naturally, no one spoke at all about us. No one dreamed of placing bets on our victory. On July 25, I issued my order for mobilization. But we

---

[5] A 'triple hash' mark, the conventional symbol for the Iron Guard.

were exhausted. We even lacked the money to pay the registration fees for our list. The Iesanu family took care of that and the cost of printing electoral flyers.

On July 30, I was in Piatra-Neamt, awaiting the arrival of our campaigners. Everyone came as best he could, on foot, by train, by wagon. It was at this time that we formed units within the Brotherhoods of the Cross, under the command of veteran legionnaires. I assigned each team to a certain sector. Altogether we had 100 campaigners. They left on foot, in boundless faith, though they knew no one—not what they would eat or where they would sleep from then on. God would provide for them; and need would teach them.

These teams worked as day laborers on farms in order to earn their keep. Soon they became endeared to the peasants. The National-Peasants came into the county by many carloads. There were seven former cabinet members who came into the county to campaign on their behalf. Likewise the Liberals came in great numbers. Of all social categories, the priest showed us the least understanding. In a country in which the crosses on church steeples have been falling down before the politician's mastery, atheistic and Judaized, in a battle in which we were the only ones coming in the name of the cross—our chests bared before the pagan monster—the county's priests, excepting three or four, were against us.

During the last week, I had to organize my forces in preparation for the final battle. We had now six strong sectors and ten weak ones. Discussing this with my team leaders, they opined that since we have six strong sectors, we could transfer our teams into the ten weak sectors to strengthen them. I thought this was an erroneous view, one that could lead to losing the battle. I proceeded on exactly the opposite course, concentrating more forces in our strong points and leaving only small units in the others.

Our adversaries committed the error I had avoided; they concentrated their effort in the points where we were stronger. Thus, we fought in our strongest points whereas they fought in their weakest ones. They were annihilated. I took in 1,000 votes in each of the six sectors, while they had 200 to 300 maximum. At the same time, their strongest sectors, left with an inadequate defense, were halved by our teams.

On voting day, beginning early in the morning, accompanied by Totu in a powerful vehicle, I covered 15 out of 16 voting sections. At 12 o'clock that night, we learned the results of the election, amidst the great enthusiasm of peasant masses and the teams of legionnaires and in the indescribable depression of politicians and Jews. The Guard: 11,300 votes; the Liberals, 7,000; National-Peasants with Averescans, 6,000 between them; the others, even fewer.

And so, in our first battle, in an open field against the coalesced forces of the politicians, legionnaires, though small in number, with incomparably smaller means at their disposal, succeeded in winning a victory, and in spreading panic among all our adversaries.

CHAPTER 7

DEMOCRACY AGAINST THE NATION

In Parliament

As a result of this election, I entered Parliament. I was alone in the midst of an enemy world. I lacked the experience of this parliamentary life and the talent of democratic oratory, which is full of empty, but pompous, shiny phraseology, of mirror-studied gestures, and a large dose of impertinence. The characteristics that help one to succeed, to rise, God had not endowed me with—perhaps in order to prevent my being tempted to climb the political ladder.

For my entire time in Parliament, I never exceeded the laws of propriety and respect for those older than myself, be they even my greatest enemy. I had not ridiculed, sworn at, laughed at, or offended anyone, which meant I could not become a part of that life. I remained isolated, not only due to the fact that I was one against the others, but altogether isolated from that kind of life.

One evening, rather late, when deliberations were nearing the end and benches were almost empty, I was granted the floor. I tried to show that our country had been invaded by Jewry; that where the invasion is the greatest—in Maramures—human misery is most frightening; that the beginning of Jewish existence on our soil foreshadowed the death of Romanians; that as their numbers increased, we would die; that, finally, the leaders of the Romanian nation, the men of the century of democracy and of political parties, have betrayed their people in this fight by placing themselves at the service of great national or international finance.

I showed that in the portfolio of the Marmorosch-Blank Bank—that Judaic nest of conspiracy and corruption—exist a great many politicians to whom this bank has "lent" money; Mr. Brandsch, Undersecretary of State, 111,000 lei; Mr. Davilia, 4,677,000 lei; Mr. Iunian, 407,000 lei; Mr. Madgearu, 401,000 lei; Mr. Filipescu, 1,265,000 lei; Mr. Raducanu, 3,450,000 lei; The Raducanu Bank, 10,000,000 lei; Mr. Pangal (the head of the Scottish Rite Masonry in Romania), 3,800,000 lei; and Mr. Titulescu, 19,000,000 lei—all of them leaders in Romanian public life. In addition to these, there are others, very many, but I could not get my hands on the list of them.

Someone interrupted me saying: "This is borrowed money; it will be repaid." I answered: "Whether this will be repaid or not, I do not know. But I tell you one thing: when someone borrows money from such a financial source, he is under an obligation when he comes to power, to satisfy it, or even if he is not in power, to support it, but in any case, not to expose it when it should be exposed."

I then read a list from that I showed, removing any possibility of denial, how, since the war, the Romanian state had been defrauded of some 50 billion lei under democracy—the most honored and most perfect form of government of the "people" and by the "people"! The leadership of "democracy," having the basic idea of the permanent control of the people in which the people, the great controller, had been robbed during 15 years of government of the fabulous sum of 50 billion lei. Then I made several critical observations regarding democracy.

In the end, I made seven demands:

1. We demand the introduction of the death penalty for the fraudulent manipulators of public funds. At this point, I was interrupted by Mr. Ispir, professor at the Faculty of Theology: "Mr. Codreanu, you call yourself a Christian, a propagator of Christian ideals. I remind you that the idea just put forward by you is anti-Christian." I replied: "Professor, when it is a question of choosing between the death of my country and that of the thief, I prefer the death of the thief, and I think I am a better Christian if I do not permit the thief to ruin my country and to destroy it."
2. We demand the investigation and confiscation of the wealth of those who have bled our poor country.
3. We demand that all politicians who may be proved guilty of having worked against the interests of our country by supporting shady private speculations or in any other fashion, be brought to justice.
4. We demand that in the future, politicians be barred from the administrative boards of the various banks and financial enterprises.
5. We demand the expulsion of the hordes of pitiless exploiters who have come here to drain the riches from our soil and exploit the work of our hands.
6. We demand that the territory of Romania be declared the inalienable and irrevocable property of the Romanian Nation.

7.   We demand that all campaigning agents be sent to work, and that a single command be established, that will inspire the whole Romanian Nation with one heart and one mind.

These were the first efforts to publicly formulate several political measures that I considered most urgent. They were not the result of some prolonged thinking or ideological search, but the result of momentary reflections over what the Romanian people needed then, without delay. Six months later, several quite popular movements appeared that had my three initial points in their program:

1. The death penalty
2. The investigation of wealth, and
3. The prevention of politicians from getting on administrative boards

—which meant that others also observed these points to be necessary.

Several Observations Regarding Democracy

I wish, in the pages to follow, to present several conclusions of my daily experience in such a manner that they can be understood by any young legionary or workingman. We live in the clothing, the forms, of democracy. Are they good, I wonder? We do not yet know. But one thing we do see: we know precisely that part of the greater and more civilized European nations discarded these clothes and put on some new ones. Did they shed them because they were good? Other nations too, make strong efforts to shed them and change them. Why? Could it be that all nations went mad? That only Romanian politicians remained the wisest men in the whole world? It seems I cannot quite believe that. Certainly, those who changed them or who wish to do so, have their own reasons.

But why should we be concerned with someone else's reasons? Let us better be concerned with the reasons that would make us Romanians shed these clothes of democracy. If we have no reasons for discarding them, if for us they are suitable, then we should keep them, even if all Europe discard them. However, they are not good for us either, because:

1. Democracy breaks the unity of the Romanian people, dividing it into parties, stirring it up, and so, disunited, exposing it to face the united block of Judaic power at a difficult moment of its history. This argument alone is so grave for our existence that it would constitute sufficient reason for us

to exchange this democracy for anything that could guarantee our unity: namely our life. Our disunity means death.

2. Democracy transforms the millions of Jews into Romanian citizens, by making them the equal of Romanians and giving them equal rights in the state. Equality? On what basis? We have lived here for thousands of years; with the plow and with the weapon; with our labor and our blood. Why should we be equal to those who have been here for hardly 100, 10, or 5 years? Looking at the past, it was we who created this state. Looking at the future, it is we Romanians who hold the entire historical responsibility for Greater Romania's existence; they have none. How could Jews be made responsible before history for the disappearance of the Romanian State? To sum up: they have neither equality in the labor, sacrifice, and fighting that created the state, nor equality of responsibility for its future. Equality? According to an ancient maxim, equality means treating unequal things unequally. On what basis do the Jews demand equal treatment, political rights equal to those of Romanians?

3. Democracy is incapable of continuity in effort. Divided into parties that govern one, two, or three years, it is incapable of conceiving and accomplishing a long-range plan. One party nullifies the plans and the efforts of another. What was conceived and built by one today is demolished next by another. In a country in need of construction, whose historical moment is that very construction, this drawback of democracy constitutes a threat. It is as if, on a farm, the owners would change yearly, each coming with different plans, doing away with what the predecessors did, their work only to be done away with by the next owner coming tomorrow.

4. Democracy makes it impossible for the politician to do his duty to his nation. A politician of the greatest good will becomes, in a democracy, the slave of his supporters; he either satisfies their personal appetites or they destroy his backing. The politician lives under the tyranny and permanent threat of the electoral agent. He is placed in the position of choosing either the renunciation of his lifetime's labor or the satisfaction of his supporters. And then the politician satisfies their appetites; not out of *his* pocket, but out of *the country's* pocket. He creates jobs, positions, missions, commissions, and sinecures, all of them loading down the national budget that burdens more and more the bowed backs of the people.

5. Democracy is incapable of authority. It lacks the power of sanction. A party, for fear of losing its supporters, does not apply sanctions against those who live through scandalous business deals running into the millions, through thievery or embezzlement; nor does it apply any sanctions against political adversaries, lest *they* expose *its own* shady deals and wrongs.

6. Democracy is in the service of great finance. Because of the expensive system and the competition among various groups, democracy needs a lot of money. As a natural consequence, it becomes the slave of the great Jewish international finance that subjugates it by payment. In this fashion, the fate of a people is given into the hands of a caste of bankers.

Election, Selection, Heredity

A people is not led according to its will (per the democratic formula); nor according to the will of one individual (per the dictatorial formula); but according to laws. I do not talk here of manmade laws. There are norms, natural laws of life; and there are norms, natural laws of death. Laws of life and laws of death. A nation is headed for life or death according to its respect for one or the other of these laws.

There remains one question to be answered: Who, in a nation, can understand or know intuitively these norms? People? The multitude? If this were the case, I believe that too much is expected. Multitudes do not understand much simpler laws. These must be explained to them by repeated insistence in order to be understood—yes, even by punishment, if need be.

Here are a few examples of laws that are imperatively necessary to the life of the people, which multitudes understand only with difficulty:

- that in case of contagious illness, the sick must be isolated and a general disinfection is needed;
- that sunlight must enter homes, therefore a house should have large windows;
- that if cattle are better fed and cared for, they yield more for man's nutrition, etc.

If the multitude does not understand, or understands only with difficulty, several laws that are immediately necessary to its life, how can it be imagined by someone that it—which in a democracy must be led through itself—could understand the most difficult natural laws? Or that it would know intuitively the subtlest and imperceptible norms of human leadership, norms that project beyond itself, its life, its life's necessities, or which do not apply directly to it but to a more superior entity, the nation?

For making bread, shoes, plows, farming, or running a streetcar, one must be specialized. Is there no need for specialization when it comes to the most demanding leadership, that of a nation? Does one not have to possess certain qualities? The conclusion: *a people is not capable of governing itself.* It ought to be governed by its elite. Namely, through that category of men born within its bosom who possess certain aptitudes and specialties. Just as the bees raise their "queen," a people must raise its elite. The multitude likewise, in its needs, appeals to its elite, the wise of the state.[1]

Who chooses this elite—the multitude? Supporters could be found for any "ideas," or votes for anyone running for public office. But this does not depend on the people's understanding of those "ideas," "laws," or "candidates" but on something entirely different: on the adroitness of individuals to win the goodwill of the multitudes. There is nothing more capricious and unstable in opinions than the multitude. Since the World War, this multitude was, in turn, Averescan, Liberal, Nationalistic, National-Peasant, Iorgan, etc. hailing each, only to spit on each a year later—thus recognizing its own error, disorientation, and incapacity. Its criterion for selection is: "Let's try someone else." Thus, the choosing is done not according to judgement and knowledge, but haphazardly and trusting to luck.

Consider two opposite ideas, one true, the other a lie. Truth—of which there can be but one—is sought. The question is put to a vote. One idea polls 10,000 votes, the other 10,050. Is it possible that 50 votes, more or less, determine or deny the truth? Truth depends neither on majority nor minority; it has its own laws, and it succeeds, as has been seen, against all majorities, even though they be crushing.

Finding truth cannot be entrusted to majorities, just as in geometry, Pythagoras' theorem cannot be put to the multitude's vote in order to determine or deny its validity; or just as a chemist making ammonia does not run to multitudes to put the amounts of nitrogen and hydrogen to a vote; or as an agronomist, who studied agriculture and its laws for years, does not have to turn to a multitude trying to convince himself of their validity by their vote.

Can the people choose its elite? Why then do soldiers not choose the best general? In order to choose, this collective jury would have to know very well:

---

[1] This is essentially identical to Plato's ideal system of government (an aristocracy), as detailed in his *Republic*.

a) The laws of strategy, tactics, organization, etc. and

b) To what extent the individual in question conforms, through aptitudes and knowledge, to these laws.

No one can choose wisely without this knowledge. If the multitude wishes to choose its elite, it must necessarily know the national organism's laws of leadership and the extent candidates to this leadership conform by qualifications and knowledge of said laws.

However, the multitude can know *neither* these laws *nor* the candidates. That is why we believe that the leading elite of a country cannot be chosen by the multitude. To try to select this elite is like determining by majority vote who the poets, writers, mechanics, aviators, or athletes of a country ought to be.

Thus democracy, based on the principle of election, choosing its elite itself, commits a fundamental error, from which evolves the entire state of wrong, disorder, and misery in our villages. We touch here upon a capital point; it is from this *error of democratic conception* that we could say all the other errors originate.

When the masses are called to choose their elite, they are not only incapable of discovering and choosing one but choose moreover, with few exceptions, *the worst* within a nation. Not only does democracy remove the national elite, but it replaces it with the worst within a nation.[2] Democracy elects men totally lacking in scruples, without any morals; those who will pay better, thus those with a higher power of corruption; magicians, charlatans, and demagogues, who excel in their fields during the electoral campaign. Several good men might be able to slip through among them, even politicians of good faith. But they would be the slaves of the former.

The real elite of a nation would be defeated, removed, because it would refuse to compete on that basis; it would retreat and stay hidden. Hence, fatal consequences for the state. When a state is led by a so-called "elite," made up of the worst, most corrupt, most unhealthy it has, is it not permitted to ask why the state is headed for ruin?

Here then is the cause of all other evils: immorality, corruption, and lust throughout the country; thievery and despoilation in the state's wealth; bloody exploitation of the people; poverty and misery; lack of a sense of

---

[2] Compare to this statement by Socrates: "And upon my word, fellow Athenians, I truly did experience something like this: I found those held in the highest esteem were practically the most defective" (*Apology,* 22a).

duty in all functions; disorder and disorganization in the state; and the invasion from all directions of foreigners with money, as coming to buy bankrupt stores, whose wares are being sold for a pittance. The country is auctioned off.

"Who pays more?" In the last analysis, this is where democracy is going to take us. In Romania, particularly since the war, democracy has created for us, through this system of elections, a "national elite" of Romano-Jews—an elite based not on bravery, nor love of country, nor sacrifice, but on betrayal of country, the satisfaction of personal interest, bribery, trafficking of influence, enrichment through exploitation, and embezzlement, thievery, cowardice, and intrigue to knock down any adversary. This "national elite," if it continues to lead this country, will bring about the destruction of the Romanian state. Therefore, in the last analysis, the problem facing the Romanian people today, on which all others depend, is the substitution of this fake elite with a real national one based on virtue, love, and sacrifice for country, justice and love for the people, honesty, work, order, discipline, honest dealing, and honor.

Who will make this substitution? Who will place this real elite in its place of leadership? I answer: *anyone but the multitude*. I accept any system except "democracy," which I see killing the Romanian people.

The new Romanian elite, as well as any other elite in the world, must be based on *the principle of social selection*. In other words, a category of people endowed with certain qualities that they then cultivate, is naturally selected from the nation's body—namely from the large healthy mass of peasantry and workingmen, which is permanently bound to the land and the country. This category of people becomes the national elite meant to lead our nation.

When can a multitude be consulted, and when must it be? It ought to be consulted before the great decisions that affect its future, in order to say its word whether it can or cannot, whether it is spiritually prepared or not, to follow a certain path. It ought to be consulted on matters affecting its fate. This is what is meant by the consultation of the people; it does *not* mean the election of an elite by the people.

But I repeat my question: "Who indicates everyone's place within an elite, and who sizes up everyone? Who establishes the selection and consecrates the members of the new elite?" I answer: "The previous elite." The latter does not choose or name, but consecrates each in his place, to which he elevated himself through his capacity and moral worth. The consecration is made by the elite's chief, in consultation with his elite. Thus a national elite must see to it that it leaves an inheriting elite to take its place—

an elite not based, however, on the principle of heredity but only on that of social selection, applied with the greatest strictness.

The principle of heredity is not sufficient in itself. According to the principle of social selection, continually refreshed by elements from within the nation's depths, an elite keeps itself always vigorous. The main historical mistake has been that, where an elite was created on the basis of the principle of selection, it dropped the next day the very principle that gave it birth, replacing it with the principle of heredity, thus consecrating the unjust and condemned system of privileges through birth. It was as a *protest* against this mistake, for the removal of a degenerated elite, and for the abolition of privilege through birth, that democracy was born. The abandonment of the principle of selection led to a false and degenerate elite, which in turn led to the aberration of democracy.

The principle of selection removes alike both the principle of election and that of heredity. They cancel each other out. There is a conflict between them; for, either there is a principle of selection, and in that case the opinion and vote of the multitude do not matter; or the latter votes in certain candidates, and in that case selection no longer operates.

Likewise, if the principle of social selection is adopted, heredity plays no part. These two principles cannot go together unless the heir corresponds to the laws of selection. And if a nation has no real elite, a first one, to designate the second? I answer by a single phrase that contains an indisputable truth: in that case, *the real elite is born out of a war with the degenerate elite, the false one.* And that, also on the principle of selection.

Therefore, summing it up, the role of an elite is:

a) To lead a nation according to the life-laws of a people.
b) To leave behind an inheriting elite, based not on the principle of heredity but on that of selection, because only an elite knows life's laws and can judge to what extent people conform by aptitudes and knowledge to these laws. It is like a gardener who works his garden and sees to it that, before he dies, he has an inheritor, a replacement, for he alone can say who among those working with him is best to take his place and continue his work.

On what must an elite be founded?

a) Purity of soul.
b) Capacity of work and creativity.
c) Bravery.

d) Tough living and permanent warring against difficulties facing the nation.
e) Poverty—namely, voluntary renunciation of amassing a fortune.
f) Faith in God.
g) Love.

I have been asked whether our activity so far has followed along the same lines as those of the Christian Church. I answer: We make a great distinction between the line we follow and that of the Christian Church. The Church dominates us from on high. It reaches perfection and the sublime. We cannot lower this plane in order to explain our acts.

We, through our action, through all our acts and thoughts, tend toward this line, raising ourselves up toward it as much as the weight of our sins of the flesh and our fall through original sin permit. It remains to be seen how much we can elevate ourselves toward this line through our worldly efforts.

Individual, National Collectivity, Nation

"Human rights" are not limited only by the rights of other humans but also by other rights. There are three distinct entities:

1. The individual.
2. The present national collectivity, that is, the totality of all the individuals of the same nation, living in a state at a given moment.
3. The nation, that historical entity whose life extends over centuries, its roots imbedded deep in the mists of time, and with an infinite future.

A new great error of democracy based on "human rights" is that of recognizing and showing an interest in only one of these three entities, the individual; it neglects the second or ridicules it, and denies the third.

All of them have their rights and their duties, the right to live and the duty of not infringing on the right to life of the other two. Democracy takes care of assuring only the rights of the individual. That is why in democracy we witness a formidable upset. The individual believes he can encroach, with his unlimited rights, on the rights of the whole collectivity, which he thinks he can trample and rob; hence, in democracy, one witnesses this rending scene, this anarchy in which the individual recognizes nothing outside his personal interest.

In its turn, national collectivity exhibits a permanent tendency to sacrifice the future—the rights of the nation—for its present interests. That is why we witness the pitiless exploitation and the alienation of our forests, mines, and oil reserves, forgetting that there are hundreds of Romanian generations, our children's children to come after us, who likewise expect to live and carry on the life of our nation. This upheaval, this breach of relationship brought about by democracy constitutes veritable anarchy, an upsetting of the natural order, and is one of the principal causes of the state of unrest in today's society.

Harmony can be reestablished only by the reinstatement of natural order. *The individual must be subordinated to the superior entity, the national collectivity, which in turn must be subordinated to the nation.* "Human rights" are no longer unlimited, but limited by the rights of national collectivity, these in turn being limited by those of the nation.

Finally, it would seem that in a democracy, at least the individual enjoying so many rights lives wonderfully. But in reality—and this is democracy's ultimate tragedy—the individual has no right, for where is the freedom of assembly in our country, the freedom to write, the freedom of conscience? The individual lives under terror, a state of siege, censorship; thousands of people are arrested, some being killed for their faith, as under the most tyrannical leaders. Where is "the right of the sovereign multitude" to decide its fate, when meetings are forbidden and when thousands of people are prevented from voting, maltreated, threatened with death, even killed? You will say: "Yes, but these people want to change the Constitution, limit our liberties, enthrone another form of government!"

I ask: "Can democracy claim that a people is not free to decide its own destiny, to change its Constitution, its form of government, as it pleases; to live with greater or fewer freedoms as it chooses?" This is the ultimate tragedy.

In reality, man has no rights in a democracy. He did not lose them for the benefit of either the national collectivity or the nation, but in favor of a politico-financier caste of bankers and electoral agents.

Masonic democracy, through an unparalleled perfidy, masquerades as an apostle for peace on this Earth while at the same time proclaiming war between man and God. Peace among men and war against God. The perfidy consists in using the words of our Savior "Peace among men" in order to change into an apostle for "Peace" while condemning Him and showing Him as mankind's enemy.

And more, this perfidy consists also in that they pretend to want to save people's lives while in fact they lead them to their death; feigning to save their lives from war, condemn them—devilishly—to eternal damnation.

The Nation

When we say "the Romanian nation," we mean not only all Romanians living in the same territory, sharing the same past and the same future, the same dress, but all Romanians, alive and dead, who have lived on this land from the beginning of history and will live here also in the future.

The nation includes:

1. All the Romanians presently alive,
2. All the souls of our dead and the tombs of our ancestors,
3. All those who will be born Romanians. A people becomes conscious of itself when it attains an awareness of this whole, not only of its own aims.

The nation possesses:

1. A physical, biological patrimony—her flesh and blood.
2. A material patrimony—the soil of her country and its riches.
3. A spiritual patrimony, which contains:
    a) Her concept of God, the world, and life. This concept forms a domain, a spiritual property. The frontiers of this domain are determined by the horizons to which the brightness of her concept reaches. There exists a country of the national spirit, a country of its visions obtained by revelation or by her own efforts.
    b) Her honor, which shines to the extent that the nation has conformed during her history to the norms stemming from her concept of God, the world, and life.
    c) Her culture, the yield of her existence resulting from her own efforts in the domain of arts and thought. This culture is not international. It is the expression of national genius, of the blood. Culture is *international* as far as its luminescence may reach, but *national* in origin. Someone made a beautiful comparison: both bread and wheat can be international as consumption items, but they carry everywhere the stamp of the earth in which they grew.

Each of these three patrimonies has its importance. A people must defend all three. The most important however is its spiritual patrimony, for only it carries the stamp of eternity, it alone endures through all the centuries. The ancient Greeks are not remembered because of their physique—nothing but ashes is left of that—nor their material riches, had they had any, but because of their culture. A people lives in eternity through its outlook, its concept of honor, and its culture. That is why the nation's leaders must reason and act, not only according to the physical or material interests of the people, but also by taking into account its historic honor, its eternal interests. In other words, not bread, but honor at any price.

The Final Aim of the Nation

Is it life? If it be life, then the means people use to assure life does not matter; even the worst is good. Therefore the question must be raised: Which are the principles guiding nations in their relationship with other nations? Should they be guided by animal instinct, the tiger in them, as fish behave in the sea or beasts in the forest?

The final aim is not life but resurrection—the resurrection of peoples in the name of the Savior Jesus Christ. Creation and culture are but a means, not a purpose as it has been believed, of obtaining this resurrection. It is the fruit of the talent God planted in our people for which we have to account. There will come a time when all the peoples of the Earth shall be resurrected, with all their dead and all their kings and emperors, each people having its place before God's throne. This final moment, "the resurrection from the dead," is the noblest and most sublime one toward which a people can rise.

The nation then is an entity which prolongs her existence even beyond this Earth. Peoples are realities even in the netherworld, not only in this one. St. John, narrating what he saw beyond the Earth, says:

> And the city has no need of sun or moon to shine upon it, for the glory of God is its light, and its lamp is the Lamb. By its light shall the nations walk; and the kings of the earth shall bring their glory into it. (Rev 21:23-24)

And again:
> Who shall not fear and glorify thy name, O Lord? For thou alone art holy. All nations shall come and worship thee, for thy judgments have been revealed. (Rev 15:4)

To us Romanians, to our people, as to any other people in the world, God has given a mission, a historic destiny. The first law that a person must follow is that of going on the path of this destiny, accomplishing its entrusted mission. Our people has never laid down its arms or deserted its mission, no matter how difficult or lengthy was its Golgotha Way.

Even now, obstacles high as mountains appear before us. Shall we be, I wonder, the weak and cowardly generation, to drop from our hands, under pressures of threats, the line of Romanian destiny and abandon our mission as a people in this world?

Monarchy and the Law of Monarchy

At the head of peoples, above the elite, one finds the monarchy. I reject the republic. We know some monarchs that were good, some very good, others weak or bad. Some enjoyed honors and the love of their people to the end of their lives, others were beheaded. Therefore, not all of the monarchs were good. Monarchy itself, however, has always been good. One must not confuse the man with the institution and draw false conclusions.

There can be bad priests; but can we, because of this, conclude that the Church must be abolished and God stoned to death?

There are weak and bad monarchs certainly, but we cannot renounce monarchy because of this. In farming, there is occasionally a bad year following a good one, or one good and two bad; even so, no one thinks about quitting farming.

Does a monarch do as he pleases, whether he be great or small, good or bad? A monarch does not do what he wants. He is small when he does as he pleases and great when he does what he must. To each nation, God has traced a line of destiny. A monarch is great and good when he stays on that line; he is small or bad, to the extent that he wanders away from this line of destiny or opposes it. This then, is the law of monarchy.

There are also other lines that may tempt a monarch: the line of personal interest or that of a class of people or group; the line of alien interests (domestic or foreign). He must avoid all these lines and follow that of his people. Stefan the Great has shone in history for 500 years and Romanians remember him because he identified himself perfectly with the destiny of his people. King Ferdinand, in spite of pressure from outside interests and influences, placed himself on the line of the nation's destiny; he suffered with her, sacrificed side by side with her, and won with her. It is by virtue of this that he is great and immortal.

The Battle of Tutova (17 April 1932)

Only four months had passed since the election in Neamt, and the young legionary army engaged in a new battle. At the beginning of January 1932, a congressman's seat was declared vacant in Tutova. I had weighed the situation. In the previous general elections, we got only 500 votes there. The county was weak; but it was framed in by the stronger counties of Covurlui, Cahul, and Tecuci, so that we could easily bring in legionnaires.

It seemed to me that we could possibly win. I was thinking of the impact an echo of a new victory would have. Two consecutive victories of the youngest generation against all political parties would have considerably enhanced its prestige in the eyes of the country. I decided that my father should run, as he was most necessary for me in the movement, both in Parliament and out of it, for organization and propaganda. The election was fixed for March 17. On January 9, I sent out a manifesto to the whole county. My father, with a first electoral team, arrived on January 10. Then came the teams from Iasi, Tecuci, Beresti, and Cahul. During the first three weeks, the speed and the bravery of the small legionary forces had set off a current of sympathy in our favor throughout the whole county. In a bad winter with heavy snows and cold weather, the political parties could not go out. They waited for better weather. But during this time, over hills, through waist-deep snows, through blizzards, legionnaires traveled from village to village.

Around the beginning of February, fighting the enemy became more difficult. A coalition of Liberals, National-Peasants, Lupists, and Cuzists was facing us with a fierceness we had never met before. The government resorted to truly terroristic measures and the Jewish press attacked us vehemently.

I felt the need of new reinforcements, so I sent the last reserves from Iasi, led by Totu. I had none others except in Bucharest, and these could not be secured for lack of funds. So I convoked a meeting of the legionnaires and proposed a heroic step: that they start off on foot from Bucharest to Bariad, a distance of nearly 200 miles, explaining to them that this march would mean more for our victory than 100,000 manifestos. It alone would constitute a great heroic discourse addressed by legionnaires to the Romanians of Tutova.

The legionnaires received my suggestion enthusiastically. A week later, a team of about 25, led by Stelescu, Caratanase, and Doru Belimace left Bucharest on foot for Tutova. At the end of a ten-day march through stormy weather, they arrived at Bariad where they were warmly welcomed by the whole populace. But the persecution had escalated to nerve-shattering tenseness. Mr. Argetoianu, Minister of Internal Affairs, sent out the gendarmes Col. lgnat, with large forces, and orders to carry the legionnaires out of Tutova county on stretchers. It was impossible for small teams to advance further. So I formed two strong teams under the command

of Victor Silaghi and Stelescu which, supporting one another, should advance on the Puesti-Dragomiresti line, supporting my father. I sent another
smaller team in the direction of Bacani. These two were the only two
routes that remained uncanvassed. They constituted the northeast half of
the county. The other half, the south, was adequately worked by my father,
Mr. D. Popescu the county head, Victor Silaghi, Teodor Tilea, and Ion
Antoniu, with the first teams.

The two teams in the North advanced nearly 30 miles, fighting the
bitter cold and ending up with several wounded, Tocu among others. In the
northern part of the county, they were met by large contingents of gendarmes. The teams barricaded themselves in the attic of an abandoned
house where they resisted for 48 hours without heat, food, or water. In the
end, they were able to retreat through a difficult overnight march, executed
in conditions truly heroic, only because of Victor Silaghi's stubborn persis-
tence in encouraging the exhausted, starved, and frozen legionnaires to the
last possible resistance.

Finally, these teams were surrounded by superior forces, captured,
and brought to Bariad. My father was arrested and locked up in a regimental prison.

The third team was completely decimated in the battle of Bacani.
There, in a valley before entering the village in the evening, it was attacked
by a large contingent of gendarmes. The team's leader, legionary Lascar
Popescu, struck over the head with a rifle, was the first to fall unconscious
in a pool of blood. The other legionnaires refused to retreat. They counter-
attacked with bare chests, nothing in their hands, trying to get into the village. One by one, they all fell unconscious. The last one standing, attacked
alone. Under blows, he fell on his knees, got up, attacked again. He fell
near his comrades. The entire team lay unconscious in a pool of blood.

From there, they were dragged through the snow by the gendarmes,
for better than a mile to the gendarmes' post in the village. At 1 o'clock
that night, a rider brought the news to Bariad of what happened at Bacani.
The team from Iasi led by Totu, which arrived in Barlad that midnight, left
immediately on foot to aid their wounded comrades. Following a battle
from 3:30 to 5 o'clock in the morning, during which the gendarmes fired
all their arms, the legionnaires occupied the gendarmes' post, finding inside, still unconscious and lying on the ground, their comrades fallen in the
battle of Bacani. They carried them to the hospital in Barlad.

But things did not rest here. Jewry launched a mammoth press campaign, attacking us with revolting cynicism and injustice. A wave of lies,

insults, and calumnies came our way. All the political groupings coalesced to put us out of the battle.

The Second Dissolution of the Guard (March 1932)

Kicked by the gendarmes, attacked by the Jewish press, we were hit by a new dissolution of the Guard ordered through a simple ministerial decision. Although we were within the framework of perfect legality, the Iorga-Argetoianu government, in defiance of laws and Constitution, dissolved the Guard arbitrarily. Our headquarters all over the country were again taken over and padlocked, and the Iasi print shop closed down. Attacked in the press, we were placed in the impossible position of not being able to defend ourselves, as all our publications had been suspended. In Parliament, I tried to speak, but I was prevented by the din of the majority, who did not permit me to defend myself.

However, the candidacy in Tutova could not be stopped. The team from Bucharest was expelled from the county. Likewise the others, one by one. Our Iasi team of about 30, under Totu's command, as it was being taken to the depot for the same evacuation operation, broke the cordons and occupied the waiting room in which, barricaded, it resisted for 24 hours, until it was gassed out. In the end, it was loaded on the train and taken out of the county. Only Ibraileanu, Nutu Esanu, and my father who was arrested, remained in town.

The persecution was then switched to the villages. Peasants, school teachers, and priests were arrested and beaten; their homes broken into. The election was postponed one month, until April 17.

My father was released. The elderly legionnaires then came into town to step into the battle: Hristache Solomon, Col. Cambureanu, Ventonic, Ifrim, Father Isihie, Peceli, Potolea, etc. I assigned them to various sectors. Each slipped to his post under the cover of night. Our teams from the neighboring counties again entered Tutova at several points. Gh. Costea's team crossed the Barlad river, water up to their necks, for all roads were patrolled; they arrived at the polling station dripping wet.

Voting began the morning of April 17, continuing into the night. On April 18, at 5 o'clock in the morning, the legionary victory was announced: 5,600 votes; Liberals: 5,200; National-Peasants: 4,000; the other groups: less than 2,000; Cuzists: 500 votes.

This second legionary victory, against the coalition of all the Romanian politicians, won through the dauntlessness and the iron will of the legionnaires, through their heroism and blood, defying obstacles, insults, blows, and persecution, stirred up an indescribable enthusiasm throughout the country.

New General Elections (July 1932)

My father was validated the last day of the parliamentary session. But our rest lasted only one week, for the Iorga government had fallen. A National-Peasant government was formed, headed by Mr. Vaida.

Exhausted both physically and financially, we went into a new battle. That was June 1932. Ever since 15 December 1929, we had been in a constant fight: December 1929 to April 1930, the campaigns in Covurlui, Cahul, Turda, Tecuci; the summer of 1930, the preparation, then interdiction of the march in Bessarabia, followed by my imprisonment until that fall; in October and November we were in Maramures—that winter imprisoned again; the spring of 1931, battle preceding general elections; summer of 1931, elections in Neamt; winter 1932, elections in Tutova; and now we were again about to come to the general elections.

In spite of all these fights, we continued the organizational work in the rest of the country. The year before, we entered electoral lists in 17 counties; this year we entered 36. All political parties engaged in the same quarrels, full of intrigues, for the naming of their candidates. This lasted a whole week. But I, alone, in one night, fixed all our candidate lists in 36 counties. No one among legionnaires fights over his place on the list; if anything, he asks to be put last.

The difficult problem for us is financial matters. Most of the counties have been able to meet their own expenses out of legionary contributions. Others have not. I needed 50,000 lei only to cover electoral taxes. I walked as in a daze until the last day. I tried one thing, I tried another. Nothing.

I went to see Mr. Nichifor Crainic, the director of *The Calendar*, in the hope he might have money, but in vain. With his journal, which had been published for five months, he supported our struggle, following the bravery of our legionary teams, step by step; however, he could not help us financially. Finally, I borrowed from Pihu and Caranica, who, by running to all the Macedonians, found the necessary sum. Several counties were supported by the county of Focsani and Ilristache Solomon.

The campaign commenced. A new persecution befell our ranks. Being spread over a large front, our thin ranks were everywhere violently attacked. Legionnaires Savin and Popescu were wounded at Tighina. At Barlad, scores of teachers and priests were dragged into cellars and maltreated by orders of Mr. Georgescu-Barlad. At Vaslui, our small teams were wounded. Likewise at Podul-Iloaiei and throughout Iasi county. At Focsani, the aged Hristache Solomon, engineer Blanaru, and ten others were attacked on orders of attorney Neagu by armed bands of National-Peasants in the village of Vulturul. Legionnaires fell to the ground wounded by bludgeons and knives. One only remained on his feet like a mountain, Hristache Solomon, whom no one dared touch. He fiercely defended himself, but in the end, fell in the middle of the road, overwhelmed by blows. There on the ground, he was bludgeoned over the head by these beasts who always made an issue—then as they do now—of legality, civilized methods, freedom, etc.

The Guard obtained 70,000 votes, double that of the previous year. The counties of Cahul, Neamt, Covurlui, and Tutova where my father ran, came out strongest. Then followed Campul-Lung with Mota; then Turda, Focsani, Ismail, Tighina. We won five seats, and now we must make our choices to fill them. I stayed in Cahul, in order to let Nutu Esanu enter Parliament. I decided that my father should remain in Barlad in order to let Stelescu, a 25-year-old student, enter Parliament; I wanted thus to give the youth of the country encouragement and a stimulus. The trust and love I showed this youth, however, was not returned to me.[3]

In Parliament for the Second Time

All the time in Parliament, I fought against the government and its measures that I considered contrary to the wellbeing of the Romanian people, just as I fought all the former administrations that took turns at the state's helm. The country had nothing to expect from all these governments. Nothing of any sanity for the future of our people was being forged there. All measures and laws were but some palliatives that prolonged, from day to day, the bitter and sad existence of our country.

When Romanian workers were shot by orders of the Ministry of Internal Affairs, sickened to the bottom of my heart by the attitude of the pro-communists within the National-Peasant Party who were applauding the government's step, I took the platform and deemed it my duty to speak as follows:

> It is bad that the unfortunate workers went out into the street,
> but it would be worse if they and our people, faced with the

---

[3] Mihai Stelescu (1907-1936) eventually broke with Codreanu and betrayed the Legionary movement. He was killed by Legionnaire sympathizers in 1936.

injustice that cries out to heaven, would not go out, but resignedly bend their head under the yoke, leaving the country in the hands of some exploiting politicians.[4]

I quote here from the Official Minutes of this session:

> *Mr. Corneliu Zelea Codreanu*: Mr. President, fellow congressmen! In the name of the group to which I belong, I demand that, in addition to the investigation which is normally made by competent authorities, another parliamentary investigation be conducted, composed of representatives of various political groups in this Parliament. I demand this because I doubt the veracity of Mr. Minister of Internal Affairs' statement; I doubt that for a very good reason. On January 24, when Romanian students, nationalist and Christian, went to the tomb of the unknown soldier to place a cross, the State Securitate leaked the information to a newspaper in Bucharest that that action was engineered and financed by Moscow.
>
> If the information you have, regarding the Grivita affair also comes from such a source, then I understand very well how right you are in taking steps of this nature as you did yesterday and today. Secondly, I wish to state that I, as well as all people of common sense in this country, am not afraid of Communism or Bolshevism. We are afraid of something else, of the fact that those workers have nothing to eat; they are hungry. Some of those workers make only 1,100 lei a month and have 5, 6, or 7, children.
>
> *Dr. V. Lupu*: It is true.
>
> *Mr. Corneliu Zelea Codreanu*: Having 5, 6, 7, children, such wages are not enough even for their daily bread. I, on the other hand, am also afraid of something else: of their thirst for justice.
>
> *Dr. V. Lupu*: Very good!
>
> *Mr. Corneliu Zelea Codreanu*: Therefore, you will have to satisfy these two needs: hunger, and thirst for justice, and this country will enjoy complete order.

---

[4] Codreanu refers to the workers' strike at the Grivita Rafiway Works in Bucharest on 4 February 1933.

One of the hardships putting the brakes on parliamentary activity is the thousands of demands to the ministries for intercessions of some kind. This constitutes a real punishment for us from our constituency, (1) because parliamentarians must waste most of their time satisfying these demands. This system is dangerous to the life of an organization, for it paralyzes its entire activity; it can lose the whole battle. You must abandon the fate of your country in order to serve your supporters. After a while I noticed that there were no legionnaires among those coming to me with such demands. All were either professional beggars or specially sent adversaries seeking to paralyze us.

(2) This system placed us in the touchy position of coming to, and seeking favors from, the men we were fighting against. For these reasons, I personally refused to intervene for anyone. During all my serving in Parliament, I asked nothing of any minister.

Another category was made up of those coming to ask us for money. Out of the hundreds knocking on our doors daily, there were no legionnaires. Some were truly sick or fallen into misfortune, but some turned this system into a real profession.

Finally, our group was a small organization, in formation, on the move, in constant battle. This demanded particularly from me uninterrupted attention to all enemy moves; it involved the uncovering and parrying of enemy plans, the winning and organizing of new positions—in other words, a permanent survey, day and night, of the battlefields nationwide. But before anything else came the supervision of legionary education, so as not to wake up and find ourselves being gradually changed into a political category of moral infection from which we would not be able to extricate ourselves and in which the legionary spirit would die.

Parliament took from me the time I really needed for leadership.

The Condition of the Legionary Organization in 1932-1933

In the fall of 1932 and the winter of 1933, legionnaires could breathe. Three and a half years of fighting were over. These youth now deserved their rest.

It had been almost two years since I set up residence in Bucharest. In Iasi, to take my place, Banea, aided by Totu, Cranganu, Tasca, and Stelian Teodorescu, stayed to handle questions relating to students, print shop, our home, etc. The legionary student group increased, comprising now more than half of the militant students. In Cluj, a healthy start toward organization was accomplished by Banica Dobre; likewise in Cernauti, where Lauric legionary life was budding nicely under the spiritual guidance of Professor Traian Braileanu, around whom Professor Toppa and others gathered. In the whole of Bucovina, the legionary current and organization were growing under the able command of the veteran and distinguished nationalist Vasile Iasinschi.

The youth raised in the Brotherhoods of the Cross were prepared by the time they entered university. A nationalist newspaper of great courage and excellent direction had begun publication in Bucharest, *The Calendar*, under the directorship of Mr. Nichifor Crainic and with the collaboration of a handful of intellectuals headed by Professor Dragos Protopopescu. This paper courageously cut a new and wide path in the Romanian intellectual world, along the Christian and nationalist line. Mr. Crainic's articles particularly were real cannon fire that caused devastation within enemy ranks. Within the student movement in the capital, legionnaires occupied the front lines. Traian Cotiga held the presidency of the student center, having a legionary committee.

The intellectual youth of the capital felt that a change had come. Their consciences were preoccupied with the great problems affecting the life of our nation. The healthy Macedonian youth, pure as a tear, and brave, came ever closer to us. However, we thought it unwise that the mass of Macedonians in the Quadrilateral be received into the Guard, because, so recently resettled in the country, we would expose it to too many persecutions. The Macedonian university youth however, in its entirety, joined the legionary movement. At the head of these Macedonian youth were three distinguished men of culture: Papanace, Caranica, and Sterie Ciumeti.

I consulted often with the first two of these, both of whom had admirable judgement supported by irreproachable purity and sincerely, great love and courage. I do not believe that a day has passed since 1931 without meeting with them. During this time of persecution, we discussed for hours blow after blow, injustice after injustice, treachery after treachery. Each bit of news of a new torture of a legionary was a knife piercing our hearts. The pain we suffered for all maltreated legionnaires tormented our souls; and particularly the impossibility of seeing ahead any hope for justice.

Sterie Ciumeti was living with me day and night. He was a young man of great righteousness and doglike faithfulness. He became the chief treasurer of the Guard. All his days—as many as he will have—he will think only of the Guard, will be concerned and will act only for the Guard, will not live his life for anything else but for the Guard.

CHAPTER 8

AN OFFENSIVE OF LIES

"Anarchic and Terroristic Movement"

The legionary movement was visibly growing, especially among the high school and university youth, and among peasants in all the Romanian provinces. It grew more slowly, however, in towns where the Romanian element was state-employed and thus prevented from expressing their views, or economically enslaved by Jews. The same muted persecution that we have known since we started this fight back in 1922 increasingly haunted us, all the fighters and their families. If you were a young graduate, you could not get a state job unless you reneged on your conscience and your faith. Hundreds of youth were sought out to be lured with money, promises, honors, and positions. The state became a school of treason in which men of character were murdered while treason was abundantly rewarded.

If you were a Romanian merchant, the only one among Jewish merchants, and you happened to believe in the Legion, everyone, from street officer to mayor and prefect, turned into your enemy. They harassed you day and night; taxed you more than they did the Jews; fines were continually levied against you; you received blow after blow until they destroyed you. If you were a peasant, you were handcuffed and taken on foot from one village gendarmes' post to the next, and the next, and the next, for scores of miles, being beaten every day. You went hungry four to five days; they looked at you like savage beasts and everyone slapped you in the face. If you were a workingman, they threw you out like a piece of used cloth from every factory and enterprise.

This is because, in this country, a man holding our beliefs must starve to death, together with all his children. All of us are considered enemies of our people and country. But we have maintained ourselves within the most perfect order and legality, so that no trouble could be imputed to us. But this does not mean a thing. The reasoning of our governments is: "We cannot destroy you because you broke the laws? No matter, *we* will break them and then destroy you! You do not want to act illegally; well, *we* will act so!" So that, in this fashion, we have entered into a truly Talmudic system. On one hand, we were accused through the press and by all political agencies of "illegality," and on the other, staying perfectly within the law.

We were ground down by the most odious and illegal procedures by all governmental and state representatives, themselves flagrantly illegal.

Dragged before tribunals, juridical decree after juridical decree throughout the country confirmed the Legion movement's line of legality and order. There was not one decree condemning us. Yet the basic argument of the politicians and the Jewish press remained invariable: "A movement of disorder," "anarchy," "lawlessness," "terroristic." The Jewish press constantly incited politicians against us, pushing them to lunge at us to rip us apart, to annihilate us.

"The Iron Guard in the Service of Foreigners"

After a while, at a loss for new accusations, the Jewish press stated that we were taking money from Mussolini; that we pretended to be nationalists but in fact our purpose was to squeeze money from anyone we met. Now we "found" Mussolini, whom we were squeezing. One by one, we learned with astonishment that: "We were in the service of the Hungarians who were awakening…" "We were in Moscow's service…" "We receive money from the Jews…"

As ridiculous as the last accusation is, it was not spared us. Here I quote a passage from the Jewish newspaper *Politics* of 10 August 1934, in an article titled "Max Auschnitt and The Iron Guard":

> In our country too, then, the phenomenon had been verified exactly, as it is a known fact that the most important movement of Romanian Fascism, the Iron Guard, was created and financed by the big capitalists. And here comes the not-at-all sensational sensation: the Jew Max Auschnitt has supported and financed the Iron Guard directly. This fact was stated by two quite serious and responsible people, Mr. Minister Victor Iamandi and the known publicist Scarlat Calimachi. According to these explanations, the fact appears as very natural. Who does not yet know that Hitler too, was financed by the great Jewish capitalists of Germany?

"The Iron Guard in the Pay of the Hitlerites"

Lately in Germany, Hitler won against the Judeo-Masonic hydra of the entire world. The German people, with an extraordinary determination and unity, fought and put down the Judaic power. The Jews print lie upon lie in their press, seeking to confuse the minds of the people:

1. Adolf Hitler is a painter, stupid, incapable. Who is going to fall for him in a civilized country like Germany? But Hitler moves ahead.

2. Adolf Hitler is not going to win because the German communists are going to oppose him. But Hitler gets closer to power.

3. Hitlerism has broken into two, or three. Great dissatisfaction within the party, etc. But Hitler is not phased.

4. Hitler went crazy. He went into the mountains, etc. But Hitler is in good health and gets ever closer to victory.

5. Should he win, the next day, Germany will have a revolution. Communism will start a general uprising and Hitler will fall. But Hitler wins power and the dreamed-of revolution by the Jews does not erupt. He will go from majorities to unanimity never before encountered in history.

6. All countries will economically boycott Germany and Hitlerism will fall. But Adolf Hitler moves ahead victorious.

7. "Dictatorship," "Hitlerist terror" throughout Germany. "The vote is snatched by terror." But the German people march on behind him enthusiastically.

8. Hitler wants to take our Transylvania. And we, all Romanian nationalists, who wish to rid ourselves of the Jewish calamity, are "Hitlerites"—namely, we want to give our Transylvania to the Germans. But we answer: "Let us presuppose that Hitler wants to make war on us to take our Transylvania. In order for us Romanians to be able to defend Transylvania against the Germans, we must get rid of the Jews; we, too, must solve this Jewish problem, must strengthen the position of our people squeezed by Jewry and sucked of its strength until it has been made quite unable to defend itself. Saddled by the Jewry, which poisons our souls and sucks our blood, we will have neither weapons, nor soul, nor meat on our bones."

9. Finally, we "receive money," are financed, and are "in the pay" of the Nazis. We answer: "A. C. Cuza has been fighting the Jews since 1890; we, since 1919, when we had not even heard of Adolf Hitler. Venomous snakes!"

Printing Counterfeit Banknotes in Rasinari

Before long, a new politico-Jewish campaign was launched against us. Not wanting us to be content with money from Mussolini, Hitler, Moscow, and Auschnitt, our enemy found for us a new financial source in the printing of counterfeit banknotes of Rasinari. The sensational discovery filled the columns of Jewish and party newspapers. We give below, out of that period, several passages meant to illustrate the system of perfidies that attempted our annihilation in the eyes of the nation. The newspaper *The Fatherland* of July 22 published this:

The Iron Guard and the Printing Plant of Counterfeit Money from Rasinari

- Source of propaganda funds -

Cluj, July 21 - At Rasinari, a village near Sibiu, a sensational discovery was made, of a kind which presents an entire political organization in the ugliest light and against which the government now has in hand the most damaging proof to proceed with all severity.

A press for counterfeit money of the Iron Guard

Specifically in the village of Rasinari, one of the many plants of counterfeit money was discovered. From the investigation made it was established however, to everybody's astonishment that this time we are not talking about a band of Gypsies or misfits who defy the rigor of the law in the hope of a quick enrichment, but of the Iron Guard, Mr. Corneliu Zelea Codreanu's political organization, which lately has indulged in the most abusive campaign against our government and generally against all political parties in Romania.

The Iron Guard and its propaganda in villages

But for those who know the activity of the Iron Guard a little better, with its bands of guardists which cover the whole country from one end to the other, this thing seems very natural. For in such circumstances, money is needed first of all.

In fact it has been known that the Iron Guard propagandists lately had large funds, which permitted their travel through the villages as well as the printing of newspapers and the arming of its devoted members with everything necessary to copy the system 'a la Hitler.'

How the counterfeiting was discovered

The Ministry of Internal Affairs had for a long time been informed that some of the Transylvanian leaders of the Iron Guard, particularly those in Brasov and Sibiu, had at their disposal large sums which they then distributed to local organizations throughout the country. At the beginning it was suspected that the money was supplied by who knows what similar foreign organization, but as a result of surveillance, it was established that the suspicion was unfounded. The discovery of the money printing press at Rasinari supplied the police authorities with a new lead, and the result of the investigations was most startling.

Sibiu finances the entire organization

Immediately the Bucharest authorities delegated investigating Judge I. Stanescu of Bucharest to begin the customary investigation. Accompanied by Chief-Prosecutor Radu Pascu and Prosecutor Mardaric, he left for Sibiu, making his first search at the home of attorney Bidianu, who headed the guardist organization, where sensational compromising material was discovered, from which it was evident that the money press served exclusively the political and subversive aims of the Iron Guard. Among the confiscated correspondence, letters of various local organizations were found, particularly from the Iasi organization in which Mr. Banea was asking for a large sum of money in order to buy a panel truck and to intensify propaganda in Moldavia.

The police effected a series of arrests and confiscated all compromising material together with the equipment used in counterfeiting. Investigations continue assiduously and an attempt is being made to establish the ties between the press and guardist organizations, and in particular the amount of funds distributed to the latter.

The moral value of the Iron Guard

When the Iron Guard's organization, which succeeded in creating nuclei over the whole country, was so shamefully caught red-handed, it made a profound impression throughout our country and caused real consternation within the Guard's ranks of partisans. It was known that agitation in villages was done in the name of justice, honor, decency, respect for the law, etc., nothing but claims now proving to have been only empty words of the Iron Guard, when, in fact, it sought only unscrupulous power when it came to the means used.

In view of these discoveries the government seems disposed to proceed with all severity. Mr. V. V. Tilea, Undersecretary of State, declared to an intimate circle that in view of the gravity of the acts committed by some members, the Iron Guard will have to be dissolved.

In *The Romanians' Call* of 6 August 1933, one read the following:

Love of Money and the Counterfeiting of Money

Newspapers have reported these past days how lackeys of the Iron Guard were caught by the authorities counterfeiting money. We know that these kinds of men began lately to go through all our villages promising people all kinds of things and demanding the death penalty for lawbreakers. We are young men who have waited for quite a while to learn for ourselves what the aims and purposes of these people are.

Preaching with ardor, love of country, its wise administration and the extirpation of foreigners, for a while we thought they were well-meaning. When we read in the papers that they began working to the country's detriment by counterfeiting money, we began to realize that we had been mistaken and that now we have come to know them. They are part of the clique of professional pillagers of our country and, for the great lawlessness they committed, we would not

advise the government to do anything but to judge them according to the manner in which they demanded the judgement for such deeds: the death penalty. To the gallows with
the counterfeiters!

This odious campaign lasted three weeks.

It was in vain that Caranica, Steric Ciumeti, and Papanace, the three
elite legionnaires, desperately knocked at newspaper offices to obtain a
denial. These young men, ever since 1931, in view of their qualities of
clear judgement and great sincerity, have lived with me daily, sharing with
me the same tormenting worries and helping me, step by step, in the difficult burden of leading an organization on the battlefield. Futile efforts, for
all these infamies thrown against us were ordered.

They will have only one effect: that of amassing in our souls injustice
after injustice, calumny after calumny, blow after blow, pain after pain.
Our youth has stood them all, burying them in its soul. Now, so many
years later, if I wanted to give the world advice, I would shout: *Beware of
those who endure it for too long!*

The Death Team

But in the face of these obstacles, blows, intrigues, and persecutions, as-
saulting us from every direction, having this terrible feeling of loneliness,
having nowhere to turn, we opposed all this with a firm determination to
die. "The death team" is the expression of these inner feelings of the legionary youth throughout the whole country, to receive death; its determination to go forward, through death.

At the beginning of May 1933, a team was formed, consisting of Father Ion Dumitrescu, Nicolae Constantinescu, Sterie Ciumeti, and several
others. Before setting out to travel through half the country, they dubbed
themselves "The death team." "The Doe" was driven down from Iasi for
their use. They had to cover the route of Bucharest, Pitesti, Ramnicul-
Valcea, Targul-jiu, Turnul-Severin, Oravita, and Resita. They were to be
accompanied also by Father Duminica Ionescu. Then to Timisoara, Arad,
and back to Bucharest. They were on the threshold of the biggest legionary
expedition, and they left with only 3,000 lei in their pockets for gasoline;
for the rest they trusted in God and in what people on their way would give
them. They took along a code of the country's laws in their hand. They
would stay within legality but would defend themselves against illegal
measures.

At Tg. Jiu, Turnul-Severin, Bozovici, they were followed by police and gendarmes and attacked. They knelt in front of the truck to protect the tires, baring their chests to the revolvers. On the outskirts of Oravita, they were met by machine guns, then arrested. A day later, Prosecutor Popovici released them, finding them innocent; for they were not doing anything, were not giving speeches, were not holding meetings. They were just traveling and singing—that was all. But people understood, and greeted them with flowers. They were given food and gasoline for their panel truck. Wherever they went, a trace of enthusiasm remained.

At Resita, I came out to meet them. There we decided to hold a public rally. It was within our rights to do so. Since I was a member of Parliament and had entered a legionary list of candidates in the county of Caras, winning 2,000 votes, I was coming to get in touch with our supporters in order to give them a report on our activity in Parliament. It is legal; it is perfectly legal. But when it comes to us, laws no longer exist.

Not even during the war did Resita see so much military power. It was brought in from nearby towns to occupy the town and encircle it. I realized the government was setting a trap for me. It would have liked for me to try an irrational move, to lose my temper, in order to give an excuse for repression. They said, "That is why we stop these gentlemen. That is why they must be abolished. Wherever they pass, they rouse the populace against our measures of order, against the military and the authorities. They want to bring on a revolution."

Such an error on our part would have been exploited by the government and the Jewish press. For this reason, I did not give them this opportunity, but by drowning all rebellion within myself, I avoided any clash. It would have been exactly in just such a clash that they would have scored a victory. We preferred to give up our rally.

The team went on, passed through Timis-Torontal county and entered the county of Arad. There in the village of Chier, the gendarmes together with the Jews stirred up the peasants, shouting that the "Red bands from Hungary" had crossed over into Romania. The peasants, armed with pitchforks, axes, and bludgeons, fell upon the legionnaires who had no time to identify themselves. The blows covered them with blood. Ciumeti's right hand was broken and he fell at the edge of the road, unconscious. Adochitei was lying by him. All of them were wounded. Then they were arrested, transported to Arad, and put in separate cells in the city jail. They were brought to trial for rebellion ten days later. Our lawyers from Arad, Mota, Vasile Marin, and myself defended them and they were all acquitted.

The Romanian populace of Arad gave them a warm demonstration of sympathy.

As a result of this incident, I decided to go along with them. Part of the team went on by panel truck, while I, accompanied by four of them and the peasant Fratila, left on foot, going through all the villages, all the way to the tomb of Avram Iancu in the mountains, some 80 miles. Peasants received me joyously everywhere.

In Tebea, we parted ways. They continued their route through Hunedoara County and I left for Teius.

At Teius

My father was scheduled to deliver a speech here. As I arrived that evening, I found my father in the home of a peasant; he was covered with blood. A large number of gendarmes entered the hall where the people were assembled and began using their rifle butts on everyone. My father was hit over the head.

Legality! Legality! A Romanian parliamentarian, enjoying guaranteed immunity and rights, goes to deliver a speech and the representatives of public force enter the hall, cracking his head with rifle butts. Peasants, teachers, priests are all shocked. I decided then and there that we would hold a protest meeting two weeks later in the same place.

On the eve of the meeting, "The Death Team" arrived in Teius as well as legionnaires from Cluj and Bucharest, but the meeting could not be held. An infantry regiment and a gendarme battalion surrounded Teius, preventing the peasants from entering. It was the same as in Resita. I tried to avoid a confrontation, deciding that my father and all the legionnaires should leave town but me; because the presence of a number of men, however few, could generate a conflict, while the presence of a single man before such large forces could not cause a rebellion, nor a glory for the many, should they bear down on him.

Yet the peasants of Mihalt and surroundings tried to forcibly cross the bridge already occupied by the army. "We, the peasants of Mihalt, conquered this bridge from the Hungarians in heavy battles. We do not admit that today Romanian gendarmes prevent us from crossing over it," said these brave and undaunted peasants from Mihalt. A battle ensued that lasted over two hours. Shots were fired. One peasant was killed, and from "The Death Team," Tocu, Constantinescu, and Adochitei were seriously wounded for the second time. The entire "Death Team" and other students, a total of 50, were brought back by the authorities to Teius during the day.

They were told that they would be put on a train, but as they did not have train tickets, they had to go to Alba-Iulia to get them.

But there, instead of getting their tickets, they found themselves thrown, without any arrest warrants, into the famous prison where Horia had been thrown. All their protests were futile. They protested in vain that their detention was illegal; that no detainee may be imprisoned without an arrest warrant; that the authority who threw them there was committing an illegal act. At 2 o'clock that night, they broke down the prison gate, formed a column, and went to the prosecutor's home. They reported events to him. There they stayed in the yard until the next morning when, together with the prosecutor, they returned to the prison. This time arrest warrants were issued for "having forced the prison's gate."

In the trial that followed, they were acquitted because, lacking arrest warrants in the first place, they were being detained illegally. They conformed to legal dispositions. By informing the prosecutor, they were just following regulations. Once again it was proven in court that those who provoked disorders were not the legionnaires but the very authorities who, instead of upholding the laws, broke them with sovereign disdain.

"The Death Team" returned to Bucharest after two months of campaigning. Its battles, the suffering to which it was subjected, and its wounds, stirred the soul of the whole of Transylvania. Now, at this moment, we can say that the legionary movement had spread throughout the country, despite all opposition of authorities and in spite of all persecution.

Beginning now, we will stop, we said. We will begin to deepen legionary education by life in work camps. Who could be disturbed by this silent activity, particularly when it was outside the political framework?

The Visani Dam (10 July 1933)

Yet during the previous winter, the pharmacist Aristotel Gheorghiu, legionary leader of Ramnicul-Sarat, forwarded to me a report in which he described the situation of the village of Visani, where the Buzau River annually flooded the fields of farmers over an area of several thousand hectares. And he said that the entire village was begging us to come help them by building a protective dam. I approved this request and took all necessary steps by sending out specialized engineers, making plans, and issuing an order that all legionnaires in that region were to be present at Visani on 10 July 1933, when the work camp was to be opened.

Over 200 young legionnaires gathered at Visani, coming on foot from Calati, Focsani, Bucharest, Buzau, Tecuci, Iasi, Braila, under the leadership of Stelian Teodorescu, Nicolae Constantinescu, Pavaluta, Doru Belimace, Stoenescu and Bruma. But instead of being joyfully received and given something to eat and a resting place, tired and hungry as they were on arrival, they were surrounded by several gendarmes companies, attacked with the brutality of savage beasts, and knocked to the ground under the blows.

The gendarmes were so instructed by their officers, by orders from the Ministry of Internal Affairs—where Mr. Armand Calinescu[1], according to his own statements, played a major role in the measures for our torture and suppression. They rained their blows upon these young Romanians with as much hatred as if they were striking the greatest enemies of the Romanian people.

Among those wounded and humiliated to the very limit of humiliation were legionnaires Stelian Teodorescu, Bruma, Doru Belimace, Father Ion Dumitrescu, Stoenescu, Pavaluta, and Nicolae Constantinescu, gravely wounded for the fourth time in two months.

The news of this unheard-of cruelty against some young people coming to do a good deed, and of all the indignities to which they were subjected, spread like a black veil over the crushed and worried hearts of all our youth—who, for their faith and their love of country, felt betrayed by the politicians of the country to their alien enemy. I understood then, that all avenues were closed to us, and that henceforth we must prepare for death.

We experienced a state of general depression in which we felt that all our reserves of patience and self-control were at the breaking point. I realized that everything around me was cracking and that, above all else, if one single slap in the face would occur, it would lead to irreparable misfortune. I felt like crying out from the depths of my soul: We can no longer stand it!

In this depressing atmosphere, I addressed myself to the Prime Minister in the following letter that was published in the newspaper *The Calendar* of 20 July 1933:

---

[1] Calinescu, then Undersecretary of State at the Ministry of Internal Affairs, had only begun his series of persecutions of the Iron Guard. Later he would leave the National-Peasant Party (in February 1938) and become—by virtue of his personal hatred of Codreanu—Minister of Internal Affairs and right arm of King Carol II of Romania. Calinescu was a true hero of the Jews, promoting their interests for the following six months, and culminating in his carrying out an order by Carol to assassinate Codreanu in November 1938. In March 1939, Calinescu became Prime Minister of Romania—serving only six months, until he himself was assassinated by members of the Iron Guard, in retribution for Codreanu's death.

The Persecution of the Iron Guard
The Letter of Mr. Corneliu Z. Codreanu
to Mr. Prime-Minister Al. Vaida

Mr. Prime Minister,

Following the incidents in Visani, of such moral gravity that they make my heart bleed, I decided to write you the lines that follow:

I am moved to do this neither by momentary impulsiveness nor by any wish to see my letter published in newspapers in order for my friends to applaud, or in order to easily meet the customary formal obligation of 'protesting' the infamy perpetrated in Ramnicul-Sarat.

I am urged to address this letter to you by my troubled conscience, telling me that this path that you pushed us into, is—for any man of honor—the path of fatal misfortunes that can no longer be avoided.

Mr. Prime Minister,

I shall not be able to describe to you here, in a few lines, our martyrdom during the last ten years, in our own country, for our Romanian and Christian faith. I shall only tell you that for ten years, Romanian governments have grown tired striking us. There was the Liberal administration that crushed us under blows; there followed Mr. Goga, and he too crushed us in 1926; then Mr. Mihalache, who likewise gloried, along with the alien masters, in barbarously hitting us, in exterminating us; there was then the Iorga-Argetoianu administration that again struck us until it tired; finally, you came to power, continuing the blows.

None among these has asked himself, Mr. Prime-Minister, whether we could support the unending moral and physical tortures that often surpassed our powers of resistance. During all this time, we have supported everything with great strength. We are full of wounds, but we never bent our heads. We bore them because no matter how trying our torture might be, at least our sentiment of human dignity and our honor were respected. However, lately, under your administration, our persecution and tortures have entered the toughest phase.

What happened at Teius where my father was hit and bloodied, and what happened particularly at Visani, are incomparably graver than all our suffering up to now. These abuses attack our very honor. I will not present to you too long an account.

You certainly remember that two months ago—when I came to ask you what wrong we had done to deserve the persecution that you began—you told me: 'Why do you not start something constructive?'

'Mr. Prime Minister,' I replied. 'I decided to build a dam on Buzau's shore. Do you have any objections?' 'No. Very well. Very nice.'

I presented a petition to the Ministry of Public Works one month before anything was to get underway; I consulted the most distinguished professional engineers in the field, and on July 10 work was to begin.

This was not to be only some youth recreation; it was the call of our youth in the service of the great need for healthy accomplishment; it was to be the education of 1,000 young men in a constructive direction.

It was to be an example for other scores of thousands of youth. It was to be a school for the great popular masses who for years had gone along with their bridges and roads in disrepair, waiting for the state to come fix them, when in a single day their work in common could have repaired them. It was an encouragement for the whole country and an example for those who mistakenly imagine that a strong Romania could emerge out of someone's pity and not from the labor of us all.

Several days before work was to begin, I sent to Visani three distinguished young men to prepare the lodging and the provisioning for those to come. But they were picked up on July 8, transported to Ramnicul-Sarat, then chained together by their handcuffs and sent home like the lowliest of thieves in this state of ridicule, demeaning their human dignity.

Two other youth from the University of Bucharest, spotted in the town of Ramnicul-Sarat, where they arrived to enthusiastically work, were picked up, taken to police, trivially insulted and slapped by the town's police chief and two police commissars—brothers Ionescu—then, with hands tied behind their backs, they were walked through the middle of town to the depot, and by train taken back home.

Finally, on July 10, 200 youth arrived in Visani, most of them students. There, instead of being welcomed with open arms for their good intentions, they were met by the county prefect, the prosecutor, gendarmes Col. Ignat, Cten. Cepleanu, gendarmes Lieut. Fotea, several hundred gendarmes with weapons at the ready, and an infantry company with machine guns set up. They were called on to immediately leave the locality in a tone of unjustified insulting aggressiveness. Faced with such a predicament of threats, the 200 youth lay down in the six-inch mud, and in that humble position, began singing "God is with Us."

The gendarmes were ordered to swoop down on them. Several hundred rushed at them, trampling them, crushing with their boots their chests and heads; the youth endured this whole calvary in a martyr-like silence, offering no resistance. At the head of those kicking the students were Prosecutor Rachieru and Col. Ignat who, with his own hand, pulled out the hair of student Bruma, and Lieut. Fotea, who rained blows with his fists on the cheeks of the innocent youth.

At the end, rope was brought; the hands of the 200 youth were barbarously tied behind their backs, after which they were kept thus in the rain for half a day. In the meantime, Father Dumitrescu arrived and the prosecutor asked him: 'What are you doing here?' 'I am a priest. I came to say Mass before work starts.' 'You are not a priest. You are an ass,' replied the prosecutor. 'Tie his hands behind his back right away.' The priest's hands were tied just like the others and then all of them, in this humiliating position, were marched to Rarnnicul-Sarat and locked up at the gendarmerie, where again they were insulted and horribly tortured by the prosecutor, gendarmes, and policemen. Some, taken out of those torture chambers and then beaten with ox-vein whips, fainted.

Following four days of such an ordeal, they were freed, for there was nothing of which they could be accused. Others, apprehended on their way to Visani, were locked up at Buzau and Braila, whence, hands tied, they were sent home. There are 15 more who, up to today, have not yet arrived. They were taken on foot from Buzau to Bucharest, from

gendarme post to gendarme post, for four days: unfed, insulted, and beaten.

Mr. Prime Minister,

These are not isolated events, but, by the government's
order, reach across the country. For two weeks, without any
guilt—and the incontestable proof of this is all the decisions
of justice handed down—we have been struck and insulted at
each step; at Bucharest, at Arad, at Teius, at Piatra-Neamt,
and at Suceava.

Mr. Prime Minister,

I call your attention in the most respectful manner, that
we who know history and the sacrifices made by each people—we, Romania's present-day youth, do not refuse this
sacrifice. We are not cowards, to avoid the sacrifice due a
new Romania.

But, I again call it to your attention that I taught these
young men the sentiment of human dignity and that of hon-
or. We know how to die, if need be, as we shall prove. You
may lock us up; our bones can rot in the prison's depths. We
may be shot to death. But we may not be beaten, we may not
be cursed, and we may not have our hands tied behind our
backs. We cannot recall any time in our proud Romanian
history that our people tolerated being dishonored.

Our fields are full of the dead, but not of cowards.

Today we are free men with an awareness of our rights.
Slaves we are not, and never were. We receive death, but not
humiliation. Rest assured, Mr. Prime Minister, that we cannot accept these days of humiliation and indignity.

Rest assured, I beg you, that after ten years of suffering,
we have sufficient moral strength left to find an honorable
exit from a life we cannot support without honor and dignity.

Accept please my sentiments.

— Corneliu Zelea-Codreanu

The Liberal Party is Responsible for Exterminating the Iron Guard

Yet, the torments of this youth were not to end. Before our eyes, the hori-
zon grew ever darker. Other trials, even greater, were being prepared for

us. Hardly had the torture of Visani ended when I heard that I. G. Duca, the head of the Liberal Party, left for Paris. We were astonished to read in Parisian newspapers the declarations he made; that "The Iron Guard" is in the pay of Hitlerites; that the Vaida government is weak because it does not destroy us; and that he, I. G. Duca and his party, have assumed the responsibility for preparing our death, for exterminating us.

At home, *The Future*, the party's official paper, would bear down on us on the basis of the same arguments: "anarchical movement," "subversive movement," "a movement in the pay of the Hitlerites;" and on the Vaida administration, accusing it of "weakness" and "tolerance" toward our movement, and of "flirting" with our "anarchical" and "sold-to-the-Nazis" movement.

As a nation, we would fall to the lowest levels of humiliation. Two Romanian statesmen, I. G. Duca and N. Titulescu, would arrange, with the Romanian political front of the Paris Jewish bankers' trusts—interested on one hand in the merciless exploitation of our country's riches, and on the other, in assuring as happy as possible a situation for their co-religionists in Romania—the coming to power of the Liberal Party.[2] This, on the formal condition, the *obligation*, to exterminate the legionary movement by any means. A young, strong, proud Romanian legionary nation, ready to spit them out of the country, with all their predatory capital, does not sit well with the foreign bankers.

And thus—as the completion of our more than a decade of suffering, without being guilty of anything—they prepared our crown of death.

Please allow me, at the end of this series of battles, to turn my thoughts toward my mother—she whose soul has followed me year in and year out, and hour by hour, trembling at each blow struck at me and shuddering at each threat thrown at me by fate. Search after search, conducted by brutal and indecent prosecutors and police commissars, disrupted each year the tranquility of her home, from which any trace of joy and peace had long since disappeared. What a reward from a people debased by its politicians, to a mother who, in the bitterest privation, raised seven children in the love of their country!

Let these few words be a tribute to all mothers whose children have fought, suffered, or died for the Romanian nation!

---

[2] Members of the Iron Guard assassinated Duca on 29 December 1933.

Comrades

Comrades: With these last narratives concluding this volume, my youth, and that of many among you, has ended. We will never again traverse its paths.

If these last 14 years of our youth have not been too full of good times and joys, a great satisfaction lights my conscience now. A legionary Romania has thrust its roots, like those of a tree, into our hearts. It grows from pain and sacrifice, and our hungry eyes watch it bloom, lighting the horizons and the future centuries with its splendor and majesty. This majesty overwhelmingly rewards not only our small sacrifices, but any human suffering, no matter how terrible.

Dear Comrades: To you, who have been struck, maligned, or martyred, I can bring the news that is much more than a casual rhetorical phrase: *Soon we shall win.*

Before your columns, all our oppressors will fall. Forgive those who struck you for personal reasons. Those who have tortured you for your faith in the Romanian people, you will not forgive. Do not confuse the Christian right and duty of forgiving those who wronged you, with the right and duty of our people to punish those who have betrayed them and assumed for themselves the responsibility to oppose the peoples' destiny. Do not forget that the swords you have put on belong to the nation. You carry them in her name. In her name, you will use them for punishment—unforgiving and unmerciful. Thus, and only thus, will you be preparing a healthy future for this nation.[3]

At Carmen Sylva,
5 April 1936.

---

[3] In the 1937 parliamentary elections, the Legion finished in third place with 15% of the vote. But elections would soon be irrelevant; in February 1938, King Carol II declared himself royal dictator. Working at the direction of the king, Calinescu arrested Codreanu on 16 April 1938. He was held in prison for seven months until, on further royal orders, Codreanu and 13 other legionnaires were murdered, on 29 November 1938; he was 39. It was said that the bodies were dissolved in acid.

With Codreanu gone, the Legion split into three factions. By late 1940, the group headed by Horia Sima emerged dominant. In alliance with military leader Ion Antonescu, Sima and the Legion rose to power in September of that year, forcing the abdication of King Carol II (he fled in exile, eventually dying in Portugal in 1953). The Legion's power was short-lived, however, due to constant quarrels with Antonescu, and Sima was driven out of office by January 1941. He fled to Italy, was captured and sent to Germany in 1942, imprisoned for a time at Buchenwald, released at war's end, and then relocated to Spain, where he died in 1993.

BIBLIOGRAPHY

Codreanu, C. 2005. *The Nest Leader's Manual*. USA: CZC Books.

Codreanu, C. 2011. *The Prison Notes*. USA: Reconquista Press.

Crisan, R. 2008. *Istoria Interzisă* ("Forbidden History"). Bucharest: Editura Tibo.

Crisan, R. 2006. *The Secret of the Fire Sword*. Bucharest: University Book Publishing House.

Haynes, R. and Rady, M. (eds.). 2011. *In the Shadow of Hitler*. Palgrave.

Evola, J. 1938/2004. "The Tragedy of the Romanian Iron Guard: Codreanu". Thompkins & Cariou.

Nagy-Talavera, N. 1970. *The Green Shirts & The Others: A History of Fascism in Hungary and Rumania*. Hoover Institution Press/Stanford University Press.

Ronnett, A. and Bradescu, F. 1986. "The Legionary Movement in Romania." *The Journal of Historical Review* 7(2), pp. 193-228.

Ronnett, A. 1995. *Romanian Nationalism: The Legionary Movement*. Romanian-American National Congress.

Sima, H. 1982-1990. *Era Libertaţii - Statul naţional-Legionar, vols. 1 and 2* ("It was Freedom - National Legionary State"). Madrid: Editura Miscarii Legionare.

Sima, H. 1994. *Istoria Mişcarii Legionare* ("History of the Legionary Movement"). Timişoara: Editura Gordian.

Sima, H. 1993. *Guvernul National Român de la Viena* ("Romanian National Government in Vienna"). Madrid: Editura Miscarii Legionare.

Sima, H. 1995. *The History of the Legionary Movement*. Liss, England: Legionary Press.

Sturdza, M. 1968. *The Suicide of Europe*. Western Islands Publishers.

www.ingramcontent.com/pod-product-compliance
Lightning Source LLC
Chambersburg PA
CBHW051506120626
46551CB00012B/800